BOUNTIFUL PRAI

A PLENTIFUL H

D0730698

🔲

"Recommended reading . . . useful . . . clear and accessible."
—*Publishers Weekly*

"Sure to enrich the lives of all women . . . .Upon finishing it, I felt refreshed, like a brand-new person. . . . The perfect gift for women not only seeking to create balance in their lives, but also women struggling to maintain it."
—*Black Issues*

"A PLENTIFUL HARVEST is uniquely refreshing and is a welcome addition to the current works of inspirational literature."
—James McBride, author of *The Color of Water*

"Refreshing . . . perfect weekly reading . . . Terrie Williams is at the top of her game . . . .Her writing is fresh, witty, sassy, and hilarious at times."
—*Black MBA Magazine*

"Practical and purposeful . . . an inspiring, working journal guide."
—*Quarterly Black Review*

"A spiritual feast of knowledge, served by words of wisdom, tranquility, and inspiration."
—Faith Evans

"Terrie gives you a complete and realistic game plan for discovering and becoming your whole self."
—India.Arie

"Replete with encouraging words for folks who lead brisk lives . . . this book is a gentle reminder of life lessons."
—*Turning Point Magazine*

"Addresses core issues that so many African-American women face today . . . the perfect gateway through which women may seek and find the solace so often missing in this all-too-busy world."
—*Black Elegance*

more . . .

READERS LOVE

⅍ *A PLENTIFUL HARVEST*

"This book is important and deep. It will empower *anyone* who reads it. There is an amazing and empowering energy to it that is fierce. Your book is a call to action. You went for strong: let's get down to it: let's do the work and make the change. No grey here, it's just do it!!! For those of us in the trenches who have not been able to just do it, make necessary changes, this book is like a *fire*. It gives hope and new ways of thinking. It is powerful and I thank you. There is just no way someone will read this book and not do something about the things in their life that need changing or attention."
—Jan Goldstoff, New York, NY

"A PLENTIFUL HARVEST has already made an indelible print on my life. I have at least five people on my 'I must get this book for' list."
—Sharon Charles, New York, NY

"I devoured this book in one sitting and found it to be enriching, enlightening, and inspirational. Reading it was a profoundly growing experience for me. This book is an exemplary chart of the 'lessons of life.' Thank you for writing it."
—Ginny Tavis, Brick, NJ

"I sat there after reading and said to myself 'Has this sistah been living in my house?' You touched on everything I am feeling."
—Sojourner McCauley, New York, NY

A PLENTIFUL HARVEST

CREATING BALANCE *and* HARMONY THROUGH THE SEVEN LIVING *V*IRTUES

TERRIE WILLIAMS

WARNER BOOKS

An AOL Time Warner Company

Copyright © 2002 by Terrie Williams
All rights reserved.

Warner Books, Inc., 1271 Avenue of the Americas, New York, NY 10020
Visit our Web site at www.twbookmark.com.

W An AOL Time Warner Company

Printed in the United States of America
Originally published in hardcover by Warner Books, Inc.
First Trade Printing: November 2003

The Library of Congress has cataloged the hardcover edition as follows:

Williams, Terrie.
    A plentiful harvest : creating balance and harmony through the seven living virtues / Terrie Williams.
        p. cm.
    Includes bibliographical references.
    ISBN 978-0-446-69120-8 ISBN 0-446-52715-7
    1. African American women—Conduct of life. 2. Virtues. 3. Kwanzaa. I. Title.

BJ1610 .W53 2002
170'.44—dc21   2002071354
ISBN: 0-446-69120-8 (pbk.)

Book design by Giorgetta Bell McRee
Cover design by Diane Luger
Cover illustration by Zita Asbaghi

To my mother and best friend, Marie K. Williams,
and to all my sistahs who are striving
to take time out of life to live.

We are hard pressed on every side, but not
crushed; perplexed, but not in despair; perse-
cuted, but not abandoned; struck down, but not
destroyed.

2 CORINTHIANS 4:8–9

To God be the Glory

Stay Strong

Contents

◩

Foreword by Susan L. Taylor, Editorial Director, *Essence* Magazine

⊡

We forget that pain is information and can be a powerful teacher. We forget that discomfort isn't always a bad thing, but often a directive. We forget that our emotions are friends we should never deny, but come to know intimately. In some way, all in life is instructive and good. All of our experiences are meant to help us grow in wisdom, faith, and courage, and they are always right on time.

Terrie Williams reminded me of these powerful truths on a business trip we had taken some years ago to Richmond, Virginia. What I gleaned from Terrie in just a few hours has had a profound and lasting impact on my life. Terrie led me to the path of self-acceptance and greater self-confidence. She taught me not to fear or run from the things that challenge me, but to see them as God's invitation to grow.

The trip came soon after I became editor in chief of *Essence* magazine. Our publisher, Ed Lewis, had promoted me over a host of highly skilled and credentialed sisters who were senior to me. Some were upset and quit. Several of Ed's business associates told him he was nuts to give so important and challenging a job to a lightweight who was a cosmetologist, not a journalist, and who hadn't written or edited anything but fashion and beauty stories. But the magazine was in trouble. Readership had tumbled the year after our beloved editor in chief, Marcia Ann Gillespie, left the publication. Much to everyone's amazement—

including my own—I got the job and wisely surrounded myself with the smartest women I could find to help turn the magazine around. Part of our circulation director's strategy to increase readership was for me to do a media tour of a few markets where the downturn had been most dramatic.

Ed had hired a young public relations director, Terrie Williams, who'd become well known in New York City's media circles as a top-notch professional. With a fully booked schedule in place, Terrie and I hit the road. I was looking forward to fielding questions about the new *Essence* we editors were creating and to promoting the exciting stories we had in the works. With all of the newspaper, radio, and TV interviews Terrie had lined up, *Essence* was sure to attract tens of thousands of new readers.

On the flight to Richmond, the first stop on our four-city tour, I reviewed the itinerary, which for weeks had been continually updated, and was horrified to discover that I was scheduled that evening to speak to students and community guests at Virginia Union University. I broke out in a cold sweat. *No way I can talk to an auditorium full of people—and certainly not on a university campus! I didn't even go to college! They'll see that I'm a fraud and in way over my head.* By the time we landed, I was panic stricken and trying to hide my wrenching anxiety from Terrie, who, though a decade younger than I, always seemed the poster girl for confidence and competence.

During the ride to the hotel I never stopped talking, nervously inventing one excuse after another about why we had to cancel that evening's appearance and any other talks scheduled for the tour. We were heading west along Highway 64, past ancient pine forests, flatlands, and lush rolling hills, silent witnesses over the seasons and centuries to both the suffering and strength of our people. Here we were, two African American businesswomen rolling into Richmond, in the air-conditioned comfort of a limousine, just two miles from the James River, which had carried our ancestors into lifelong servitude. It's a drive I've taken many times since. I have heard those distant voices calling from the river. I've seen their ghosts barefoot in the land, running from Richmond with real reason to panic, but also with great faith and determination. But on that day I was too busy talking, not listening, and too much blinded by my own fear to see how far we had come.

Turning her attention from the beautiful, haunting terrain, Terrie's soft brown eyes searched for mine, her smile and spirit so bright they seemed to light up the limo's dim interior. In that very direct and loving way of hers, Terrie said she could feel my fear, but that I mustn't turn back. "God will never challenge you beyond your capacity," she stated with simple certainty; "just be yourself, Susan, you are enough." She seemed to be speaking to my soul, giving me the faith and clarity I so needed at that moment.

You are enough. The truth in Terrie's words is unfolding in me still. *You are enough.* Over the years I have worked to believe this and to have this truth inform my thinking and my life. I've learned that although that day of revelation in Richmond was an extraordinary one for me, it was an ordinary day in the life of Terrie Williams. This is how she serves the many people in her universe. This is how she walks the earth. Rarely have I seen so seamless a line between what a person says and does. Trained as a social worker, it is her compassionate heart that guides her overscheduled life. Terrie's a healer, a teacher, and a believer in the dauntless power of love. Love stands, she has proven, where all else falters. No matter what our drama, Terrie believes we can heal and become bright, new, and whole again. These are the seeds she is planting each day in our great garden universe.

And so, like so many others, from the hip-hop community to Hollywood and from major players in politics, in business and sports to college students and kids in crisis, I lean on Terrie Williams, on her humanity and wisdom. There's been a long line of us over the years, a diverse procession of grateful souls— Eddie Murphy and Master P, Janet Jackson and Jesse Jackson, Johnnie Cochran, Michael Jordan, Charlie Ward and Stephen

King, Al Sharpton, David Dinkins, Star Jones, Sean Combs, and Sally Jessy Raphael. Plus legions of everyday folk, and the hungry, homeless people she leaves food for atop mailboxes throughout New York City, the thousands of kids her Stay Strong Foundation is helping to keep secure. Sis is on a mission; I am a witness.

Since that day in Richmond, Terrie and I have grown close as sisters. And that talk I gave that evening? Once I let go of my need to be perfect, I felt quite comfortable standing before the audience, comfortable just being myself. And off to the side I found Terrie, her bright eyes and loving smile supporting me through every moment. And I realized that I do have lots to say. That evening Terrie helped open the way to my busy public-speaking career that I love as much as I do writing, editing, and running a business. Also, I gained the confidence I needed to go back to school, and I graduated from college in 1991.

God wants to give you so much more than you're asking for, Terrie would say, so stop doubting and fearing and get on with the building and the living and giving. She believes that this is a land of plenty and encourages us to hold a grander vision of who we are and what we can do. Her unwavering faith in life and love raises the bar for us all and encourages profound change. Our gifts and talents and many privileges, Terrie's life has shown me, are made valuable by what we do with them, and she continues to develop hers and to use them to help others.

A Plentiful Harvest is a guide for the generations searching for love, a meaningful life, and inner peace. It is the offering I have longed for my beloved friend to write. All you need bring to meet Terrie on the path is commitment. Terrie Williams's blessing is her wisdom, clarity, and training. Our blessing is that she shares it all so generously.

May the powerful truths you learn from her here live in your heart and help to heal your life as they have mine.

Foreword by Iyanla Vanzant

It's still hard to admit that the adults in my life knew what they were talking about when they warned me about life. As I attempted to rush through my experiences of puberty and adolescence, my family watched over me protectively, constantly giving advice: "Slow down! Take your time! Don't overdo it." When I fell flat on my adult face, I finally recognized that all of the warnings and precautions could be condensed into a single statement, "Straighten up and fly right!"

Flying requires balance. There must be an equal distribution of weight and a steady flow of energy throughout the aircraft. When the pilot is skilled and focused, and the aircraft is mechanically sound, the takeoff flight and landing, we can assume, will be successful. We are all built to fly. In fact, with the equipment we've been given and a good tailwind (a little help from the universe of life), there is no reason we cannot soar to unexpected heights.

It's the balance thing that usually gets us. We are resistant to the slow start. We become frightened or overexcited with the initial liftoff. The excitement can make us careless or negligent about the equipment checks and mechanical requirements that ensure a safe flight and smooth landing. Unfortunately, few of us realize that without step-by-step preparation and methodical maintenance in all respects of our lives, we cannot achieve or sustain the balance and harmony required to get off the ground and fly safely.

A Plentiful Harvest is a mindful and masterful contribution that will help you get your flight plan and flying instructions in order. Terrie Williams teaches us how to fly with an open mind and heart. She shares her own trials and triumphs, which is a demonstration of how to fly with your eyes wide open in order to maneuver through turbulence and imbalance. She offers us "seven living virtues," which can be your guide for a successful liftoff, flight, and landing. Most important, the virtues Terrie offers will help you fine-tune your inner equipment to attain a greater outward expression, which leads to a more *Plentiful Harvest*.

Terrie has soared to success in public relations, a field littered with careers that were here today, gone tomorrow. She has achieved what most people only dream about, and she has done it in a way that hasn't compromised her spirit or principles. It is no easy feat to excel in an industry that is often more impressed with *who* you know rather than *what* you know. So how does she keep the who and the what together without losing sight of who she is and what really matters? Terrie is successful because she knows that creating balance and harmony is the key to yielding the "plentiful harvest" that so many of us desire. Remember the proverb "As you sow, so shall you reap"? Terrie understands that you harvest *exactly* what you plant and cultivate, and she reaps plenty because she sows plenty. She knows that the more you give the universe, the more the universe gives back to you. And now, with the book you're holding, she's sharing what she knows. I invite you to pay close attention to the loving instructions offered in *A Plentiful Harvest*, because like Terrie, I know all God's children have wings.

A Plentiful Harvest

Introduction:
My Basket Runneth Over

I woke up in the small hours one morning, when even the most dedicated lovers or party people have called it quits. The world was as quiet and calm as New York City ever gets (if you can ignore the far-off car alarm or the sound of a five-ton truck barreling down the avenue . . .).

But my mind was racing a hundred miles an hour with things I did and didn't do, "gottas" and "shouldas," doubts and suspicions. The typo I spotted in my pitch letter just before the phone rang (again)—did I remember to fix it when I got off the phone? The two talks I'd be giving in the next couple of days—what could I possibly say that would mean something to kids living in a juvenile detention center? Or to three hundred white guys in expensive suits? How long is it since I called my dad? Will the brilliant idea I came up with for a client's new project still seem brilliant by our eight-thirty staff meeting? That new receptionist cuts off more calls than he connects. Is Shellie's birthday this week or last week? Is there any Häagen-Dazs in the freezer? And on and on . . . you know how it goes.

It was pitch dark outside, I didn't have to be at my first meeting for hours yet, but I was totally awake. I flipped my pillow over to the cool side and realized my heart was going as fast as my thoughts. I groaned in frustration—I couldn't remember the last time I'd slept through the night, and tonight obviously wasn't about to change things.

I took a deep breath. Forget the little things—what was happening with my *life?* After years of making zero money as a social worker, I had switched tracks to public relations, and now I was head of the best known African American publicity agency in the country—not bad for the daughter of North Carolina sharecroppers. And yeah, it was sure enough paying the bills, but emotionally and spiritually? Let's just say my soul was about as healthy as a pile of bleached bones in the middle of the desert.

Sure, I had achieved the business goals I started out with, but do you think it brought me happiness? And what about the other goals I was nowhere near checking off my list—like finding love, and becoming a mother? I wasn't in a relationship; my biological clock was about to sound the final alarm; and I knew I couldn't be a single mom—not with my fourteen-hour workdays. I wasn't giving up on finding a man to share my life with, but I had to face facts: The joys (and heartaches!) of motherhood that I'd always assumed would be mine "once I get it together" were just not going to happen for me. No one was ever going to call me Mom. And when that hit me, when I finally looked at the reality of my life today and not the fantasy of someday, it shattered me like a wrecking ball destroying a building.

Needless to say, the stress of my daily life coupled with the heartache of unfulfilled personal goals left me feeling empty. I had been dealing with that emptiness for the past several years with my mood-altering drug of choice—food! Instead of eating when I was hungry, I was eating when I felt empty, and that was most of the time. I knew I was putting on weight, not just because my clothes were getting tighter, but because my friends had been giving me the Look of Concern lately. Whenever they asked me, "Are you okay?" I knew they were thinking, *Girl, you and food are way out of control!* But I kept saying I was "Fine, fine, fine . . ."—I just couldn't talk about the pain in my heart. The few hours each week that I wasn't at work or asleep, I just wanted to lie in bed. It had gotten to the point where I tried taking Prozac. But that night, feeling so low I couldn't fall off the floor, I suddenly understood there was nowhere to go but up. Prozac wasn't helping because my ailment wasn't biochemical—it was spiritual.

When I sat up in bed that night, I didn't have a grand plan for changing my life. As a matter of fact, I didn't have a clue about where to start! All I knew is that I was bottoming out, and I had to start somewhere. As I got up, I knocked over a handwoven basket I used to keep on the nightstand to collect clippings, letters, and scraps of paper I wanted to do something with "someday." Kneeling on the floor to pick up the mess, I noticed something with a pretty border: a Kwanzaa greeting card.

I remembered keeping the card because I liked having a handy reminder of the principles Kwanzaa promotes, but it had disappeared in a day or two under the pile of scraps. Looking at it fresh, months after the noise and rush of the holiday season, I finally really heard the message of those principles. This was a list of what I aspired to. These were *living virtues* I wanted in my life. It's what I was working toward when I met my first Big Brothers/Big Sisters partner, when I brought a new intern into my office, when I coached a young NBA recruit on how to function in the public eye. It's what I'd liked about being a social worker, before it got to the point where I was jumping through so many administrative hoops that there was no time to really touch people's lives. It's what I felt each time I saw someone's dream ignite from a small spark in one of my talks.

That's what it's all about, I thought. It's what *I'm* all about—or want to be about. As I translated the values into the language of my daily life I knew that my best self yearned for these things. Sometimes I hit the mark. But too often I was just putting out fires—whatever burst into flames was what got my attention, and "little" life-affirming things never got paid any mind. With this new framework in my head, I could see just where and how I'd gone off course—*and* how to get back on!

That morning I sat down and wrote out these seven virtues for myself. Calling, Responsibility, Thrift, Love, Community, Spirituality, Creativity. Each week for the next year I would commit seven days of intensive reflection, meditation, and action to one of the principles. I began that week with thrift. I knew that running my own business was a strong economic stance—but my personal finances were a mess. I approached knowledgeable friends, made a very basic financial plan, and organized my financial records. Soon I was paying off my debts and learning how to invest my savings intelligently. It wasn't easy, but it wasn't even half as bad as I thought it would be.

After the first week I felt like my attitudes were changing. Within a month I couldn't believe the difference in my life. I let go of the Prozac because I realized I didn't need it, and never had—I had found a way to be emotionally honest about what I was missing or neglecting, and was taking concrete steps to change it. I realized that if my first book had been about helping sistahs and brothers in business, the next stage of my life would be about caring for our souls and spirits and bodies. The approach to life that I was blessed to discover that sleepless night was working for me, and I wanted to start sharing it.

Just three months after committing to and doing this plan, I realized how powerful it was. Not just because each principle was powerful, but because taken as a whole the seven virtues added up to a balanced life. Going from times when the ground is parched or frozen, when nothing takes root or grows, into times of fertile soil and abundant sun and rain, is part of staying in balance. You have to know that even after the coldest winter comes the spring. And knowing the cool weather will always come around after the summer can help keep us real.

The seven virtues will help you create a balance between giving and taking, saving and spending, looking inward and reaching outward, between planting and harvesting, between passing judgment and doing justice. Then, and only then, will you be able to feel the full power of this way of living.

Living up to the virtues was the beginning of a lot of changes for me. I refocused the agency to concentrate on the kind of work that excited me, and began to feel I was serving my clients more effectively than I ever had. I admitted I wasn't able to do my best work for anyone, including me, as long as I kept trying to be all things to all people. I poured more time and energy into my speaking career, looking for ways to connect with more people and ways to make that connection at least as much about sharing the virtues as about work. I gave myself permission to do things for *me:* I started working through my food issues, made my therapist appointments a priority, and started working with a trainer. Many of these things had been under my skin for a long time, but once I fastened on to these virtues, I found I could finally take action.

I made all this up as I went along, but I kept wishing I had a guide to reconnecting with these virtues each day, a book to map my journey—and that's why I'm writing this book. A guide can be a great help, and I'm hoping the guidance you find here will speed you on your way, making you more comfortable in the process.

The living virtues are the cornerstones of right living, no matter what your cultural heritage. They are among the good and true things that don't get upgraded every year *because they are already perfect.* For me, they're the anchors that keep me grounded and the wings that lift me higher. Wisdom like this used to come to us through our church or our community—but many of us no longer feel connected like that, and others of us so thoroughly bend the rules to match our lifestyles that they don't mean anything anymore.

This book is for you, if you are someone who ever feels overwhelmed and unfulfilled, as if you've lost sight of the plenty in your life. In simple and straightforward ways, it shows how you can reconnect the truths of our heritage with the needs of your soul. And it takes you there, by the hand, every step of the way.

I've worked hard at this way of living over the last few years, but the story's not over yet, and it probably never will be. Balance, after all, isn't stationary—it's dynamic. A lot of the time—say walking down the street—you stay in balance naturally, automatically. But some balancing acts are harder than others. Stand on one foot for a minute, and you'll know soon enough that staying in balance demands constant small shifts—and a lot of muscle work. You've got to move to stay in balance. That's why I like to remember that these principles sprang out of *harvest* ceremonies. Life is constant movement, but not always in a straight line. Too often we expect that, when the reality is that it's a cycle. It comes with seasons, both literal and metaphorical. As we read in Ecclesiastes (and the Byrds sang into our minds): "To every thing there is a season, and a time to every purpose under heaven."

May the reading of this book help you to sow, to reap, and to enjoy your own plentiful harvest!

How to Use This Book

There is joy even in the hardest work.
ANONYMOUS

This book is structured around the seven living virtues. Each chapter reflects on one of the seven virtues, with the seven principles rotating throughout for a total of fifty-two chapters. We will concentrate on each virtue for at least seven weeks. Some virtues will take longer to work through than others, but all are equally important. The last week of the year I emphasize "celebration" to focus one day on each of these living virtues. This will mesh with Kwanzaa for anyone who cares to observe it (though this book won't be the place to learn the specific rituals that go with it), or provide an opportunity to review everything on your own, or with any other kind of celebration you want to stage.

The structure, then, reflects the cyclical and seasonal nature of life. As we rejoice in our harvest, we must also gather our seeds, setting them carefully aside for after the thaw. Even as we enjoy the fruits of our labors, we must prepare for the next time of planting.

Each week will end with a set of exercises to help you work through that week's lesson. Most call for writing in a journal or notebook of some sort. If you don't have one, I encourage you to make or buy one. Your thoughts and ideas deserve a special place to be recorded. Journaling has been an important way for me to explore and record my growth. I believe this process will help you, too.

What Are
The Seven Living Virtues?

---

1. CALLING.

Knowledge of your life's true purpose. If your principles and goals are clear, you never have to fly by the seat of your pants. Even in situations you never imagined, events that send you reeling, you'll find your course is clear if you know your calling.

2. RESPONSIBILITY.

Accepting the duties and obligations in our life *today*. We all have the impulse to advise the people we care about, even to try to "fix" their lives, often because focusing on others is easier than focusing on ourselves. It's not selfish to cultivate your own garden—it's the only way you can be strong enough even to begin helping others.

3. THRIFT.

Thrift is not penny-pinching or austerity—it's thinking before you spend. How many times has the week or the month mysteriously outlasted your paycheck, forcing you to borrow money or "put it on the plastic"? If you take the time to be aware of the money you have, what's coming in and what needs to go out, you can really *choose* where your money goes. Before you know it, you'll have less debt and more savings than you ever thought possible.

4. LOVE.

The self-determination that grows from, even depends on, self-love. Only by believing ourselves worthy of life and love regardless of where we come from or what we look like can we calmly and wisely make the choices and take the actions that will bring us deep and lasting benefit.

5. COMMUNITY.

The group you see yourself as part of, which you constitute by choice. Being a member of the same race or gender or ethnicity or neighborhood or sexual preference as other people doesn't *make* you part of the same community; only by embracing a group and its values do we *make* community ours.

6. SPIRITUALITY.

This doesn't mean going to church, though there's nothing wrong with finding spiritual expression in formal worship. Spirituality as a vital virtue means connecting with the power or energy beyond ourselves that infuses the best in us to do our best in *any* situation. It's not just that every one of the other vital virtues can be grounded in spirituality—they *must* be!

7. CREATIVITY.

We constantly hear people talk about the "creative impulse," but the key virtue of creativity is much more than that—it's the honoring and channeling of that impulse in our daily lives. We don't have to sculpt or write symphonies or novels to be creative (not that we shouldn't do those things if we can!); we can buy a disposable camera and take pictures of anything that catches our eye, bring in flowers from outside, put pebbles in a bowl of water, press leaves in a frame, sing to someone we love, dance around the living room . . . As soon as we start channeling our creative impulse, we'll find it flowing through almost everything we do.

Living Virtue 1

Calling

This is the true joy in life, the being used for a purpose recognized by yourself as a mighty one . . . the being a force of Nature instead of a feverish selfish little clod of ailments and grievances complaining that the world will not devote itself to making you happy.

GEORGE BERNARD SHAW,
from *Man and Superman*

As a child, I once listened to a minister tell a story about how he had been called by God to preach. He cried as he told us about being healed of his addictions and "carnal" living and compelled to worship God and serve the community. Wow, I thought, to be handpicked by God to do something special must be awesome.

Sitting on that cold, hard pew, I wondered, Did God only call preachers? Did He ever call regular folks like me? I wanted God to handpick me for something important, too. I wanted to feel special.

In the past we used to believe that "callings" were reserved for our religious leaders. A calling was generally understood as a commandment from God to do divine work, whether as a missionary, evangelist, or church head. The mystery of the calling made these powerful people seem larger than life, and they enjoyed respect and obedience from their followers.

Regular folks supposedly didn't get callings. They may have been faithful laborers in their churches and communities; they may have loved their jobs; they may have had hobbies that gave them intense pleasure. But these activities were seldom given the same respect and divine association as a calling.

Baby boomers changed all that. They introduced a new idea into our work ethic: All people, not just religious figures, are "called" to do something special. In true democratic fashion, we began to believe that everyone had a calling, not just a select few. This idea is both empowering and revolutionary. It's empowering because answering a calling brings meaning and satisfaction to our lives. And it's revolutionary because if we achieve a critical mass of folks committed to living their calling, society will change for the better.

What is calling? A calling is not just a job, although if you're lucky, it's what you do from nine to five. A calling is not just a career; it goes way beyond that. Calling is that seed of something big within that just won't let you be. It just grows and grows, seeking the sun of your right place in the world.

My definition is simple: *Calling is your divine assignment.* Our jobs may wear us out, but calling feeds the spirit. Our jobs pay the bills, but following a calling is the key to the treasure chest. Your calling is that thing you've spent your entire life loving and trying to do to the best of your ability. Each one of us has a calling, and I believe it comes from God. When you're living your calling, you are happiest and most fulfilled. Calling gives our lives meaning.

I don't have a scientific survey to back me, but my instincts tell me that most of us have not tapped into this powerful aspect of life. Why? Because calling is a mystery. Discovering our calling is not as simple as looking in the want ads for a job. If only it was! Mysteries take a bit more time and willingness to investigate, but if we keep our minds and hearts open, calling will slowly and beautifully reveal itself, unfolding like the petals of a flower over a lifetime.

To discover calling, we must search our souls, not once, not twice, but daily. It's a sweet obsession, this pursuit of calling. We must go within and listen to the Still Small Voice, even when the loud noises of daily survival threaten to distract us and throw us off course. We may not think we can afford the luxury of meditating on calling when the roof is leaking, the kid's got the flu, and back-to-back meetings have been scheduled for the rest of the day. Not only can we afford it, but we owe it to ourselves to explore our life's calling. Somehow, some way, we *must* find the time and the energy.

Of all the living virtues that challenge me every single day, calling is the one that, puzzle piece by puzzle piece, is finally *(thank God!)* falling into place. I hesitate to write these words because I don't want to give the impression that it's been an easy journey. It hasn't. Today I'm finally clear that my calling is to help others reach their true potential, but that knowledge did not come to me fully birthed. For so many years I wrestled with indecision, self-doubt, and clouded vision. All too often depression prevented me from seeing opportunities that were inviting me closer and closer to my calling. Countless times I've taken one step forward only to fall two, three, and four steps back.

As I search my memories, I realize that there was seldom a time when my calling was not beckoning me. Growing up in Mount Vernon, New York, I absorbed the lessons of giving that my parents provided just in living their daily lives. We were your typical working-class family. My dad was a truck driver whose route ran throughout upper New York State. My mom devoted much of her time to school and community activities.

Both my parents love to help people. That's when they're happiest. My dad would come home tired on the weekends, but still find time to spend with us and a foster kid we had taken in on weekends. Their earliest lessons in helping others planted a seed deep within me. Only time would reveal just what kind of special blossoming would occur. My parents taught me that life's not centered on me alone. Doing service work was an important part of my week, whether I tutored kids after school, participated in charity fund-raising events, or helped out at church. It mattered that I gave back. They believed that if you want to have a fulfilling life, you can't just sit on the sidelines. You've got to get involved.

It seemed only natural that when I got to college I'd major in ways to help people. I got my undergraduate degree in psychology and sociology from Brandeis University and a master's of science degree in social work from Columbia University. Fresh out of graduate school, I got a job at New York Hospital working with terminally ill, "at risk," and physically challenged patients. I didn't know exactly what I wanted to do, but figured this would be the best way for me to help.

I should have been in heaven. Here I was, actually working in my chosen field. How many people get to do that? But during the two years I was there, it became glaringly, painfully obvious that I'd made a big mistake. Instead of healing others, I was killing my own spirit. I couldn't separate myself emotionally from the pain and suffering of my patients. I took the job way too personally. Soon after accepting the job I began to realize that my work didn't make a difference. I was disturbed. I had spent so many years preparing for this, only to find that I wasn't effective.

There were so many things about the job and the hospital setting that bothered me. I'm a free spirit and very independent, but the job forced me into a relentless nine-to-five rut. I'm a creative thinker and a problem solver, and you just can't put those things on a schedule. Some of my best thinking is done late at night when I'm alone. All these compromises were actually molding me into a person I didn't want to be.

Today I know that I'm an entrepreneur at heart, but back then that knowledge hadn't blossomed within me yet. All I knew was that I was frustrated. I had creative ideas, but there was no place to plant them so they could take root and grow. Heaven forbid I make a suggestion or stand toe to toe with my supervisor. It's hard to buck bureaucratic regulations designed to break spirits, subdue creativity, and maintain control over the activities of employees.

To make matters even worse, I was barely making enough money to meet my basic needs.

I wanted the job to live up to all my fantasies, but talk about a square peg in a round hole! I just didn't fit in, and I was miserable. I had to admit to myself that I'd made a mistake about my choice of profession, and this depressed and confused me. Hadn't I studied the right courses in college? It never occurred to me to major in business or communications. Those weren't "helping" majors (or so I thought). Yet with my "correct" degrees and "ideal" hospital gig, I wasn't effectively helping anyone.

This was too deep. How many of us have misread the clues to our passions and interests? People who seek justice become lawyers, but can't find the justice in their profession. True healers leave medicine when after years of study they realize that treating the whole person does not mesh with the corporation's bottom line. I'm not knocking these professions; they weren't right for me. And as I travel and speak to more and more folks around the country, I realize that many people are making the same mistake I made—doing work that doesn't make them happy.

Have you ever worked a job that was so unbearable that just getting up in the morning was a chore? Every morning I'd wake up with the covers over my head. The alarm would ring, and I'd hit the snooze button five or six times before dragging myself out of the bed.

When you're not loving your work, your soul suffers a slow, lingering death. Sabrina, a young, professional woman, once worked in a situation she hated so much that it caused her almost a physical sense of pain. Her new boyfriend (now husband) Jerry says that on Fridays she would come home like a "comatose person," suffering from post-traumatic *work* syndrome. On Saturdays he'd watch her detox and relax from the week, but on Sundays at 11:00 P.M. she would shut down again, steeling herself to go back to work on Monday morning.

I remember feeling the same way. All those years I'd spent in school and in internships and what did I have to show for it? A job that drained me and made me feel stuck, which made me feel guilty on top of all my other depressing feelings. How could I hate working at a hospital? People were sick, and they needed help. My guilt was overwhelming. What I didn't understand is that although I'd realized a part of my calling, I hadn't yet seen the bigger picture. I wanted to serve, but I'd have to discover better uses for my time and creative energies. Sure, the hospital seemed like an ideal place to serve others, but I wasn't happy. Didn't I deserve to be happy? I asked myself constantly. Did I have to suffer to truly be of service?

I didn't have the answers to these questions, but at least I had begun to ask, and that was the beginning of change. The first glimmer of light was a little miracle that occurred during the end of my tenure at the hospital. The buzz going around the nurses' station was that the great jazz legend Miles Davis was a patient on another floor. I had heard that Miles wasn't very friendly, but he was such a genius that I decided to take a chance and introduce myself.

Nervous as hell, I walked into his room and said, "Hi, my name is Terrie." He answered, "Hey, how're you doin'?" in that famous, raspy voice of his, and our long-term friendship was born. I'd always had friends in the arts—they may not have been famous, but they were cool, creative, high-energy people. So to me, Miles was surprisingly "normal." Meeting Miles was like meeting an old friend, and I was delighted to find that, in his own way, he felt the same way about me.

During his stay, I'd often visit him on my breaks. One time I came in just to shoot the breeze, but something about my demeanor or aura must have disturbed him because he took one look at me and told me to sit down. He stared at me for some long moments.

"What's the matter?" I finally asked.

"Be quiet," he said. He was thinking something through, so I held my tongue. Eventually he spoke. "We've talked music and life, so I know you good enough. But what I can't figure out is why you're wasting your time here." He opened his hands. It was a small gesture, but I knew he held the entire hospital in those beautiful ebony hands. "What the hell you working here for?"

I was taken aback and a little offended. "I'm trying to help people work through their problems."

He just stared at me. When Miles stared at you, it was like having a laser beam rip right through you. A very uncomfortable feeling.

"Cut the bullshit, Terrie. You're being wasted here. What is it that you really want to do?"

I opened my mouth, but no words came out. Miles had left me speechless. I wasn't sure what I wanted to do, but it sure as hell wasn't what I was doing.

He broke the silence. "I need somebody to take care of the media and things, you know? Think about it." Then he closed his eyes and softly tapped his fingers to a tune only he could hear.

I walked out of his room stunned, but strangely energized. Miles's words had shocked me out of my lethargy. What did I want to do? For the first time in a long time I actually felt a smile creep across my face. I wasn't out of the woods yet, but I had a question that I could work with: *What do I want to do with my life?*

Allowing myself to even ask the question helped me to consciously admit that I was not in my right place and that I needed to make some changes.

It's not an overstatement to say that Miles changed my life, and although I wouldn't take him up on his offer until a couple of years later, our discussion focused my thoughts in a different direction.

I wanted to do my own thing. I wanted to make my mark on the world like Miles had. I thought I'd found my thing at the hospital, but now that I discovered what a bad fit the job was I had to start over again at square one.

Sometime after that fateful conversation with Miles, I was reading the *New York Amsterdam News*, one of the country's most important Black newspapers. I happened to notice a small article about a public relations course being given at the YWCA on Lexington Avenue in New York City. If it hadn't been for my conversation with Miles, I might not have paid any attention to the article. I didn't know anyone in public relations; I'd never really heard about it. But I figured, why not give the course a try? What I didn't know was that the course would be yet one more step toward living my calling.

I can't say that the course was exciting, but it did whet my appetite. There was something about this PR thing that was interesting. I enrolled in another course and met many new and interesting people. I liked the concept of creatively packaging an idea to raise public awareness and influence lots of people. Early on I could see the potential for making myself useful. In fact, I began to apply what I was learning to help promote my artist friends. I'd create flyers, write press releases, organize events, develop mailing lists, and stuff envelopes. It was PR 101, and I was learning.

The idea of leaving behind job security and benefits was scary, but life was showing me that I had a decision to make: either I continued to work a job that drained me or I stepped out on faith. Leaving the hospital would probably mean sacrificing financially for a while, but I decided to go with my heart anyway and take the plunge—it was now or never! I quit my secure hospital job, and I've never looked back.

I took a series of jobs, and at each one I learned as much as I could. It took years of trying to find my way, but I learned PR and, most important. I learned about myself and my calling. Today I say that it was always in my blood to start my own company. It was definitely a key part of my calling. And after fourteen years of running my own agency, I've discovered that calling isn't a static thing. A job may be a dead end, but calling continues to grow—which means that you have to grow, too.

Getting the agency up and running was only one goal. Within the past couple of years I've had to rethink my personal calling and company mission. I've pruned away some old ideas and old ways of doing things so that new fruit can grow.

The search for your calling is an evolutionary process. At the heart of calling is the ability to understand, with increasing clarity, your place in the world. All the sacrifices and challenges begin to make sense.

Don't feel bad if you're still unsure about what you're supposed to be doing. Give it time. It took years for me to get to this point, and it ain't over yet. But through it all, being clear about my calling and making the commitment to pursue it full thrust keeps me centered, even when things get crazy.

Over the years I've noticed that people who are not living their calling—who are just hanging out and living for the moment—are empty inside. They hop from one activity to the next without any real sense of direction or purpose. Living your calling balances and gives focus to the many aspects of your life. It is the one thing that gives your life a sense of purpose, meaning, and direction.

In this section on calling I've selected what I believe are some of the most important aspects of discovering and fulfilling your divine assignment. As you read through the ideas and do the activities and journal exercises over the next seven weeks, you'll begin to discover your own calling. We'll be looking at how your innate talents often provide a clue to calling. You'll be encouraged to make a commitment to pursue your calling, and I'll share solid strategies to deal with the twists and turns that are bound to occur (so expect them).

I want to do for others what Miles and many others have done and continue to do for me. I'd like you to use this book to help you achieve your full potential.

Together let's harvest the joy that comes with finding our calling.

WEEK 1
A Calling of Your Own

No individual has any right to come into the
world and go out of it without leaving behind him
distinct and legitimate reasons for having passed
through it.

GEORGE WASHINGTON CARVER,
May 25, 1915

When I discover who I am, I'll be free.

RALPH ELLISON

I explore calling first because it is so important to healthy, balanced living. It is fundamental. Calling is the reason we're here on the planet.

Searching for, discovering, and living your calling is not a fad or trend. It is a lifelong commitment. No one but you can answer the question, *What's my purpose in life?* I can help guide you, but ultimately you must discover calling for yourself—and live it your own way. No one else can do this for you. Once you begin to listen to yourself—your inner voice, even your body—you'll start to receive guidance through your feelings and thoughts. There will be times when you'll feel utterly compelled to take action—and other times when the silence tells you to be still and wait.

Whether you knew what your calling was when you were a kid, or if, as an adult, you still don't have a clue, that's fine. Whenever you come to this lifelong journey is okay. No matter at what point in your life you pick up the search, you'll be right on time. It's never too late, or too early, to question your reason for being.

Maybe you think only special people are blessed by God with a calling—a unique, personal, divine assignment. I hope you know you are special—and one of a kind. I'm here to remind you that *you are*. And when you find your calling (or when your calling finds you), you'll begin to connect to the joy inherent in your creative potential. Not knowing what we're supposed to be doing can make us feel depressed and even worthless. When you commit to the journey, you begin to feel better about yourself.

Calling is our intimate connection to the divine, and we desperately need that connection. Without it we're lost. When we're simply living for the moment with no sense of destiny, we become spiritually ill and feel empty in our souls. Attempting to fill the empty spaces with addictive and self-defeating behaviors hurts us and wastes precious time. People who are disconnected from the divine and their destiny are not happy, bottom line. And they look for quick-fix ways to escape their misery and pain.

Earlier this year a friend told me that she wanted to commit suicide. After dealing with the shock of it, her statement made me think about her life and where it might have gone wrong.

How does a life get so out of balance? While suicide should never be an option, I do understand being so miserable that you don't want to be here anymore. In my darkest days I've had my doubts about life, too. This is not a popular topic of conversation at cocktail parties, but the truth is, normal, intelligent people often feel like checking out. It's too bad that in our society we don't feel comfortable talking about the things that matter the most. So many of us are walking around in silence and in pain.

Listening to my friend I realized that while she had a career, she had no calling. She was completely disconnected from any sense of destiny or the divine. She hated what she was doing, and since she had been doing it for years she felt trapped. Misery can become such a habit that you don't know how to shake yourself free.

In my travels around the country, I run into many people like my friend. They may not be contemplating anything as drastic as suicide, but they're still in pain. After a speech or workshop, without fail someone will come up to me, looking for an answer about his or her life. I tell these folks that while they too are called to do something special, I can't tell them what that something is. They must seek it out for themselves. Be wary of individuals bearing advice about your divine assignment. At the very least they may lead you down the wrong path, and at worst they may have a hidden agenda of power and control. Learning to listen to your own Still Small Voice is the safest, most reliable approach to discovering your divine assignment.

Now, there are probably many inner voices vying for your attention. Sorting through them all to hear the voice of your truth is challenging and requires that you first hush your mind. Go off by yourself. Sitting in nature is great, but sometimes all you may have is your car and a long commute to work. That's fine. Being alone and quiet is all that matters.

Next, start asking yourself questions. They can be simple questions: *What do I enjoy? Who do I like to spend time with? What did I want to be when I grew up? Did I choose my present job or did I "fall" into it?* Some people "hear" answers right away, while others receive them over time. By hear, I also mean feel, sense, intuit. How you receive the answer will be unique to you. I often just ask the question and then leave it alone and go on about my business, trusting that I'll get my answer in good time.

Trust is an extremely important component of this exercise. You'll receive answers to your questions, but you've got to trust in what you're hearing. Without trust, you won't feel confident to take steps and make changes. Maybe you're called to be a housewife and mother. Maybe on your days off from work you get a charge out of volunteering at the shelter or soup kitchen. Maybe your calling is painting and your career is teaching children art. We all have a calling, but whether or not we realize our calling depends on how willing we are to honor our heart's desire, and how courageous we are when faced with the need for change.

A calling is usually all-consuming, almost obsessive—and that can be frightening and overwhelming. We want to believe we're running our lives and not the other way around. You may wonder if you really want something taking over your life so completely. Friends and family may accuse you of being a workaholic. They may not agree with what your heart is telling you to do. Do you even have a choice about accepting your calling? And what if your true calling isn't what you want to do? What if you don't like the answer you've received?

My writer friend Donna Marie once prayed to know what her calling was, but she worried that the answer might be something she wasn't prepared to do. It turned out that her passion was writing, but she was afraid that it seemed frivolous, irresponsible. Since she couldn't imagine supporting herself as a writer, she did the "sensible" thing and worked as a secretary for many years. But the thing about your calling is this: While you're rationalizing and doing what you're "supposed" to be doing, your soul is constantly whispering, *Do this.* Your calling will not let you go. Donna finally listened to that inner voice and decided to write full time. Her passion paid off, and she's been supporting herself as a writer ever since.

Let yourself dream and believe that your dreams will come true. Children are experts at fantasy games, but as we grow older, we forget how to dream. Yet our daydreams hold important clues to our calling.

I double-dare you to dream your different and amazing dreams. Sometimes we're afraid to look at our dreams because we don't believe they can be done. Too big! But our dreams contain the essence of who we are, if only we have the courage to embrace them. Low self-esteem and difficult life experiences often keep us from looking at the person in the mirror. Well, it's time to start looking at yourself. As the saying goes, "Feel the fear and do it anyway." Face it and embrace it. Be grateful for fear, because once you get past it, you'll be strong and ready to face any challenge.

Search your daydreams. I often ask folks, "What's your fantasy gig?" The answer to that question may lie in your daydreams. Acknowledge your dreams because it's your soul talking. Say yes to the desires of your heart. Begin to believe in the "impossible." I don't care what your mother, father, teacher, or counselor told you as a child. You can achieve your dreams, and chances are, you've been dreaming about your calling all along.

J ournal time

I have a crazy schedule, but one of the things I try to do regularly is write in my journal, even if it's only for a few minutes a day or every other day. If I'm on a plane or in a hotel room somewhere, I'll take out my journal and gather my thoughts. I get a lot of insights by putting pen to paper and regularly reviewing what I've written.

Over the next few weeks and months, I'll be encouraging you to do the same. The following questions should get you thinking about your calling: Write down everything that comes to mind and be honest. No one has to read your journal but you, and it doesn't have to be an everyday thing.

The first step to discovering your calling is being able to answer the questions: *Who am I? What are my likes and dislikes?* Know yourself and you will begin to know your calling.

What's been keeping you from living your calling? Is it that you just don't know what it is? Or have you been distracted by day-to-day survival? Do you think that you're not special enough, important enough, interesting enough, or smart enough to have a calling? Are you afraid of the commitment? Do you have "too many" interests, talents, and abilities to know what your calling is? Are you all over the place—like me sometimes?

Some of you may be living your calling already and not know it. Take the time to think about what you've spent your entire life loving and doing well. Now write down in one simple sentence what your calling is. Keep this statement short and sweet and let it be your daily guide in seeking opportunities and developing positive relationships. Tape it to the refrigerator and the inside of your wallet—places you know you'll look at every day.

Part of pursuing your calling is doing your own homework! If you're not clear on your calling, if you have many interests and can't pick one, or if you're feeling burned out about your job and need a change, take heart. The following are things you can begin to do, right here and now.

1. Reflect on your childhood—many clues to your calling are there. Check out old photos and childhood treasures to stir memories. When we were children, we felt free to imagine our lives just as we wanted them to be. Then parental desires and responsibilities of adulthood crowded out our fantasies. Remember the pretend games you used to play with your friends and how much fun it was imagining yourselves as doctors, teachers, actors, and singers? I'm no Patti LaBelle, but that didn't matter. Turning my hairbrush into a microphone, I'd imagine myself onstage, singing to thousands of my adoring fans. I also used to practice signing my autograph. Little did I know that I'd end up signing as many as four hundred books in one sitting!

2. How does your childhood dream match what you're doing now? If it doesn't match, jot down the reasons why you're not living your childhood dream. What life circumstances and obstacles prevented you from achieving your dream?

3. If you could live that childhood dream today (and you can), describe how your life would change. Would you have the same friends? Live in the same neighborhood? What kind of work would you be doing? What would a typical day in your life be like?

4. According to Master Prophet Tomblin, we should always understand why certain people are in our lives—what their purpose is. Who are your friends? Do you have quality friendships, or do they leave you feeling empty? What do you generally talk about? What do you do together? The company that you keep says a lot about where you've been, who you are today, and where you're headed in the future. If you cannot figure out why a person is in your life, then he or she doesn't need to be around.

5. Assess your physical environment—your home and community. Dr. Myles Monroe says that if you place a seed on a sheet of plastic, twenty years later it will still be a seed. Why? Because it's in the wrong environment. It needs to be planted in fertile soil. Is your environment fertile enough to grow you? Does it stimulate your creativity? Do you feel safe, or are you constantly looking over your shoulder? Is there constant noise? Does your environment help connect you to or distract you from pursuing and living your calling?

6. Pray. Think of prayer as a daily call to God. There are many religious formulas for the "right" way to pray. In his best-selling book *The Prayer of Jabez*, Bruce Wilkinson writes about a guy who wanted more out of life. Jabez asked God to bless him, to "enlarge his territory," to keep His hand on him, and to keep evil away from him (1 Chronicles 4:10). If you don't know how to pray, study the prayers of wise men and women throughout the ages. (I'm working on this one, too.) I like Marianne Williamson's and Iyanla Vanzant's prayers because they speak from the heart. But you can explore contemporary inspirational writers and find one whose prayers resonate with you. Be real with God, and your prayers will be heard, and the journey to self-discovery will begin.

7. Keep a daydream journal. Daydreams may hold important clues to your calling. Whether awake or asleep, your mind never stops. This week, whenever you think about it, take a deep breath and consciously listen to what you're saying to yourself. Go into your secret place, and dream your dreams. Dealing with

your dreams is a positive act. It's like saying, *This is me, weird, wonderful, and wise.* There's no room for being cool when you're dreaming. Leave that at the door. Write your dreams down for a week and see what they're telling you.

WEEK 2
Gifts, Talents, and Skills

Find your true purpose; live it, do it, give it and
be it. You will benefit others and the by-product
is a richer, rewarding life. If you are obedient to
your natural gifts and talents, you will never get
tired of doing it. This doesn't mean it won't be
difficult or challenging, but you will be successful and fulfilled because you are finally aligned
with your purpose.

AFRICAN PROVERB
shared by KOMEKA FREEMAN

Scripture says that the kingdom of heaven is within us, and I believe that this inner kingdom contains everything we need to live
our calling to the utmost. Babies may not be born with parenting
instructions, but they do come fully equipped with the ability to
think, create, envision, make decisions, and take action.

Now if that's all we had, it would be enough to live rich, full
lives. But believe it or not, we have more, much more. We have
incredible mind power that we haven't even begun to tap into.
According to the experts, we only use 10 percent of our brain capacity, which leaves an unimaginably large universe of mysteries
residing within us, virtually untapped. If we put our minds to it,
what could we do with that dormant 90 percent of our mind
power?

You'll discover that living your calling will bring out your special genius, and who knows? You may even begin to access amazing mind powers you didn't even know you had. Meeting the

demands of our divine assignment opens us up to the vast reservoir of spiritual, creative, and intellectual gifts that make up our inner kingdoms. We each have special God-given abilities that, to paraphrase Chef Emeril Lagasse, "kick us up a notch."

Before going further, let me define my terms. Often we use the words *gifts*, *talents*, and *skills* interchangeably, but as we explore calling, I'll be using the terms very specifically.

Gifts really refers to spiritual gifts. God gives them to us unconditionally, simply because He loves us. Wrapped in our souls, spiritual gifts come in handy, during good times and bad. Some examples of spiritual gifts are strong faith, the ability to forgive, courage, a generous spirit, creativity, and compassion. We usually have one spiritual gift (sometimes more if our project is really big) that defines our personalities. Think of Ghandi's compassion, Bill Gates's vision, and Rosa Parks's courage. Although these gifts can be used for good or evil (which is why, say, a Hitler was so successful), of course I encourage you to use yours for good. Why? Because the seeds you plant will certainly grow. Karma brings us face-to-face with the mistakes we make, and we will repeat the lessons until we get them right.

Talents are abilities that we come by naturally. If you can sing, cook, dance, speak many languages, write, play the piano, fix a car, or organize a bake sale with one hand tied behind your back, then these are your talents. If we work to develop our talents, we master them. Venus and Serena Williams, Michael Jordan, Whitney Houston, and astronaut Mae Jamison come to mind.

Last but not least, *skills* are the abilities that are developed through training and hard work. The difference between talents and skills is that talents come naturally while skills take an extra effort to master because they *do not* come naturally. We often think about skills in the context of our jobs, but we also use skills in every other area of our lives. For example, we were not born knowing how to drive. We had to take lessons, and then we practiced to master the driving skill. Some folks have a natural talent for parenting, but many others must learn how to raise healthy, happy, well-adjusted kids. Some people have a talent for managing money, but others have to learn how to save and invest for the future.

This inner tool kit of spiritual gifts, natural talents, and developed skills is what you will use to pursue your calling. The greater your mastery, the greater your confidence and your ability to live your calling.

Journal time

Do you know what your special abilities are? If not, let's find out together. This week we're going to do an inventory of our gifts, talents, and skills. First, in your journal, explore the following ideas with as many examples as you can think of and how you feel about your special abilities:

- Make a list of your abilities. Write down at least ten things (from household chores to inventions) and rank them according to importance to you and practical use in the world. What do you like doing best, and how practical a skill is it?
- What do people constantly ask you to help them with? This question is very important. Sometimes a thing comes so easily to us that we're often pressed into service. If we do not value our natural talents or if we take them for granted, others will, too.
- What school subjects were easy for you? Which ones were pure torture?
- What skills would you like to develop? Why would you like to develop them? Why haven't you developed them so far? How will you go about developing them? When will you begin training?
- What type of environment nourishes you best? Rosebushes planted in sand will not grow. Do you like a structured envi-

ronment? Do you like to be around innovative, creative thinkers? Do you like working at a desk, or would you prefer to be out and about?

Now that you've got a big picture of your strengths and weaknesses, let's go deeper by exploring your spiritual gifts, natural talents, and skills.

• *Spiritual gifts.* Learning how to identify a spiritual gift can sometimes be a challenge if you're focusing on yourself. We're too close. So take a few moments this week to analyze the people you know. Think about their personalities and try to pinpoint what qualities stand out. Ask your friends to do the same for you, because often we don't see ourselves clearly. This exercise is not about giving criticism—just the opposite. Try to identify positive qualities. Meditate on what your friends tell you. Do you think they're right or not? Ultimately, you'll have to know for yourself. When we have an awareness of our spiritual gifts, we can begin to consciously (rather than unconsciously) use them as we pursue and live our calling.

• *Natural talents.* As a child, were your natural talents and interests allowed to flourish, or were you forced to pursue a different path that had nothing to do with who you are inside? List as many abilities that you can think of that come naturally to you. Which natural talents have you spent time developing? Which ones lie dormant within you? Do you want to develop them? If so, when and how?

• *Developed skills.* If you're still not clear on exactly what your calling is, you may not know what skills to develop. Still, it'll be helpful to list out the skills that you've already spent time and money developing. Jot down the skills you use on the job, at home, at church, and at play. Also, brush off your résumé and take a good, hard look at it. Most are traditional and boring. They give no sense of the individual. Although it may not be appropriate to get too personal on a résumé you'll be sending out to companies, you may want to prepare one for your own use to help you think about your calling. This week, prepare an amplified professional and personal résumé. Look at each job and list, in exacting detail, the skills you needed to do the job well. As you begin to pursue your life calling, you'll be amazed to discover how the skills you've listed in this inventory are just the ones you'll need to accomplish your goals and objectives. You were being prepared without even realizing it.

WEEK 3
Make a Commitment

回

You can begin to create your work by staying your
course, by sticking with things you don't particularly like, and by practicing a mental discipline of
focusing on, and actively preparing for, what you
want.

MARSHA SINETAR,
To Build the Life You Want,
Create the Work You Love

Confession time. Sistahs constantly complain about men not
being able to commit to relationships. I challenge you to look at
your own life. How committed have you been to your own
growth and development? The hardest part of realizing your
dream is committing to yourself.

Many of us have a "once in a while" kind of style. Once in a
while you go to church (*although He is always in my heart*—that
used to be me). Once in a while you call an elderly aunt or uncle.
Once in a while you check on a friend who's been seriously
stressed or even ill. Once in a while you get to work on time. Although we mean well, we just don't get it together to follow
through.

The first step on the road to peace and joy is to commit to living your calling each and every day. You can't run and you can't
hide. God has given you this life purpose and it's time to decide,
here and now. Are you going to live up to the promise of your life
or are you going to keep doing what you've been doing and getting what you've been getting?

It's time to commit to living your calling. Even if you don't know what that calling is, at the very least commit to the search. When you make a decision to commit, it's like a steel door slams shut on the past. Often you can't see the doors in front of you until you close the doors behind you. You can't go back. That's what commitment is all about.

In *The Spirit of Intimacy*, Sobonfu Somé adds an even deeper dimension to the idea of commitment. She says, "People think that when they say yes once, it means yes forever. But in the indigenous context, no. That's why you have to constantly renew your vows. . . ." What a great idea! Let's not just stop at the commitment to pursue and live our calling, but every few months or so, take the time to reflect, fine tune, and plan for the future. Renew your vow to live your calling.

So here's the process:

1. Seek your calling and know that although the journey may be difficult, you shall find it.
2. Every day take one step to doing what you say you want to do. That's living your calling.
3. Every week, make sure you're not merely ticking off obligations but are pursuing the things that make you happy.

Check this out: Every day this week, repeat (or think about) the following affirmation with joy and energy:

I fully commit to living my calling.
I am entitled to pursue my passions and live my dreams.

I used to hate it when people would tell me to repeat affirmations or when the preacher would say, "Repeat after me." I always thought it was hokey. But it really does work. Saying it makes you conscious, gives voice to dreams, breathes life and meaning and direction to the words, and if you say it is, it is.

I'd also like you to think about what you can do this week to demonstrate your commitment to yourself. Take a tiny step to show yourself that you really mean it this time. Call the office of admissions at that college you've wanted to attend. If you're a mom with young children, find a baby-sitter and take three or four hours a week to pursue your passion to start a home business, for example, or simply to do more thinking about your calling. If your kids are older, involve them in your quest for a calling. They could do basic research for you—and sharing the pursuit of your dreams is a great model for them. Request information from the Small Business Association if you know you're supposed to be starting your own business. Talk to your boss about the possibility of a more flexible schedule. More time away from the office just might be the thing you need to start living your calling more fully.

*J*ournal time

Commitment starts with the self. If you don't commit to yourself, you cannot commit to others. Calling is the first important commitment you'll make to yourself. As you stay true to the commitment to seek your calling (in sickness and in health, for richer or poorer), you'll become more disciplined. You'll find that you'll be able to endure any challenge. Self-esteem will become more than nice words and a nice sentiment. Commitment will transform self-esteem into self-acceptance, strength, and self-love.

This week let's write down our commitment to stay on the path of discovering calling. Wedding vows are excellent examples we can use to help us understand the importance of the promise we'll be making to ourselves.

Have fun with this exercise. Make it as flowery or as solemn as you'd like *("I, Terrie, do solemnly swear to ask for what I deserve")*. Write your ceremony as a poem or a short story—however you want to do it. Here are some thoughts to get you started:

- What does commitment mean to you?
- Why is making this commitment important to you?
- You know yourself best. What are some of the challenges in the past you've had with keeping promises to yourself? How do you plan to overcome them?
- How does making the commitment to pursue your unique calling make you feel inside?

WEEK 4
Power in Your Passion

When I stand before God at the end of my life, I would hope that I would not have a single bit of talent left and could say, "I used everything you gave me."

ERMA BOMBECK

What is loved will survive.

ALICE WALKER

I'm fortunate to work with women and men who seem to have bottomless energy. From politicians to celebrities, I'm surrounded by driven and motivated people who spend their lives accomplishing important things. Unfortunately, I don't always feel energetic, positive, and optimistic. I have days when I feel physically tired, or spiritually and emotionally burned out. For many of us, such feelings can last weeks, even years. It's taken me a long time, but I've finally recognized that I'm most drained when I lose touch with my sense of personal power. In other words, when I've lost sight of my passion. Much of our self-confidence comes from tapping into our passion and harnessing all that energy. And one of the truest expressions of that passion should be our calling.

Passion is not a cheap thrill, or an easy fix like sex or drugs. It's not even the intense ups and downs of an early romance. Passion means attempting to express and realize our heart's goals through the everyday practices of our life. Passion is the combination of love, hope, and compassion we bring to our thoughts and actions.

It is the cornerstone of a meaningful life. I talk about passion in this chapter because our calling is the lived expression of our passion in daily work. It can sustain and nurture us in both the most rewarding and the most difficult of times. When we realize the power of our passion, we realize that happiness alone is not our goal. Our goal is to live the fullest life possible, to harness our potential and use it to enrich the world.

If your life's work is feeling kind of flat and uninspired, it could be because you haven't found the passion in what you do. For years, my friend Diane worked as an editor at a publishing house. She'd loved books ever since she was a little girl, and she figured building a career where she got paid for reading would fill her up, no problem. But after a few years, she got to feeling bored and tired with her daily routine. Editing books just wasn't firing her up the same way reading them once had. So when a girlfriend asked her to join in on a weekend writing workshop, Diane figured it might help reawaken her love of words.

As soon as she got to work with that pen and piece of paper, Diane realized what had been missing in her job and in her life. She just didn't love editing books; she loved creating them. Her calling was to be a writer. Just the discovery was enough to build a fire under her again. She kept on at her publishing job, but she also started working on her own novel on the weekends. It took a whole year to complete, but in that year Diane not only became a writer, but also found her passion again. She was able to tap into that fire inside her heart. These days she's a successful author and a teacher, showing others how to tap into their passions and express them on the page. Her life still revolves around books and reading, only now it revolves around passion as well. She feels fulfilled, but even more important, she feels powerful. She knows she's leaving her mark on the world.

J ournal time

Tapping the power of your passion is a three-step process: Identify energy drains, rejuvenate your spirit, and claim your power. First, let's investigate ways in which we've been turning off passion and power in our lives.

Let's start with the basics. The biggest energy drain for many of us is poor nutrition. Start using your journal to record what you eat and how it affects your mood. Write down what time of day your energy levels rise and dip. Based on what you learn, try starting to add some foods that give you long-term energy, like fruits and nuts. See what happens if you eliminate those quick fixes, like coffee and chocolate bars, that ultimately make you crash.

Are you exercising, sleeping eight hours, and taking care of yourself? If the answer is no, start journaling about it. Write down the reasons you're not getting to bed by 11:00 P.M. Start making some small changes, things like turning off the TV or not bringing home so much work. Now try the same thing with exercise. Write down some of the reasons you're not doing it and come up with ways to motivate yourself. Find an exercise buddy or start walking to work.

Also, take a look at the key relationships in your life. The people we spend our time with can have a serious impact on how we feel. Who makes you energetic and excited? Who validates your ideas and projects, and who doesn't? Start cutting back on time with folks who bring negative energy to the table, even if it means spending more time alone. The more you validate yourself, the more you'll feel empowered to make changes and pursue your goals.

Now that we've identified some energy drains, let's start rejuvenating our spirits:

Two are better than one. Modern life can feel a little overwhelming when you've got to face everything on your own. Instead, make an effort to pool resources with your friends. Share baby-sitting time, share vacation homes, take turns cooking dinner at each other's homes, find ways to increase your bounty—and your energy level—by working with the positive people in your life.

Taking a vacation can be the quickest way to jump-start our spirits. Be creative here. A vacation isn't just a week away from work. It can mean all sorts of things. Maybe you need a girlfriend holiday, where you and your best friend spend a few days relaxing, talking, and window-shopping away from your hometown. Maybe you need to get away for a few weekends in a row. Is there a cute bed-and-breakfast near your home, or a campground you can use in the summer? Or perhaps you and your husband could exchange houses or apartments with good friends in another city. Home swapping cuts down on hotel bills and makes weekends away much more affordable.

Now claim your power!

As your energy starts to increase, make one commitment to yourself, and stick to it! If you commit to searching for a new job, don't put it off any longer. Get out those résumés, call up those contacts, and buy a new interview suit. Whatever your commitment is, make a pledge to yourself that you will pursue it for three months no matter what else arises to distract you.

Also, make a point of taking the time to visualize your goals for five minutes every day. See if they don't seem more realistic and accessible after two weeks. Surrender to the guidance of the voice within. Trust it and take action. As Toni Morrison says, "If you surrender to the wind, you can ride it." This is the truest path toward finding the passion in your life.

WEEK 5
Twists and Turns

No one said it was going to be easy.
ANONYMOUS

Life happens, even when you're living your calling. You lose your job. A loved one leaves or dies. New job opportunities cross your path. Just when you thought you had it all figured out, the universe throws you a curveball. These challenges are so difficult to deal with because they are impossible to predict and therefore beyond our control.

Why is it that so few things go according to our plans? We eventually get to where we want to go, but what an adventure, with all the twists and turns along the way! My partner and friend Xavier reminds me that the path is already ordained—it's written, even the curves—and it's taking you to exactly where you're supposed to be. Know to expect the challenges so that you are prepared. This thought helps me get through the tough times.

One thing I've learned all too well is that the best-laid plans often change. Nature has many lessons to teach in this regard. When the warmth of spring arrives after a cold and difficult winter, the first thing many folks want to do is reacquaint themselves with their gardens. It's spring, and it's tulip time. So clean up the flower beds, then wait with eager anticipation for those green shoots to grow and beautifully colored heads to bloom. They make your lawn so pretty, and they make you feel good. Having something living in your yard is a good barometer for how you are caring for yourself.

But then, guess what happens? If you live up North like I do, a winter storm happens and freezes out your garden. If only you had waited. But how were you supposed to know what the crazy weather would do? You're so worried about your young plants.

What you don't know is that those tulips are tougher than you think. As soon as the cold front passes and the sun comes out to warm you and the ground, those strong shoots will probably resume their upward stretch.

Tulips are strong, but you're even stronger. Yes, life throws you curves after you've laid down your plans, but you can handle this. Say to yourself the phrase that gets tulips through the worst flash frosts: *This too shall pass.*

It helps to let go of the need to control all things and just accept the fact that life is full of twists and turns. Maybe the surprises are tests to see how much you want a certain thing. Maybe they're designed to make you stronger. One thing's for sure, no weakling tulips will be growing after a surprise spring frost. They will be strong and they will be beautiful. Just like you.

Still, we're emotional beings and a curveball can make us depressed, especially if a lot of work went into our plans. You might cry (which, by the way, is a good release). But try not to stay down. It can be too hard to climb out of depression. Learn from the tulips. I imagine those little guys saying among themselves, "Be still. Frost coming. No more growing until it passes." They huddle together, keep warm as best they can, and they wait. When the sun comes back out, they know exactly what to do. They continue their upward growth.

When things get really crazy, sometimes you need to just stop a moment and regroup. Sometimes it's best to do nothing at all. Sometimes your inner wisdom will tell you, "You're going down the wrong road. Back up and start over again."

The calling path is seldom a straight one, so just know that the twists and turns are coming and that they have a purpose. Pastor Rick Godwin says, "Adversity is the breakfast of champions. You want to eat those challenges like nutritional supplements. You will weather the storms if you recognize that they will come and

---

if you have built your house on a rock instead of sand. After the storm, you will be still standing."

When all my personal and professional projects seem to need attention at once, I've found it helpful to cultivate an attitude that helps me go with the flow. I can't always control what happens in my life, but I can control my attitude. "Attitude stands as the one area of your life where you are in complete and total control," says Dr. Arthur Caliandro, author of *Simple Steps: Ten Things You Can Do to Create an Exceptional Life*. Especially in team projects in which relying on one another is key, you can't always control how others will perform. You can only do your thing to the best of your ability. I've also learned that if the project is calling-related, somehow, some way, the work will get done.

Expect the twists and turns, the disciplining, the pruning. Allow room for variation in your plan. Let's say your calling is to be a writer, and you've spent months writing the Great American Novel. You've sent it out to sixteen agents and editors—and you've gotten sixteen rejection slips. "But my calling is to write," you say. How could this happen?

The very first *Chicken Soup for the Soul* was rejected forty-eight times, but today it is a phenomenal success, a multimillion-dollar industry. They've got chicken soup for everything! Let their success be a lesson to us all: Never give up. Draw inspiration from others and how they went through the fire.

Living your calling will be an adventure, but not necessarily an easy ride. Think of the wildest and craziest roller coaster and you have the idea. So why would any of us want to live our calling if it's all about ups and downs?

While there will be times when things won't go as smoothly as you'd like, there will be more times when everything's right with your world. Mostly calling is a lot of fun. It's satisfying, like a good meal or good sex. When you're working on your divine assignment, you get into a creative zone and you're happy. There's a feeling of positive energy and serenity all at once. You're calm, centered, and excited about the work you're doing. And when it's all done at the end of the day, you feel a tremendous sense of accomplishment.

If you believe you've found your calling, dealing with the rejected manuscript, the failed audition, the job interview that almost happened can be tough. But you must keep trying. You cannot quit. You could be five minutes away from your miracle! Everything is just as it should be—I promise!

When you've been disappointed, it may be tempting to think, *Failure.* I've experienced many disappointments in my personal and professional life, and every time I have to remind myself not to beat myself up. We make mistakes and things often don't work out the way we'd hoped. Don't let disappointments undermine your self-worth. From this moment forward, throw that word *failure* out of your vocabulary! It's simply, *Back to the drawing board.* So things didn't work out the way you planned. Learn from what went wrong and go from there. Bounce ideas off mentors and friends. Take a break, take a vacation. Sometimes you need to just get away, and when you come back, you'll tackle the challenge with a fresh perspective. You've only failed if you don't get up again.

There is another type of twist and turn on the calling path. Sometimes you have to get to your calling through the back door. You might work two or three major jobs to prepare you for your calling. Shirley Chisholm, that amazing sistah who had the nerve to run for president of the United States, was an educator first and then a community organizer before she became one of the finest stateswomen in Congress.

I know many successful folks who came from humble backgrounds. They put themselves through school by doing odd jobs, and then when they graduated, some were still seeking their rightful place. But they kept at it; they didn't stop. Looking back, they can see how all the twists and turns were simply puzzle pieces that were falling neatly into place (although it sure doesn't feel neat while you're going through it).

It is only in reflecting back on a life that you can clearly see how the twists and turns made sense in the greater scheme of things. The many connections and opportunities and crossroads and forks in the roads will all lead to the fulfillment of your calling.

---

*J*ournal time

From time to time things will happen that are beyond our control. When this occurs, it is important to manage your stress, because panic and depression can undermine your ability to perform your calling effectively. This week, let's practice stress relief.

- When you're in the middle of a crisis, do something physical to relieve stress. Take a long walk. Turn on your favorite music and dance. Pound a pillow.
- I'm a big fan of talking out problems, but that doesn't always help. Sometimes the best thing to do in the middle of a crisis is to take a time-out. This is one of those times when having a journal can be a godsend. Spend some time just writing about your feelings. Use the journal to vent and grieve. Once you let the feelings out in a safe place you can take a step back and figure out how your best self wants to address the issue. Whenever I have time to deal with my feelings in writing first I feel blessed. Once I've journaled on an issue I'm much more likely to facilitate a swift, just, and clear solution to whatever issue I'm presented with. Writing out my feelings often gives me the courage to talk about them. Bottling things up is a sure way to increase the drama of life's little curveballs—so purge those feelings in your journal and then address them in your life.
- Never, ever look at yourself as a failure. Talk about a dream killer! It helps me to read about others who have struggled

and overcome. Not only do they inspire me to keep moving forward on my path, they help me think through my own challenges and even provide strategies on how I might deal with them. Give it a try, and see how it works for you.

WEEK 6
Calling, Service, and Kindred Spirits

There is in every person something that waits
and listens for the sound of the genuine in herself. This is your assignment. . . . Can you find a
way to hear the sound of the genuine in yourself?
HOWARD THURMAN

Sharing the company of kindred spirits is one of life's pleasures
and can provide healing to your soul. Being able to talk, brainstorm, plan, set goals, share responsibilities, or just chill together
can make life truly worth living.

Kindred spirits are like soul-mate relationships. They differ
from ordinary friendships in that two people share the same attitudes, beliefs, and feelings. They come together for a short time
or a lifetime, and there is usually a specific work that binds them
together. Either they share the same calling, or their callings are
complementary and supportive of one another. Churches,
mosques, temples, workshops, art galleries, classrooms, the
workplace, and even health clubs are places where kindred spirits meet, form fellowships, and work together toward a common
cause.

Discovering and living your calling usually involves a dramatic
shift in values and beliefs. When your values change, your perception changes. And when your perception changes, your old
friends will begin to look different to you. While there will always be those friends who are in our lives just because we love
them, we may have to reconsider other relationships that may no
longer support us.

You may feel as if you're growing apart, and your friend may resent you for it. Or you may feel disappointment because your friend is not keeping up with you. This often happens as we fully embrace our calling. We change. This can be an extremely lonely time. Who can you call when you need to talk about a new idea? Victories and setbacks are meant to be shared. We were not meant to live this life alone, but there may be transitional times when we have to.

Reaching out to others and developing new relationships will get us through the transition. Think about how your calling intersects with the social world, and then check out organizations that are related to your calling. Join a professional association and volunteer to serve on a committee. Go to a place of worship. Volunteer to work at a homeless shelter, help out at a soup kitchen, or mentor a young person. There are so many ways to meet people who are aligned with your interests and values.

We come into each other's lives to accomplish goals and also to fill in the gaps in our personalities. Looking back, I can see why certain people came into my life and why I came into theirs. You've heard the old saying, "Opposites attract"? A quiet man hooks up with an outgoing social butterfly. Or in the case of my longtime friend and financial adviser Ray and myself, it was social worker meets bottom-line businessman.

Smart, wonderful, all-about-business Ray. I don't consider myself a hard-core businesswoman, and I absolutely needed him early on to take the company to the next level. Although he's active in the community (he chairs the New York–based Association of Black Charities), I didn't perceive him as a people person in the helping sense, and I believe he needs me to develop that aspect of his personality. When we started working together, you can imagine the conflicts.

I volunteer a lot of my time and resources to Kaplan House, a group home for young brothers (ages fifteen to twenty-one). Often I'll bring them to work or an event to shadow us, or I'll hire someone who's just been released from jail to give him a start. Ray just looks at me and shakes his head.

On the other hand, Ray often has me pulling out my few hairs. For some years he had me focus on planning for the future of the business. He taught me to create a business plan and he made me stick to the goals and objectives we developed together. He'll say, "It's not in the budget to take this person on," and I'll say, "We'll just have to find the money." He watches the financial bottom line, and I watch the human bottom line. Having the agency's best interest as our common calling balances us out, and our respect and fondness for each other keep us united.

Calling does not and should not take place in complete isolation. There will be times when you'll need to work alone, and other times when you'll work with others. As I learned in the development of this book, you don't have to know how to do everything. Finding the right partners is half of the battle. I couldn't have written this book on my own, and I'm not ashamed to admit it. Although I had the vision for *A Plentiful Harvest,* a few kindred spirits lent their special abilities to the process and helped me grow it into the gift you now hold in your hands.

Ideally, kindred spirits can also meet up in the romantic realm, but often this is not what happens. Instead, you might meet a love interest at a time in your life when you have no clue about calling. As time passes and you become more interested in finding your life's purpose, you may find that your changing values may or may not be in sync with your partner's. In fact, your love life can't help but be affected. Unless he or she is growing with you, this can be a time of much confusion and sadness. Your partner, not understanding your new interests, may feel threatened and left out. Growing apart has split up many a relationship. If the relationship is worth saving, communicate what's going on and be patient with the other person. I would never recommend divorce or breaking up with someone just because you're moving to a new phase of life. When you're moving in opposite directions, however, sometimes it can't be helped. Only you know what you're capable of enduring on a day-to-day basis. Everything happens for a reason—in its own time and the way it's supposed to.

Some people get so caught up in the intensity of living their calling that the needs of those who mean the most to them become secondary. Folks can be brilliantly living their calling while neglecting their personal lives. All too often the spouse is lonely and depressed and the kids are running wild. That's not balanced living.

If this sounds like you (be honest with yourself), this week consider turning off the cell phone and having a nice dinner with your family. Calling should never be mistaken for workaholism. In fact, if your relationships are in trouble, that's a sign that you may be working too hard. Sit down and do homework with the kids. Talk to your spouse. Call up a friend and chat.

If you're not in a relationship but would like to be in one, I encourage you to bond with people who have similar interests and values. Look into your heart and spirit. Don't worry about the outer package of dress, looks, type of car, and so forth. Ideally, you want to share your discoveries and activities with your partner. There's nothing worse than lying next to someone night after night and not being able to share what's in your heart.

Look at marriages or relationships that have survived the test of time. Why are they successful? Look closely and you'll probably find that friendship and mutual values have strengthened the bond. The stronger the bond, the better you'll both be able to withstand change. I've known more than a couple of relationships that didn't survive because one partner found his or her calling and the other felt threatened or resentful of the changes.

If you can find someone who shares your calling, you may have found your life's soul mate. Shared calling is as powerful as love and sex. Think of all the things you can do together: making music, raising a family, worshiping, making a home, collecting, restoring old things, traveling . . . Think of the support you can give one another. This type of romantic relationship is an ideal, but it is one worth striving for. If you don't reach it, that's okay, but do try to be in a relationship in which both partners respect and are interested in what the other does. Whether one is a brain surgeon and the other a stay-at-home parent, both partners' callings need to be respected and valued.

Journal time

This week, let's write about the relationships in our lives that have a purpose, that touch our hearts, whether at work or at home. Assign each person his or her own page. Draw a line down the middle. On the left side write examples of "caring," and on the right, "uncaring." Now think of every single meaningful relationship in your life right now and fill out those columns. Which of your friendships are strong and positive enough to help you move to the next level of your life? Which relationships are working and which ones aren't? Which relationships are full of ego, doubts, and disappointments? Which relationships offer support, caring, and encouragement?

WEEK 7
Calling Will Change Your Life

Things are changing around here. . . . Maybe we
need to change and do things differently.
SPENCER JOHNSON, M.D.,
Who Moved My Cheese?

What you can tolerate, you will never change.
RICK GODWIN

The universe is in a constant state of motion and change. Planets, moons, stars, and galaxies are born, grow, and die. Because we're part and parcel of the universe, we too are born, grow, and die. So do our most sacred institutions, societies, nations, and civilizations.

Although change is an inescapable fact of life, we seldom seem prepared to deal with it well. Either we seek out change for change's sake in an attempt to escape the ruts and pits of our lives, or we resist change with every ounce of our being. It's like forbidding a flower to grow. We can try, but it's going to grow anyway. Developing a healthy respect for change will help us deal with the inevitable. We've got to learn when to dig in and stay put, and we've got to learn "when to fold 'em" and go on to the next adventure.

We are all called, but few accept the challenge of a calling. Why? Because accepting your calling will change your life. All of us tend to deal with change in our own unique ways, some empowering, some not, but being serious about living your calling means learning how to welcome and manage change.

As our calling becomes more intense and complex, change works its magic on our critical thinking abilities and emotional maturity. If we ask God, as Jabez did, to enlarge our territories, then we must expect some deep shifts to occur in our basic psychology. We would never expect a child to run a large company. She must grow in wisdom and maturity, and she must develop the vision and management skills to take on such a task.

When change occurs within the context of calling, it will rattle your old defense mechanisms. If you have low self-esteem, finding your calling will require you to think more highly of yourself.

When you begin to act on what you believe is your calling, you will receive insights about your life's mission. You'll learn new things about your gifts, talents, and skills that you may not have known while you were going about your established routine.

My friend Gloria dropped out of college her junior year to move across the country with the man she loved. Well, the man turned out to be no good, but by the time he left she had a three-year-old and no means of support. The failure of her relationship coupled with the realization of what she'd given up by dropping out of college sent her into a four-year depression. When she finally began to come out of it and think about what she wanted to do, she realized that the one thing she kept loving, even when she was down, was taking pictures. She saved money for two months and enrolled in a night course on black-and-white photography. She loved the course, and taking pictures, but she had a hard time accepting criticism from her teacher and classmates. After a few weeks she wanted to drop out. That's when she had her first wake-up call. She was repeating old patterns, fearing failure and dropping out. Confronted with this truth about herself, she decided she would hang in there no matter how hard it was to present her work and get feedback. The funny thing is, the longer she hung in there, the easier it got. She started to feel entitled to show her work and believe in her work even as she took in positive and negative feedback from her classmates. After two more classes she got a job working in a professional photo studio and began showing her own photography in local venues. Far from quitting or dropping out, finding her calling let her work through her fear of failure and rejection to fulfill the promise of her talent.

Your territory will indeed be enlarged as you live your calling, but if your psychology isn't enlarged right along with it, you will miss opportunities. I cringe when I think of some of the opportunities that I've missed along the way because I hadn't fully dealt with some of my confidence issues—fear of failure, for example. The thought of failing, at anything, terrifies me. I think it's because I'm a perfectionist. I have a hard time letting work go because sometimes I don't trust my highly competent team members to do it right. Of course they can; it's just me, getting in the way of my success.

Taking steps toward calling also requires you to be gentle, patient, and compassionate with yourself. Take James Earl Jones as an example. This is a brother with one of the most beautiful voices in the English-speaking world. Imagine my surprise when I saw him in an interview one day talking about his childhood stutter. Instead of giving up because of it, he kept looking for ways to work with it. One day he tried acting—and the minute he got onstage, his stutter went away. Bingo, he'd found his calling and a way to deal with his speech impediment. Through acting he worked continually on this stutter until it went away. So part of calling is allowing yourself the space and opportunity to work with adversity in a nurturing and supportive way.

Sometimes as you change, you begin to realize that your issues are too big or overwhelming to work on alone. If that's the case, you may need to seek counseling. If you think you may need to, do it. Never feel ashamed of needing help. Therapy is a gift you give to yourself. When you get too close to your problems, you can't always figure out what to do with them. Talking to an objective person really helps. Do what you need to do. Get the help you need.

Understanding the nature of change will help us anticipate

and manage it when it comes. Sometimes change takes its own sweet time; other times we may be notified of its coming well in advance, which allows us to prepare. A friend experienced this on one of her jobs. A program had lost its funding, and her boss told her a year and a half prior to the close of the program that she'd be out of a job. She had plenty of time to look for other work. She handled the change by sending her résumé to other companies and taking advantage of an outplacement service the company provided to its departing employees.

Then there are those times when change is like the police with a warrant for your arrest, kicking down the door and demanding you put up your hands. Lord, have mercy. You stand there, trembling and in fear, in the face of such sudden, awesome, and scary change. Testing positive for a life-threatening disease is an example. You're never really prepared for such a life change. Still, joining a support group and learning how to live with and even survive the disease can help you cope with the crisis.

As we become more conscious of the process of change and how it is strengthening us, we begin to manage daily life more effectively. Say you've accepted your calling and want to quit your job in order to pursue it, but you fear the financial uncertainty that may loom ahead. Just remember that the change will move you into your calling. You'll make it through. As your territory is being enlarged, so are you!

Changes that occur because of calling will wake you up. You'll grow in understanding about life in general. As I grow older, I realize that we do not wake up all at once but in stages. Our eyes may have been wide open when we were children, but being able to see doesn't mean the same thing as being able to understand. I'm forty-eight years old and I still don't get stuff, which is why I like to talk to the elders in my community. Talking to the elders can be one way in which to find comfort and sustenance as you negotiate change. They've been negotiating a lifetime of it and usually have good tips about what to do and not do. They also have perspective. They can sometimes see the bigger picture when we can't.

We will change and we will be transformed by our calling. How well we manage the change is up to us.

J ournal time

Within us is an inner compass that will keep us from getting too lost, steer us in the right direction, and keep us on our calling path. To help us manage the many changes that are occurring in our lives, this week let's point that compass to the future. Let's try to get a handle on where all these changes may be leading us.

- How are the changes you are experiencing impacting your home life, work life, personal relationships, and so on?
- Are you beginning to know what you'd like to be doing in the next one, five, ten years, and beyond? If so, are the changes that are taking place in your life moving you forward? Or are they setbacks?
- Take time to talk to your parents, aunts, uncles, elders in your community whom you respect. Sometimes the perspective of those older and wiser than us can be enlightening and helpful. They've probably been where you are now, and might have the benefit of hindsight to help you.
- Changes often present new opportunities for growth. Think about what your calling is and what changes you're going to have to make. If you've already been making changes, what has been their impact on your home life, personal relationships, job? Write down your thoughts about how the changes that are occurring right now might be used to take you to the next level of your calling. For example, if you've just been laid off from your job, think deeply about what

your calling is before going into another job. This could be a great opportunity to pursue a new career or go back to school.

Living Virtue 2

Responsibility

The longest journey is from the mind to the
heart. Longer still is that very journey that takes
us back from the heart to the mind.
MACKI RUKA,
Maori elder

In my never-ending quest for balance, moderation, and peace of
mind, I've learned that your strongest, most positive values can
sometimes turn around and hit you upside the head. One of the
characteristics that I'm most proud of is my strong sense of responsibility toward others. I take my responsibilities to family,
friends, business, and community very seriously. In fact, "taking
care of others" used to be my working definition of *responsibility*.
If I wasn't helping or supporting others, I felt like I wasn't living
right. When it came to the living virtues, I figured responsibility
was one area where I was already earning straight A's.

Wrong again.

Notice that I didn't mention helping or supporting *myself.* Oh sure, I know that I'm supposed to take time out for myself, but when other needs demand my attention, I tend to put myself last. All this self-sacrifice can sound like a good quality. But look a little closer and what do you find? You find me spread so thin I can't give any one person all my energy and support. You find me too sick or too tired to be 100 percent present with those I love. I'd be the first one to tell a friend that while taking care of folks is good, neglecting yourself is bad. So what have I been doing my entire life? Taking care of others and neglecting myself. Not until I started applying the living virtues to my life did I truly begin to understand that if I don't take care of myself, I won't be able to help others. It's been a rocky road (I can be pretty hard-headed at times), but I think I'm finally getting the message. Responsibility starts at square one, with taking care of you.

Sistahs tend to have this problem across the board. Maybe the brothers too, but mostly I see women running around, multitasking, trying to do everything. Sure, the brothers work hard, but when it's time to chill they play ball with their buddies or watch the game on TV. Not us. My friend Tanya is a single mother working full time managing a restaurant plus taking care of two teenage boys, and let me tell you, I'm surprised she even stops long enough to breathe. Last year she felt so wasted she decided to hole up under the covers instead of going to her own birthday party. Turns out, she'd been running around with a case of walking pneumonia. She wound up in bed for three weeks with no choice but to let everyone else wait on her for a while. It's a tough way to learn a lesson.

Unfortunately, I can relate to Tanya a little too well. Hard as it is for me to admit, I've been irresponsible, *especially* when it comes to taking care of my body. I *know* exercise is good for me, but I still have a hard time taking action. I've read all the studies. I know that exercise and good nutrition will make me healthy and strong and add years to my life. But when it comes to health and fitness, I continue to make poor choices around what I eat, and I just can't seem to make it to the gym.

I'm overweight and, according to researchers, that puts me at risk for all kinds of ailments. Being overweight makes me tired, which leaves me open to colds, flus, and viruses, not to mention more serious health concerns down the road. I'm also in danger of not being able to maintain my hectic schedule because I'm so tired all the time.

In the back of my mind I always knew that not tending to my own health was irresponsible. Not just because of the risks to my body, but because carrying around all that extra weight was taking a major toll on my self-esteem. The hard, cold truth is that people (the brothers especially) treat you differently when you're carrying a few extra pounds. Remember that routine of Sinbad's, the one about the sistah whose butt was so big it was dragging in the sand? Ouch. I've understood all this for years, but did I make the responsible choice and get my rear in gear? No way. Instead, I ate even more. I felt paralyzed. And depressed. I was spiraling downward fast. And as I was falling, I was still rationalizing my behavior. I wasn't all that heavy, I'd tell myself. There were always people way heavier than me.

As with most people, my weight problem was tied to emotional issues. I wasn't always heavy. When I was a girl, I was kind of skinny. I started gaining weight in college and my early adult years. I ate when I got stressed, and it just spun out of control. Food became my outlet to deal with all the pressures of work and relationships. So I closed my eyes to my compulsive eating. Now, every car has a blind spot, and if you don't look over your shoulder periodically to check what's there, you're going to hit something. When I'm driving, I never forget about that blind spot. But in my life I failed to do periodic checks to see what was going on with my body. I didn't even acknowledge there *was* a blind spot. Instead, I just kept ignoring the woman in the mirror, buying bigger clothes, and doing a whole lot of complaining about things "shrinking" in the wash.

Deciding to think deeply about responsibility made me take a closer look at everything, including my weight. I think the real moment of realization came while reading a magazine article by Ronna Lichtenberg in which she said, "If you were to meet me, I would probably sense, in that initial moment of assessment, that you don't think I'm the 'right' weight. I've struggled with that moment for years. It's a moment that matters. . . ."

Reading those words, I finally understood that this secret I'd been keeping from myself was no secret to anybody else. I was so deep in denial that this hit me like a bolt of lightning. People knew I was heavy. And "they" (the ones who count) were still in my corner. They still talked to me. They still did business with me. They still asked my advice, requested me as a speaker, bought my books, invited me to events, and accepted my notes and calls. Some were worried about me, and they called to encourage me to take care of myself, but they didn't drop me because I was overweight.

They cared about me, but *I* hadn't been giving my body the love and respect it deserved. I had been irresponsible with .the person who mattered the most—me! I'd done it because at the time it just seemed easier than facing up to who I was. Making the decision to lose weight involves a whole lot of soul searching, and I didn't know if I felt up to the job. Sometimes neglecting yourself is just more convenient than taking responsibility for what's going down. But if I was going to achieve peace and balance in my life, I had to get healthier. *I was worth whatever it took to do it.* Time, money, sacrifice. I wasn't aiming for Tyra Banks thin or Jackie Joyner-Kersee strong, but surely I could make it to healthy and fit. I wanted to stick around. I owed it to the people I loved.

So when my friends Michael and Shellie asked me for the hundredth time to go with them to the gym, I finally agreed. I remember that first visit. The way I walked through the doors, you would have thought I was heading for the electric chair. It's a wonder I even made it down the hall and into the right room. Of course, once I got there I didn't do a thing. Just sat and watched people sweating and grunting. I wanted—make that *needed*—to exercise, but I couldn't make myself lift a weight if my life depended on it (and, of course, it did). So while Shellie and Michael were doing their thing, I sat on the sidelines and watched.

"Terrie!" said Shellie, speed-walking over to me in her sweats. Shellie is such a great role model for me. She's fit *and* full figured.

"Yes?" I said.

"Come on, let's walk a couple of laps."

"Okay," I said. "You go on. I'll catch up."

Naturally, I didn't budge. So next came Michael. He grabbed my hand and yanked me onto my feet. "C'mon, Terrie," he said. "You've gotta start sometime."

"Just give me a minute," I said.

"Okaaaay," he said, staring at his watch as if counting down the seconds.

I slumped back down into my chair. What was the matter with me? I wasn't a lazy person. A procrastinator couldn't have run a business the way I had over the years. Why was I letting a little thing like exercise get the best of me? Where did my resolve go? What was my problem?

Michael sighed dramatically, then gave me a quick kiss on the cheek.

"You'll exercise when you're ready. No pressure. Just let me know when you really want to get started, okay?"

I nodded, totally ashamed of myself. Clearly, I was at a cross-roads. One direction led to a walk around the track with Shellie, the other to my freezer with its full carton of Häagen-Dazs ice cream.

As I watched my friends work out, I thought about my doctor. Every time I saw him I got the weight lecture. He told me that the weight was going to kill me if I didn't deal with it. Black folks suffer more obesity-related ailments than everyone else, he reminded me. Did I want hypertension or diabetes? Did I want aching joints for the rest of my life? When you're overweight, it's hard walking up a flight of stairs. Not only does it hurt your hips and knees, but you get out of breath easily. I assured him that I wanted to be healthy and fit and that I would do better. If only he could see me now, I thought—finally made it to the gym but too chicken to work out.

It's not as if I wasn't capable of losing weight. Six years ago I lost thirty pounds by walking to and from work and by eating healthily. Simple. Unfortunately, I gained it all back plus some. Why was I so bent on neglecting myself? I packed my time with so many meetings and so much work that I was convinced I couldn't possibly squeeze in half an hour of workout time. That's irresponsible. I was always on the run, so I grabbed a few bites at the deli or junk food from some vending machine. It had to stop.

I never got up and walked with Shellie that day, but it was important to at least be there at the gym. I gave myself a pat on the back for a tiny movement forward.

Unfortunately, that tiny movement forward didn't come soon enough. A few months later my doctor called me in for a general checkup. All the tests came back negative except for the one that I dreaded the most. Turns out I have diabetes. Years of inactivity, poor eating habits, and family genetics have caught up with me. That diagnosis put the fear of God in me.

I knew I *had* to get moving, but believe it or not I still needed a push. So this time I turned to that one living virtue I thought I had conquered. Responsibility. I thought a little about my definition of responsibility as taking care. Had I done that? Not really. It's easy to think of responsibility as some big, overwhelming concept. Who's responsible for national health care? Who's responsible for that latest oil spill? But when it comes down to it, responsibility, like all the other virtues, is about individuals. If we don't take care of our personal health, how are we supposed to take care of our relationships with our loved ones?

And if we don't tend to those relationships, how are we supposed to do our part in bettering our community, and even the world?

These days I'm truly making an effort to turn my health habits around. And I'm finding out that taking responsibility can mean something as small as getting up half an hour early every morning to walk to the office. When I do that, I feel better about myself. And that happier self rubs off on everyone around me. Though I gotta admit I still dread eating skinless baked chicken and doing my sit-ups, I'm also starting to understand responsibility in a new way. I see it as a gift, not a burden. The Creator has put the world in our hands. He's trusted us with the future. We owe it to each other to take that responsibility as seriously as we can.

Responsibility is like a muscle, and during the next few weeks we're going to start giving that muscle some exercise. We cannot be responsible if we have low self-worth or are apathetic about the needs of others. The opposite of my self-neglect is total self-absorption, and we don't want to go there either. So we're going to examine the ways in which we are and aren't taking responsibility for those things that truly matter in our lives. We'll start with the personal, then move on to our loved ones, our children, and our community. Responsibility means caring and respect, for ourselves and for those around us. When we assume responsibility for ourselves, we are empowered. When we assume responsibility for others, we can make a difference. We can make the world a better place.

WEEK 8
Responsibility to Ourselves: Tending Our Own Garden

回

A human being's first responsibility is to shake
hands with himself.

HENRY WINKLER

The buck stops here.
HARRY S. TRUMAN

We're going to begin our journey toward responsibility by getting back to the basics. If you're like me, you've probably heard
all this out of the mouths of everyone from your doctor to your
favorite talk-show host. So it's time to start listening. Taking care
of yourself is important, both inside and out. But you can't even
begin working on your inner self if you aren't physically up to it.
Your body is your foundation, and we all know what happens
when you start construction on a shaky foundation. Before long,
the whole thing falls apart.

The truth is that if you feel good physically, you'll have extra
emotional energy as well. You'll have the strength to take responsibility for your own life and to enrich others'. I've always
believed that we are the ones in charge of our own destinies, and
it's up to each one of us to make positive use of the space we're
in. I love the living virtues because they wake you up to what's
been going on in your life all along. They give you guidance on
how to think, feel, and make decisions. If you let them teach you,

you'll find yourself becoming more conscious and wise about your life. You'll start taking charge.

So let's begin at the beginning. My biggest personal challenge right now is sticking to that fitness program. I make my resolutions, go strong for a month or two, and then I start to backslide. And it's getting more and more difficult to rev up the engine again after so many false starts and failures. Yet I know I've got to do it. It's a matter of life and death.

Many of us are in this same boat. Even if you're facing immediate health dangers (and I hope you aren't!), chances are you aren't taking proper care of your body. Chances are you could use more energy, not to mention more confidence about how you look and feel. So let's get practical. Let's think about ways that we can take charge of our health. After all, no one can eat well, sleep, or exercise for us. Believe me, if it was possible, I would've found a way.

First, let's make an honest assessment of our current state. Take off your clothes (that's right, butt naked) and look at yourself in the mirror. Do you like what you see? What's due for a change? Remember, be realistic here. Most of us are never going to wind up looking like Halle Berry, I don't care how many Stair-Masters we climb. Now take a health and stress inventory of the past week. How often were you bone-tired? How often did you opt for coffee and a candy bar instead of tucking into a healthy meal? Are you looking and feeling like you've got it all together? If not, you've got some work to do.

I've found that mental preparation is just as important to starting a program as actually taking action. So read all you can. Flood your mind with images of healthy-looking people. Notice I didn't say *skinny*. In this country we have no perspective on what's a healthy body size. You do not have to be rail thin to be healthy. Some folks are naturally thin, God bless 'em, but the rest of us have to honestly ask ourselves just how thin we have to be to enjoy quality health—and cute clothes. If you have any questions, go ahead and call your doctor. (It's always a good idea to check with your doctor before starting out on any fitness plan anyway.) After all, she's there to help.

Let's start with baby steps, something any of us can do anytime, anywhere. Open your mouth and breathe. We are a society of shallow chest breathers. As a result, our bodies are starving for oxygen. It's like we're slowly suffocating to death. If that sufficiently scares you, all you need to do is breathe more deeply, from your stomach. Deep breathing gives us more energy and helps us think more clearly. Try it out whenever you can—waiting for the bus to come, or lying in bed, or sitting at your desk.

I know you've heard it a hundred times but let's do our best to drink at least eight to ten glasses of water a day. Most of us are so dehydrated we don't know the difference between hunger and thirst. When you feel hunger, try drinking water instead. If you're still hungry after that, then you'll know it's the real deal. Drinking water can increase the body's metabolism and improves elimination, which is great for those of us who need to lose weight. Some researchers believe that drinking more water will boost our energy levels and even ease back and joint pain. If you're on the go all day, try arming yourself with one of those sports water bottles. Carry it around in your purse or toss it on the front seat of your car.

Another important step is doing our best to get enough sleep. I find that when I'm tired, my mind isn't as focused as it could be, little problems start seeming enormous, and I wind up eating more just to get more energy. The older we get, the more we need regular sleep. Our bodies don't bounce back from those all-nighters like they used to when we were younger (though even young people should keep all-nighters to a minimum). Not getting enough sleep will take years off your life. Years we'll need in order to do some serious good.

I know that with my jam-packed schedule, getting enough sleep can be very tricky. It means I have to practice real time management—and have enough discipline to turn off the TV. Being accountable for your life means organizing your days so that you're accomplishing everything within a reasonable time frame and not burning the midnight oil. Sure, there's always going to be one more thing that's gotta get done, but maybe sweeping the floor or sending that last e-mail can wait until morning. Do your best to make sleep a priority in your life.

If you don't smoke, don't start. If you do smoke, quit. Now. I know how hard it is to give up an addiction (I'm struggling with a few of my own . . .), but study after study attests to the lethal nature of cigarettes. They've been linked to everything from cancer to brain aneurysms and heart attacks. You owe it to yourself and those around you to stick around. This question isn't debatable. And if you have kids at home, please don't smoke around them. Second-hand smoke is deadly too.

Exercise! I know what you're saying: "Terrie, you can't even get your own butt in gear. Who are you to tell me to exercise?" But hey, aspiring to the living virtues is a constant process, and I'll be the first to admit I'm right in there struggling just like everybody else. This stuff isn't easy. If it was, it wouldn't be so important. So I'm going to say it loud and clear, for me and for you. Every day you must do twenty to thirty minutes of heart-pumping exercise. Go take a walk. Swim. Jog. Ride a bike. If that bores your socks off, then get creative: Do some vigorous housework, put on some music and dance, or go outside and pull up weeds. Whatever you do, do something. Get started. Break a sweat today and then continue for the rest of your life. Don't do what I did and wait until you're on a doctor's examining table hearing about the damage that's already been done.

Last of all, start eating healthy. Get your vegetables, get your chicken and fish, buy that whole-wheat bread. Then start cutting back on the junk food and those bad fats like butter and red meat. Again, it's important to be realistic here. As soon as you go saying "I'll never eat chocolate again," those cookies are going to start singing to you in your sleep. Start with what you think you can handle—maybe one cookie instead of a dozen. But spend some time really enjoying that cookie of yours, savoring it instead of mindlessly gobbling it down. That way you're getting maximum pleasure for the calories, and you may even find you don't want those eleven other cookies anyway. As with everything, don't expect your habits to change overnight. Taking responsibility for yourself requires a lot of patience and hard work. Be honest with yourself and do the best that you can. Remember, you're the only one who has the power to change your life.

Phew! I know, that's one long list of improvements to the machine. But don't even think I'm done yet. Bad food and exercise habits aren't the only things that take a toll on our physical well-being. We can't forget about everybody's good buddy, stress. If you're constantly stretched too thin to meet all of your obligations, you owe it yourself to take a close look at how you spend your time. Do you need to go to one more dinner party, or stay that extra hour at the office? Or would you be better off making it an early night every once in a while, writing in your journal, cooking a fine meal for someone special, or just hitting the sheets before midnight for once?

It's tough to set limits on your life, especially if you're one of those people whom others turn to when they need anything at all. Are you the type who can't say no when any old—or new!—friends come calling? I know I sure am. They need a speaker, a ride, a birthday cake, and I just feel like I can't let them down. But of course too much of the time I do wind up letting them down. Here's a perfect example:

Not long ago I found myself trapped in a meeting-packed afternoon at the office. Instead of admitting that I didn't have time to do everything I wanted to do, I'd gone and scheduled myself way too tightly. All the meetings were too short and they still wound up running late. Worst of all, I had a date that night with two of my kids from Kaplan House. Just the three of us and the Knicks. But I got so held up at the office, we missed half of the first quarter. Of course they didn't complain, but I felt like they had every right to. Instead of prioritizing, I'd made the irresponsible choice of trying to cram too many events into too little time.

I wound up too tired and frazzled to really enjoy what was supposed to be a great evening out. Just showing up is not enough;
you've gotta *be* there. And if you can't do it, that's a clear sign it's
time to take some time off, even if it's just one night tucked up
with the latest issue of *O* magazine.

It's your life, and only you can be accountable for your own
health and well-being. So many of the stresses and ailments we
suffer are preventable. We have wonderful, beautiful bodies.
Scripture calls them temples. We must treat our temples with
the respect they deserve. After all, their mission is to carry us
through this life. Our bodies cannot do their job if they are not
fed, rested, and strong. Taking care of our personal health is just
the first step toward tending to a more universal garden. If we
can't make it up the stairs without stopping to rest, how are we
supposed to go out there and change the world?

Journal time

Our bodies would just love it if we treated them as well as we
treat our cars, filling them with fuel, visiting the mechanic, and
scheduling mandatory seasonal inspections. This week we're
going to focus on making our bodies healthy and strong. Make a
list of the ways in which you tend to neglect your body. Do you
exercise regularly? Drink enough water? Eat healthy meals? Now
pick the two things on the list that you consider most important
(for me it's exercise and good nutrition). Take this week to
change those two bad habits. Write down a nutritious menu, then
actually stick to it. For one whole week, drink eight glasses of
water a day. Exercise for thirty minutes a day. Get proper rest.
Take a multiple vitamin. Use your journal to record your progress
and to keep yourself on track. Also record how these changes
make you feel. Do you have more energy? Do you feel more positive about your life?

This week, we're also going to meditate on how to reduce some of the stress in our overcrowded lives. Write down the things that cause you the most stress. Is it too much work at the office? Never getting to spend enough time with your kids or your mate? Now write down your weekly schedule. Is there anything in there that doesn't have to be? Are you putting everyone else's needs in front of your own? Pick at least one obligation that you just don't have time for and practice saying no. Be friendly, but firm. Setting priorities is the first step toward taking charge of who you are. Remember, saying no to someone else means saying yes to you.

WEEK 9
Responsibility for Our Actions: Making the Choice to Grow

回

Self-pity is our worst enemy and if we yield to it,
we can never do anything wise in the world.

HELEN KELLER

Character—the willingness to accept responsibility for one's own life—is the source from which
self-respect springs.

JOAN DIDION

I've known my friend David since back in our college days, and let me tell you not a single thing has gone right for that boy since. Every time I talk to him he's got another story about one of his colleagues getting better treatment at the office, or one of his neighbors having a finer car, or yet another girl leaving him because she just doesn't know a good thing when she sees it. Now, I try to make it a point to keep in touch with old friends, just to make sure they're surviving and thriving, but David started to be a serious drain. He never saw a rainbow or a silver lining. Everyone was out to get him, and everything that happened to him was always "someone else's fault." I do my best to be patient with people's shortcomings—Lord knows I've got plenty of my own—but a few years ago I finally decided I just couldn't take it. I told David that I loved him but if he didn't have anything positive to say about our beautiful world, I'd rather not talk as often because it was too draining.

We all have friends like David who refuse to take responsibility for their own lives. Instead of taking steps to change the things that don't make them happy, they nestle down in that victim role and stay there until their dying day. But notice you don't see self-pity listed anywhere near the living virtues. In fact, it's kind of an antivirtue. Those big old pity parties you might be throwing yourself are one of the most dangerous things around. We all have power over our own lives. We all have the right to make changes. So if something's bothering you, stop moaning and take steps to turn things around.

All of us have things going on in our lives that make us unhappy. It's our job to do something about it. Got a dream of a bigger house? What are you doing to fulfill that dream? Are you wasting precious time complaining about that girlfriend who's got three bedrooms and two baths? Or are you taking a little bit out of your paycheck every month and setting it aside for a down payment? Let me tell you, option number two is going to get you a whole lot further than complaining.

Maybe you hate your job. So stop moaning to your colleagues about that evil boss of yours. Instead, decide what sort of career path you'd like to pursue, whip your résumé into shape, and start making some calls. I don't think I've ever felt so powerful as that day I quit working at New York Hospital and launched what was ultimately my PR career. For the first time I felt like I was truly in control of my life, and let me tell you it felt *good*. Action is always better than suffering. Blaming other people for what's going wrong in your life uses up a bunch of energy that gets you nowhere. You wind up like one of those hamsters on its little wheel, doing a whole lot of running and winding up exactly where you started out.

Of course, sometimes we have a legitimate reason to blame others for what's going down. But that doesn't mean we can't still take responsibility for our lives. Although something like job discrimination is very real and happens far too often, always be careful about making the choice to play the victim. Don't let other people steal your power. The more responsible path is to fight back in whatever way you can. If that means moving to a new workplace or neighborhood, then that's what you gotta do. Think about our real heroes, people like Rosa Parks and Martin Luther King Jr. When times were tough, did they give in to self-pity? No way. Instead, they wound up changing our society. Playing the victim does nothing but get you stuck in your own mess. The rewards you may get are so minuscule and fleeting that it's just not worth it. Inspirational speaker Sidney Madwed says:

> How much better our lives would be if we would simply take responsibility for the things that happen to us. . . . No matter what or whom one can blame for the circumstances of his life, he is still stuck with the consequences of everything he thinks, says or does. . . . Until people fully realize that they are totally responsible for their lives, we as a society collectively will be operating under a false and distorted assumption of what responsibility means.

Taking charge of your life means changing those things that don't please you. That includes the outside things—like your career and your friends—but the inside things, too. Part of fulfilling your potential is being honest about your flaws as well as your visions and dreams. After all, you have a responsibility not to get in your own way.

A few years ago a former colleague of mine, Liza, was feeling stuck and frustrated in her job at an advertising agency. She couldn't understand why she was always getting handed the most difficult clients. First she worked with a cookie company, and they hated her ideas for new commercials. Then she moved on to a cruise line that refused to use her photos in their brochure. It seemed like every time she turned around, someone else had a problem with her work. She'd started getting real defensive about the whole thing; whenever anyone questioned her, more often than not she'd explode.

Liza was on the verge of quitting her job entirely when her boss called her in for a little informal meeting. He told her that, while he really valued her discipline and her creativity, she needed to spend some time improving her people skills. Apparently some of the clients had complained that every time they had a suggestion, Liza refused to listen. Her boss said he was willing to give her another chance but, even if she thought her own ideas were great, she had a responsibility to listen to clients, too, and incorporate their wishes into the campaign.

Now all along Liza had been focusing on how her work was getting dissed. It never occurred to her to examine her own behavior. But with her job on the line, she decided it might be time to do just that. And looking back, being as honest as she could, she had to admit that maybe she had been too rigid. Maybe she needed to try compromising just a little bit more. Once she started paying closer attention to respecting her clients and their needs, things started flowing a lot more smoothly. In fact, six months later she got herself a promotion. All it took was the courage to take responsibility for her own mistakes. Instead of feeling like the victim all the time, she figured out how to take charge of her future by working on herself.

When you don't accept responsibility for your life, you're robbing yourself of power—to pursue your career, to end a dead-end relationship, to get out of bed. It may be easy to blame government, society, that brother or sistah for your problems, but do you really want to believe that they have more power over your life than you do? Because in reality, that's what folks who play the victim believe.

The living virtues teach us that when you're seeking a balanced life, everything matters—the positive and the negative. Everything you think or do, all that energy you send out, is a contribution. Ever heard the saying that a butterfly flapping its wings in Beijing can cause a hurricane in New York? Little things can generate big results. So don't kid yourself that your actions won't have an effect on the world. Our first job is to tend to ourselves. The evolution of the entire human race depends on us. Picture the universe as a giant bank. Being negative is like making a withdrawal from the energy of the world. And we just can't afford to be doing that.

When we accept responsibility for our lives and roles in society, we are empowered. We make a difference. Practicing both on a daily basis gives us a strong sense of fulfillment and purpose. It makes us feel good. This being human is not easy. But we owe it to ourselves, and to the world, to stop wasting any more time.

Journal time

Make a list of the things that you don't like about your life. They can be anything, big or small. Maybe you can't stand having to do all the housework. Maybe you don't like your car. You don't travel enough. Some of your friends are sapping your energy. Then next to each thing, write a few sentences about how the problem could be fixed. Try not to blame anyone else for what's making you unhappy. Just focus on what you can do to make a change. Could you start saving for a vacation? Join a social group to meet some new people? Talk to your mate about sharing some of the cooking and cleaning? It's time to take the power for your own contentment out of the hands of others. Go ahead and reclaim your life.

This week we're also going to meditate on the page about some of the attitudes and habits we've fallen into that don't serve us well. First, make a list of five things you love about yourself. Are you hardworking, outgoing, generous? This is going to be our inspirational list. Every time you start feeling negative about yourself, go back to those five things. Add a few more if you feel like it. Remember, you are a strong and powerful force.

Now make a list of five things you don't like about yourself. Don't beat yourself up, but try to be as honest as you can. Are you a procrastinator? Do you fly off the handle way too easily? Or, like me, do you often avoid conflict, even when something has you really upset? This week, try to pay attention to these traits. Think about how they might be getting in the way of your achieving your goals, and about how you might go about changing them. Think about how good it will feel to claim responsibility for the extraordinary person you are.

WEEK 10
Because We Care: Taking Responsibility for Our Relationships

▣

Do unto others as you would have others do unto you.

THE GOLDEN RULE

R-e-s-p-e-c-t!

ARETHA FRANKLIN

Last December one of my close friends, Joanne, had what I call a relationship meltdown. A bunch of us girls had planned to celebrate the holidays together by meeting up for lunch then going to a movie. Though I was definitely looking forward to a few hours of just kicking back with good friends, at the last minute I had to change some travel plans and catch an early train to Boston. I called Joanne to explain the problem, and let her know I'd have to make it a quick lunch and skip out on the movie altogether. Joanne hit the roof. And I'm talking sky high. She started crying and saying no one cares about or appreciates her, how everybody around her just uses her and never gives anything back. Now, I felt like I'd been as kind and respectful as I could, but according to Joanne, I'd gone and single-handedly ruined Christmas. After that, Joanne and I didn't connect again for months.

Eventually it came out that Joanne was having serious problems with her mate, a relationship that had been on the skids for months but just refused to die. Add to that some tension with her mother, who couldn't bring herself to stay out of Joanne's life, and you've got a woman primed to explode. But instead of taking responsibility for what was going wrong in those other relationships, Joanne found it easier to play the victim. She decided that everyone was out to get her, including her best friends. My canceling our holiday plans wasn't the cause of Joanne's hurt but, because she refused to acknowledge where those real feelings were coming from, our relationship wound up being the one to suffer.

Though our relationships with friends and family are the most valuable things in our lives, they're also one of the most difficult things to take responsibility for. We can't always predict how another person is going to react, and too often it seems like the whole thing risks flying out of our control. But it can't fly out of control, not entirely. Because every relationship has two sides, and though you can't dictate another person's actions, you can certainly take responsibility for your own. Your first duty to those you love is to do your best with your end of the relationship bargain—to treat your friends or husband or lover with respect and generosity, no matter what kind of chaos is coming down in your own life.

What Joanne really needed to do was sit down and take a good look at the relationships in her life that were giving her legitimate trouble. Sure, it's easy to say you're being used and abused—and sometimes that's the God's honest truth, in which case the only solution is to cut and run and save yourself any further heartache. But relationships are rarely that simple. If we're having troubles, we owe it ourselves and to our loved ones to spend some time tracing those troubles back to their roots.

Every human being has needs. But sometimes we're afraid to voice those needs because we're afraid of appearing too demanding or that our friends and family won't be there for us when we ask. If you want a healthy relationship, though, that's a chance you've got to take. Both parties share equal responsibility for how a relationship unfolds. Are you and your mate bickering all the time? Instead of deciding to feel put out and spending hours complaining to your girlfriends, maybe you should to take a closer look at what lies beneath the arguments. Maybe troubles at work. Maybe worries about money or something going on with the kids. You owe it to both of you to probe deeper than just another fight over who has to drive the car pool. If you can get to the root of the problem together, then it's got a real chance of being solved.

A few years ago I was seeing a man I really cared about. When the relationship started, it was nothing but fun—dinner, dancing, a weekend trip to the coast. We were neck deep in the honeymoon period, and I refused to believe it would ever end. But once we'd been seeing each other about six months, the bliss started to fade. I had a difficult new client and I wound up feeling stressed out and depressed. The prospect of not always being in fine form for my man made me worried. Maybe he wouldn't like the real me. So I kept trying to put on a happy face. Needless to say, this got old real quick. I started resenting the man I cared about for making me pretend to be someone I wasn't. Looking back, I now realize I was the one putting most of the pressure on the relationship. I finally snapped over him leaving a bunch of dirty dishes in the sink. I completely overreacted, and out came all the anger I'd been building up toward him and the new client and the world in general. We wound up deciding to cool things off that same night.

For months afterward I steamed over how that guy couldn't take the real me. Then, as I moaned yet again to a friend who was just sick of hearing about it, she finally asked me what this man had done to make me so sure he couldn't handle the genuine Terrie. Her question made me think, and I decided to backtrack and look at my behavior honestly. Once I'd done that, I made the decision to accept my share of the responsibility for what had gone wrong. I called my ex and apologized for blowing up like I had instead of raising the real issues bothering me. He apologized for not being more sensitive toward the pressure I'd been under at work. Since then the two of us have resolved our differences and remained close friends. When you're having a conflict with someone, it's all too easy to just sound off or run away. But taking responsibility for our relationships means that we must look honestly at the role we play.

A strong relationship will last forever. It will be there when the work and parties and stresses of daily life have disappeared, and it deserves all the time, respect, and hard work we know how to invest. A strong relationship is one in which both parties contribute thought and energy, and are willing to make compromises. If you're the only one willing to do any work, that may be a red flag that you've hooked up with a creep. But some work, difficult work, is always going to be necessary.

If you care about a person, part of that investment includes accepting responsibility for how you treat him. Both of you need to spend time just keeping the lines of communication open. Are you being sensitive to your mate's needs? Are there problems neither of you is addressing that are causing tension in the relationship? Are you blaming other people for not fulfilling desires you haven't voiced? Even those people who love you the most can't read your mind. They don't know how you're feeling until you tell them about it. And no matter how angry or fed up you might be, do your best to stay calm and choose your words carefully. You owe it to those you love to both care and give them the chance to care back. Be sensitive, be gentle, be generous, be honest. Every person deserves to be treated with the same respect we want for ourselves, most of all, those people we love.

*J*ournal time

This week, take the time to examine a healthy relationship in your life. Why does it work so well? How do you and the other party share responsibility for what unfolds? What happens when there's a conflict? Is there anything you can learn from this relationship that you can apply to another that isn't going quite as well?

The best way to keep any relationship strong is to take responsibility for all aspects of it. Congratulate yourself for what's going right, and understand the role you play in what might be going wrong.

Also, meditate on the page about any rocky relationship in your life. Why is it rocky? Write down what's going wrong. If your first inclination is to blame the other person for what's happening, go ahead and write down why she or he's to blame. Then, once you're done listing your grievances, make another list of what you're contributing to the relationship. Try to be as honest as you can. Remember, no one ever has to look at this list but you. Are there ways in which you can accept responsibility for mending the wound? Are there any behaviors you might be willing to change? Are you treating the relationship with the respect it deserves? Think up one or two ideas for opening the door so that calm discussions can take place.

WEEK 11
Movin' on Up:
Responsibility for Our Successes

I try to live what I consider a "poetic existence."
That means I take responsibility for the air I
breathe and the space I take up. I try to be immediate, to be totally present for all my work.

MAYA ANGELOU

The game is my life. It demands loyalty and responsibility, and it gives me back fulfillment and
peace.

MICHAEL JORDAN

The resourcefulness and imagination of everyday people constantly amaze me. Pick up a magazine, turn on the news, or just
go out in your community and track down the latest gossip. You'll
be amazed at the incredible stuff folks are up to right outside
your front door. Used to be it was mostly the menfolk out there
climbing the ladder to success, but not anymore. Every day I
hear new stories about women achieving all kinds of remarkable
things. Thing is, you ask those women about what they've done,
and often as not they start shrugging and looking at the ground
and pretending that raising six college graduates on a secretary's
pay, getting elected to the school board, or making it on Wall
Street is no big thing. Now, humility has its place—you don't
want to go tempting fate, after all—but being a successful
woman, especially a successful Black woman, means you've got

to trumpet your achievements to everyone you know. We sistahs have a responsibility to those around us. We've got a duty to own our successes and use them to enrich the world.

One of the most amazing women I've ever known is my mother. No, she never hobnobbed with celebrities or raked in the big bucks, but she sure knew how to use her skills and achievements to give back to the world. She didn't come into this world with a lot of advantages, but she did have one fine brain and a real sense of purpose. She was the only one in her family to graduate from high school and college. And (after my sister and I had finished our schooling) she went to college and graduate school to earn her master's degree. With all that learning, my mother had only one real goal: to give back to the world around her. She became a social worker. Every year children of all ages came through her office, and she did what she could to touch their lives. She taught them how to focus their minds and chase their dreams, taught them to value their gifts and abilities, and, maybe most important of all, showed them that anyone can achieve if they set their mind to it. She's using her gifts to make a positive contribution to her family and her community, and she is one of the most successful people I know!

For a lot of sistahs who start making some money, it can be real tempting to just spend, spend, spend. You want a nice house, a fast car, exquisite jewelry, designer clothes. And there's no shame in treating yourself to some of those things. After all, as the song says, "You work hard for your money." But making it in the business world or the creative world, or any world, means you've got a responsibility to those around you who maybe didn't get the same opportunities. Part of being financially successful is learning to share. So find a charity or a cause that appeals to you, and make a donation. Even if you don't have much money to spare, you'd better believe you've got time (even if it may not seem like it!) and you've got talents. Got an eye for fashion? Volunteer at a career center to help teach first-time job seekers how to dress for the office. Computer skills? They're more valuable than hard cash. Get your butt to an adult education program or a teen center and spend one night a week passing on your knowledge.

Here's another way you can become a responsible success story: Set a good example. The people around you—your friends, your colleagues, your children—are all looking to you for clues on how to behave. What are you teaching your kids if you spend a lot of time bad-mouthing your boss? How do you expect them to learn to speak up for themselves if you're too timid to ask for a raise? There's a myth these days that success is all about being flashy and knowing the right people. It's your job to teach by example, just like my mother did for me. Do all you can to show young people that integrity, hard work, and respect for others really are the qualities that win out in the end.

Now, I know there are some of you out there who were tempted to skip over this whole section. You're telling yourself, *I'm not successful.* You're assuming just because you never started your own business or hung out with celebrities or went to college, that means you don't have something to give. Well, tell that voice in your head to shush itself right now. Everyone is blessed with success. Everyone has talents to share. Everyone has gifts to give.

Success isn't just a job title or a bank balance, it's an attitude. How you see yourself in your mind directly translates into how people perceive you in the world. If you see yourself as someone with learning and talents she wants to pass on, then trust me, that's just who you'll be. Still got your doubts? Think over all the things you've accomplished in your life. Everyone has something to give. Parenting skills can be passed on through classes for teen mothers. Five or ten dollars can make a difference to an AIDS foundation or homeless shelter. We've all achieved things we can be proud of. Part of claiming responsibility for our lives means owning our successes, then taking a close look at how our achievements can better the lives of those around us. You've been given talents, a voice, energy. Claim your success by giving back—it's what keeps the cycle going.

Journal time

This week, meditate on the page about the different ways in which you've been successful. Are you good at your job? Have you overcome difficult health or financial circumstances? Do you have your own business? Have you raised children as a single parent?

Think over what you've learned from these experiences. Are there skills and life tools you've acquired that you could pass on to others? Write down one or two ways in which you can use those skills or accomplishments to improve the lives of those around you. Then start doing it.

Also, spend some time this week thinking about those successful people who've had an impact on your own life. What have they taught you? How did they go about passing along their knowledge? How might you do something similar? Being truly successful means investing in the world. We're all in this together. Whether you're standing at the top of the ladder or still midclimb, there's always time to reach out and give a hand to the folks coming after you.

WEEK 12
Closing the Generation Gap: Responsibility to Our Youth

There always seems [to have] been someone . . . to point out the way for me to go. When I go to the next corner, there would be someone else standing there to tell me where to go. And that's how my whole life has been all along.

DUKE ELLINGTON

If you and I don't build a bridge back, throw out some strong lifelines to our children, youth and families whom poverty, unemployment are engulfing, they're going to drown, pull many of us down with them and undermine the future our forbears dreamed, struggled, and died for.

MARIAN WRIGHT EDELMAN

I've spent a lot of years working with children of all ages, watching how they react to what they see going on around them, listening to what they need. And if there's one thing I've learned it's that the most important thing parents can do is be involved in their child's life.

My friend Gloria was real tight with her five-year-old daughter, Kymberly. They spent every day together until last year when Kymberly finally took off for kindergarten and Gloria went back to work full time as a social worker. Well, things got a little hectic for a while. Gloria was spending too many nights trying to catch up on job stuff while Kymberly entertained herself, usually in front of the TV. Then, about halfway into the school year, Gloria noticed her child had started coming home *demanding* Pokémon shoes and Destiny's Child tapes and *insisting* she had to watch cartoons all day long instead of playing outside like she used to.

Now some parents would just let this slide, figuring it's part of what happens to kids when they head out into the real world. But not Gloria. She'd spent ten years as a social worker before Kymberly came along and, like me, she'd seen what happened to too many kids who wind up raised by a television set instead of their own parents. She wasn't about to watch that happen in her own home. She started making sure she and Kymberly had some real quality time together every night, doing something they both could get into like reading out loud or playing with the dog.

The payoff was clear to her the day she offered Kymberly an extra hour of cartoons while she finished up some work and Kymberly turned her down. Instead, she joined Gloria in her office and settled in for some of her own work, drawing pictures about the stories she and Gloria had been reading together. The messages Gloria'd been passing on—about work and creativity and expressing yourself—were making a difference in her child's life.

It's tough for us do-gooders to see the kids we care about basing their life philosophies on messages from the media and the streets. We can get to feeling like we don't have any power anymore. But let me tell you, that isn't true. These kids, our kids, want someone to take an interest in their lives and give them guidance and structure. If we want to reclaim their minds and souls, all we have to do is take action. Kids start out good. All of them. So do your part, and see that they stay that way.

Become a dependable presence in your child's life. Follow through on your promises. If you say you're going to take her somewhere, you have to do it. You can't forget. The generation gap is filled with broken promises and a lack of trust.

Be a positive role model. Help your kids become critical thinkers and problem solvers. Sometimes kids just need to vent (often we don't listen until their pain becomes public). After they've talked, help them take it to the next level. Ask questions that can help them think through positive solutions to their own problems, like, "So what's the lesson in this situation?" Let them see that obstacles are to be overcome. Urge them to develop a plan, and a dream, for the future.

Our responsibility to our children may begin in the home, but it certainly doesn't end there. We've got thousands of kids in our neighborhoods and on our streets who need someone to take an interest in their lives. I hear people complaining all the time about how kids these days have no respect for their elders, how gangs are taking over the streets and the schools, like teenagers have mutated into some other species of the human race. Like we sure as hell can't understand them so we might as well just give up. Well, talk like that is as irresponsible as it comes. These people don't bother to stop and ask themselves how we let this happen. We've still got experience, don't we? We've still got our voice. We owe it to those kids, and to ourselves, to see that they don't become the power. Because, tough as they like to act, they just aren't ready for it.

As adults, we forget what it's like to be young. The world is big and frightening, and sometimes young people feel like they have to take drastic steps to get control. It's up to us to stay connected to them, to let them know there's someone around who's looking out. When it comes to responsibility, there are no "other people's" children.

I've met a lot of very special young men in my work at Kaplan House. And I've seen firsthand that if you take the time to brush away the anger and attitude, odds are you're going to uncover a sweet kid who just never had a chance. My buddy Eric already had a real bad reputation when he came to Kaplan House a couple of years ago. He wanted to turn his life around, but he had a lot of forces pulling him the other direction. He'd been in jail, he'd been on the streets, and he just didn't have much faith left in anything at all. Well, I knew there was a smart and spirited young man underneath all that trouble. So I decided that, no matter what he did, he was going to find out there were some people who still cared. I gave him a job at the agency, let him know I trusted him with responsibility. I regularly checked up on what was going on in his life. It was a tough road, but the rewards were worth it. Like the letter he wrote me explaining how much I'd touched his life, and how he was already spreading the word that it's okay to care. He signed it, "I love you Terrie." Of course that letter made me cry.

But the most touching day of all was Eric's twenty-first birthday. I was headed over to Kaplan House that night and at the last minute, I decided it'd be a nice thing to get him a cake. I stopped by my favorite bakery and had them decorate one. As soon as I pulled out that cake and we all started singing "Happy Birthday," Eric—the tough-talking, street-savvy dude—burst into tears. Turns out no one had ever celebrated his birthday before. Never. Hearing that just broke my heart. How was a kid like that supposed to have a chance?

This process of closing up the generation gap begins with each of us renewing our pledge to parenting, not just our own children, but the entire younger generation. And don't think you won't get something just as rich out of the deal. This isn't about us being right and them being wrong. Each half has something to learn from the other. We can teach these kids some respect for our experience. They can open our minds to new ideas, make us relax a little, make us laugh. Hey, maybe you'll even find out you actually get into hip-hop! Don't disrespect or disregard the younger generation just because they seem different. They are different. How great is that? It's those of us who are supposed to know better who need to show them that differences can coexist, even thrive. It's our job to take the steps to unite our families and our neighborhoods.

So if you don't have kids of your own—or you do and can still manage the time—go to a local teen center, a low-income housing project, or an after-school tutoring program and just spend a few hours being with a young person. Even if it's difficult to hear what she's saying, let her talk. Listen without judgment. Listen to what she needs from you, instead of deciding beforehand what you "should" be giving her. Sometimes all kids really want is a meal, a chance to laugh and let loose, or a quiet place to think. If you can provide for them, and continue to provide, that's the first step toward making a connection. And if you don't think you have time for that, then I have one word for you. *Prioritize.* Part of taking responsibility for our lives is determining what's important. Nothing could be more important than our kids.

*J*ournal time

This week we're going to meditate on the page about how we can become better parents to all our children. First, spend some time writing about the lessons and values your own parents passed on to you. How did their beliefs shape your life? What did they teach you that you want to pass on to your own kids? Are there things you don't want to pass on? Why not?

Think a bit about your own values and how they've formed over the years. Are you passing these values on to the kids in your life? How can you do a better job of setting a good example for the next generation? (Again, I'm not just talking biological. As we should all know by now, parenting doesn't only come from the parents.)

Also, spend some time thinking about how you can serve as a better parent in your community. Talk to the kids in your area and let them know you care. Are there local teen centers? Reading programs? Mentoring opportunities? If not, what can you do to change that? Maybe it's time to organize block by block, set up some after-school programs, or look into funding for a playground or a rec center. List a few ways in which you can get involved with the kids around you. Now pick at least one of those things and *do it*. Today. There's no time left for wasting. If we want healthy families and healthy communities, it's our responsibility to create a loving, caring atmosphere for our kids.

WEEK 13
Civic Responsibility:
Expanding Our Horizons

❑

There can be no daily democracy without daily
citizenship.

RALPH NADER

Remember in elementary school how everyone, even the bad
kids, got citizenship awards? Seems like civic involvement was
easy as saying the Pledge of Allegiance first thing in the morning
with the rest of the school.

Now that we're all grown up, it's time for our involvement in
our neighborhoods, communities, and society to increase in so-
phistication. As adults, making a positive contribution means
taking action. If you don't stop hiding and start doing, you abdi-
cate your responsibility to other powers—like politicians and
large corporations—that may not have your best interests at
heart. It's our society, and it's our responsibility to participate in
how it functions as a whole.

Of course, it's a whole lot easier to just complain or worry
about the problems we see around us. After all, things like
hunger, education, and the environment can seem too overwhelming for any individual to tackle. But one person can always
make a difference.

A few years ago my friends Zeke, Doug, and Stephanie got
concerned about all the homeless people in their neighborhood
who never got a hot meal. Sure, there were shelters and soup
kitchens, but they were all underfunded and overcrowded. No

one had the resources to help those folks who couldn't even get it together to get off the streets and indoors. So instead of just sitting around and fretting over the problem, these three decided to do something. They went to local restaurants and gathered donations of plastic forks and take-out containers. Then they talked to nearby supermarkets about cutting them a deal on their tired vegetables and day-old baked goods. Every other Sunday, the three of them started meeting in Doug's apartment to cook up a couple of turkeys or chickens. They mashed potatoes, mixed salads, heated up rolls, and sliced a few pies. While the food was still hot, they dished it up into individual containers, added a fork, a napkin, and a little personal touch like a card or a flower. Then the three of them, and eventually a group of other friends who also wanted to contribute, hit the streets and spent all night passing out hot meals. These days they've got a whole crowd of hungry folks who expect and depend on them. These three people saw a problem and took action. They got local businesses to donate supplies and got their friends to volunteer their time. They got organized and they made a difference. So can you.

An important first step is educating ourselves about the issues that concern us. It never ceases to amaze me how uninformed people can be about what's going on in their communities, not to mention the world around them. Civic involvement requires that we wake up and become informed. Read the newspapers. Listen to political debates on television. Why? Because they're talking about the things that will ultimately affect you. Companies that move to other countries may mean fewer jobs in your hometown. A debate in Congress about taxes may have a direct effect on your paycheck. Cuts in education spending might mean fewer teachers or larger class sizes in your children's schools.

Once you've educated yourself, then start voting. If you haven't registered to vote, then put this book down right this second and go do it. Especially for Black folks and women, the vote is sacred. It wasn't that long ago that people died so we could have that right. The civil rights era of the 1960s was all about forcing the government to practice what it preached in the Constitution and Bill of Rights. We should never forget that those political advances were won on the blood, sweat, and tears of thousands of freedom fighters. It's worth your time to go back and revisit the stories of civil rights heroes like Malcolm X, Harriet Tubman, Martin Luther King Jr., and Medgar Evers. Ultimately, their victories strengthened the entire society, because none of us is free until we're all free. As we are all lifted up, the society becomes strong.

I am grateful for the freedoms we enjoy in America, but I do not wear rose-colored glasses. There are many problems and many divisions that come with a pluralistic society. Our historical and economic foundation was built on the unwilling backs of enslaved Africans, displaced Native Americans, and indentured Europeans and Asians. Today the inequities resulting from those divisions continue. When it comes to equal rights, equal pay, and equal opportunities, too often women and Black folks still find themselves getting the short end of the stick. Does this bother you? I sure hope so. Here's a perfect opportunity to start exercising your right to speak freely and organize around an issue that matters to us all.

How can you get involved in your community and your future? Here are just a few ideas: Form a neighborhood watch group to help keep your local streets safe. Join your block club or building co-op. If you have school-aged children, become involved in the PTA. Get to know your neighbors. Participate in community events. Plant gardens, paint schools, clean up the nearby parks. When superstar Bette Midler learned that New York City was thinking of selling its urban gardens to real estate developers, she bought up all the empty lots herself, just to make sure the city got to keep these lovely and much-needed pockets of nature. Now, most of us don't have the power or the bucks to go buying up major real estate, but we can learn from Midler all the same. If there's an issue that concerns you, move. Write to your congresspeople and let them know about it. Circulate a petition. Organize a march or demonstration. Make your voice heard.

Once you've educated yourself about what's going on in your community, go ahead and spread the net even wider. With the Internet and air transportation, we have quickly become a global community. The old saying, "Think globally, act locally," should be our motto from this day forward. Start paying attention to events going on all over the world. Read the international section of the newspaper. Watch the evening news. Something that happens in India, Africa, the Middle East, or anywhere else affects us here. Our investment in the human condition shouldn't be regulated by borders. Think about making a donation to an organization like the Peace Corps or Doctors Without Borders that's devoted to bringing health and education to every citizen of the world.

As the living virtues tell us, finding peace in this lifetime is all about achieving a balance. It's about giving and taking in equal proportions. So go ahead and spend some time thinking how you want to do your part in shaping the policies and products of this world. How do you want to be remembered?

Of course, taking up your civic responsibilities isn't just about sacrifice. It's about becoming a whole human being. Feeling helpless on a global level also leaves us feeling helpless on a personal level. It starts to seem like the issues that affect our lives have spun out of control. But we don't have to settle for that. If you're overwhelmed by the rising unemployment rate, or feeling depressed about the state of education in our poor neighborhoods, the best thing you can do about it is get out there and take a stand. Volunteer at a job placement center, or lobby your local politicians for more money dedicated to inner-city schools. Society is made up of a group of individuals, and that includes you. Getting involved in your country or community will empower you as a person. It's not just about being a do-gooder because you feel you should. It's about feeling better about yourself. When you do something for someone else, you get the gift.

Claiming a place in society can mean doing something as small as casting your vote for city council member, or as large as running for office yourself. But whatever you choose to do, know that by taking action you are making a statement that you care about this world. Everybody has the power, and the responsibility, to change the things they don't like. We've all been given unique gifts, a unique point of view, unique energies, and unique visions. If we don't contribute those gifts, then the world will suffer for it. Those who would benefit from our contributions will go without. Not contributing isn't just irresponsible, it's selfish. You matter. You're important. You are a big part of this world.

*J*ournal time

This week, spend some time considering what you can do to fulfill your civic responsibilities. Are there things in your community that you feel need changing? Are the streets safe? Are the schools good? What can you do to make a difference? Maybe it's volunteering at a soup kitchen or starting a book club. Maybe it's taking the time to learn about the members of your local government and where they stand on the issues. Maybe it's starting up a children's program at the local church or community center. Once you've come up with a few ideas, go ahead and act. Just thinking isn't enough. Get your butt in motion.

Also this week, try going more global. Meditate on the page about what you can you do to change the world. Think about what issue matters to you most. Education? The environment? Women's issues? Health care? Are you doing anything about these things? Choose three ways in which you can make a difference. If you haven't done it already, your first step should be registering to vote. Then add your name to a petition. Make a donation. Make a phone call. Organize a protest. Get involved—and make it a habit.

WEEK 14
The Big Picture:
Responsibility Equals Liberty

Being happy is not the only happiness.
ALICE WALKER,
The Color Purple

Quick, let's play one of those word association games. I say *responsibility* and what's the first thing you think of? Burden, obligation, duty? I hope not! I hope you're thinking words like *opportunity* and *growth* and *freedom*. I hope the living virtues are starting to teach you what they've taught me: that we're incredibly blessed to have a place in this world, and claiming responsibility for our lives means every moment of every day has become rich with new possibilities.

Responsibility equals liberty. Let's think for a moment about just what that means. The word *liberty* is pretty significant, especially for Black folks. It's the cornerstone of our existence. It says everything about our history, the struggles we've overcome, and who we're proud to be today. But liberty isn't something you just possess, like a designer suit or a new car. It's something you have to work at constantly. It requires time and thought and dedication. It's a responsibility, one we're very lucky to be able to undertake.

I think about responsibility every day. I think about it when I'm debating whether or not to walk the four miles to work. I think about it when I'm dealing with the young folks in my office or my foundation. I think about it while I'm reading the paper, or just hanging with close friends. Because if it weren't for the fact that I'd finally decided to assume responsibility for my life and my future, none of these things would be happening at all. I'd be stressed, depressed, unhealthy, and unhappy. I might be lonely. I might be lost. Truth is, I might not even be here at all. So you can believe I'm thanking God for the gift of responsibility every day of my life. Responsibilities don't tie us down. They're not a weight but a privilege. They give us the freedom to fly.

That day the doctor sat me down in his office and let me know I had diabetes, I had the choice to make changes in my diet and exercise programs that can keep me around for a good long while. When I felt like my business was stretching me too thin, I had the option to reevaluate which clients and projects were filling me up and which were draining me dry. Each one of these decisions was a life-changing event. Taking responsibility for my actions, my future, and my role in the world surrounding me meant taking control of my life. I'm happier and more optimistic than I've been in my forty-eight years, and believe me that's no small thing.

What have you done recently to make positive changes in your life? Take a moment to celebrate the wonderful, giving person you are and the still-better person you have the freedom to become. How does it feel to claim responsibility and control for the world around you? How does it feel to know you can make a difference? I can speak for only one woman, but I can tell you she's feeling stronger, more focused, and more powerful than ever before. I can't wait to see what new avenues continue to open up with this decision to reclaim my own life. I firmly believe that similar opportunities will rise up to greet all of us, as long as we've got the patience to search for them and the courage to take action. A lot of us—myself included—tend to go looking for the moments of high drama as evidence our lives are moving forward. We forget that it's accepting responsibility for the small details, the daily efforts, the expressions of caring and investment that really define who we are. And, in the process, finally set us free.

---

*J*ournal time

This week let's meditate on the page about the idea of responsibility as a gift. What are the most important responsibilities in your life? Do they involve your family? Your community? Your job? Your health? How many of these responsibilities still feel like burdens? (I have to admit, sticking to that exercise plan often feels like a burden to me.) Concentrate on how you might change your outlook. Think about how these same responsibilities also give you freedom. For instance, being in better shape means I'll have extra energy to devote to the people who care about me, to give back to the community, and to live a longer, fuller life.

From now on, whenever you find yourself feeling overwhelmed by your responsibilities, do your best to reshape them in your mind. Think about how they enable you to take control of your life. Remember how lucky you are to live in a time and place where you have the freedom to make your own decisions and act upon them. Never forget: Responsibility is one of our greatest gifts of all.

Living Virtue 3

Thrift

Nature is the most thrifty thing in the world; she never wastes anything; she undergoes change, but there is no annihilation, the essence remains—matter is eternal.

HORACE BINNEY

Nature can teach us a thing or two about conserving, recycling, growing, and spending our resources so that ultimately we build wealth for ourselves, our families, and our communities. In the desert, flowers bloom in infertile sand and rainwater collects in the driest, most unlikely places. In the city, flowers and weeds somehow break through the concrete cracks of sidewalks and highways. I've seen beautiful lavender bushes grow on a landfill mound and sunflowers amid the rocks and debris of a vacant lot. Nature resourcefully "stretches its dollar" so that life can continue, even under the harshest of conditions.

Having experienced many tough times, my parents' generation understood how this lesson from nature applied to money management. Many of our parents lived through the Great Depression. They had to learn how to feed an entire family on a pot of beans for a week. Families and communities huddled together to survive, often sharing food, money, clothing, and shelter with one another when times got tough. Black folks often threw rent parties when money got tight. Even if you didn't have much to spare in your own household, you'd kick in what you could—you knew that your turn could come any day. They pooled their resources, and they watched every cent carefully. From such hard times, they grew to appreciate the value of a dollar.

They also developed a healthy respect for what a dollar could do. Taking the American Dream seriously, they saved, sometimes for years, to buy homes, furniture, and cars. They carefully allocated their limited dollars to give their kids the kind of education and start on life that they never received.

My parents were raised dirt-poor in the South. My mom was a sharecropper's daughter, and Dad picked cotton. Probably more than anyone in the family, my mother had a strong desire to be financially free. She hated debt of any kind, and many of the financial decisions she made as an adult were based on her desire to be free.

My parents migrated to the North, partly to escape racism and discrimination, but also to search for jobs and economic opportunities. When I think about the quality of life my folks were able to provide for my sister and me, I am amazed at how much they were able to do with so little. We weren't rich or poor, just your basic lower middle-class family. We didn't have a lot of disposable cash, but somehow we never seemed to want for anything. We never went hungry and we lived in a safe neighborhood. We were well educated. If we lacked some of the more obvious symbols of wealth, I never noticed. As far as I was concerned, we were rich in the things that mattered.

My parents were typical of their generation in that they didn't talk a lot to my sister or me about money. Although they did encourage us to open a savings account at the bank, for the most part they believed that household finance was not a child's business. I learned about saving, sacrificing, and keeping a lid on my spending habits through osmosis, but the really big household financial issues, such as insurance policies, monthly mortgage payments, and grocery bills, were never discussed. Back then, children were to be seen and not heard, especially when it came to money.

I don't blame my parents for not talking to us about money, but in hindsight I can see how my ignorance of money matters led to many challenges in my personal finances as an adult. Money was a mystery that inspired awe and a little fear in me. When I was a little kid, I used to wonder what it would be like to be rich. What would I do with all that money? Give it away to help people? Buy a big house—and then what?

I had no real relationship with money because my folks took care of all my needs. I guess you could say that I took money for granted. I figured it would always be there.

My world and sense of safety came crashing down the day that Dad lost his trucking job. I was about twelve years old when we learned that his company had gone out of business. Although Mom and Dad tried to cushion me, they couldn't stop me from worrying. We were totally dependent on his income. I lost my innocence that day. Suddenly, money was no longer the stuff of fantasies, but a cold reality. Consciously I became aware of the fact that we needed money, not just for the nice stuff, but for survival. For the first time in my young life, I knew real money-related fear.

What would become of us? I wondered. Would we be thrown out into the streets? Would we starve? Would we have to beg to survive? My father has always been a proud man, and there was no way he'd consider begging. We had family and friends—we would make it. Until he finally decided to launch his own business, there were many terrifying days. Often during those times my parents would huddle off by themselves to work out their financial problems, still trying to shelter us. But this only gave my already overactive imagination more room to roam. I suffered a few sleepless nights.

Although I wouldn't wish such a scary situation on any child, I did learn many things from my parents during that time. I'm sure they remembered the hard times they suffered as children when their own fathers walked out, and they didn't want us to go through that nightmare. I'll always be grateful that they worked it out together. They kept a roof over our heads and food in our mouths with money they had saved for this rainy day. I learned a powerful lesson in saving and stretching dollars to take care of our day-to-day needs.

Just because you have income today doesn't mean that you'll have it tomorrow. Nothing is promised, and with the ups and downs I've experienced over the years in my business, I've kept this lesson close to heart. You must always plan for those dry, desert times.

On top of learning about savings, watching Dad get through his employment crisis taught me a ton about business. One of the things I really respect about my father is his resourcefulness. I watched him make connections, build relationships, generate seed capital, and ultimately manage and grow his company. He'd sometimes take me with him when he was going on a job, which was great because I got to watch him in action, interacting with clients. It took a while, but eventually he pulled us out of the financial crisis. And while he was pulling us out, I was absorbing the lessons of entrepreneurship.

The fear of starvation, my father's resourcefulness and willingness to take risks, and my mother's strong desire for financial freedom certainly shaped my feelings about money and my approach to money management. And yet, despite the many positive lessons I learned from my folks, I ended up with major financial difficulties as an adult.

During the first few years of my business, I would sometimes use my personal credit cards and loans from Mom to keep the agency afloat. The company was in the black, but my personal checking account was bleeding red. One day I looked up and found I was in my own sharecropping hell of credit-card debt. If you've ever gotten threatening letters from creditors, you know what I mean. I've been depressed many times in my life, but this anxiety was on another level. Money worries can give you ulcers, high blood pressure, and sleepless nights. I honestly thought I'd never see daylight.

I hated the fact that I couldn't even enjoy the money I was working so hard to make, so I swallowed my pride and decided to ask my friend Ray to help me out. I went home, got out my box of bills and bank statements, and then took them to Ray. Ray is a whiz with money, and I trusted him to not laugh at me or make me feel bad about getting myself into such a jam.

Ray's no-nonsense yet compassionate approach was so helpful that I will always be grateful. He didn't gasp in horror or make me feel stupid when he saw how much I owed Visa and Master-Card. He simply held my hand and asked me if I really wanted to get control over my financial situation. I did, and for the first time in a long time I felt hope. If I could manage my company's budget, I could do the same for my personal finances. I was starting to believe that I could do this.

First, I told Ray the truth about my personal spending habits. He made me account for every penny that I spent. I had to write down all my credit-card balances and total them up. I felt a lot of shame about how I had been spending my money. No wonder I never had enough to pay bills at the end of the month.

I have to admit to you that I hated this entire process, but I endured it because I couldn't stand the pain of not being able to take care of myself. I hated being in bondage to credit-card companies. It seemed that my only reason for working was to pay off the credit cards. So even though I hated this exercise, I knew that it was absolutely necessary. I had to do it to see where my hard-earned dollars were really going. As it turned out, apparently I had returned to the fantasyland of my childhood. My credit-card use separated me from the immediacy of a cash payment. It lured me into a false sense that I could have anything I wanted, anytime I wanted it—a sure recipe for disaster.

So Ray took my all credit cards, except for one that I was to use strictly for business purposes. Then together, we developed a budget that I felt I could stick to.

In a year I was debt-free and ready to begin the process of building true wealth. I felt like marching in my own ticker-tape parade, I was so ecstatic and pleased with myself. I was free! When I wrote the check for my last credit-card payment, the joy I felt was indescribable. Ray had helped me, but I had done the hard work. My self-esteem shot through the roof. I was free at last.

I vowed to never return to such a state of financial bondage. Ray's approach to finances—plain and simple thrift—would now be my approach to earning, spending, and growing my money.

Since then, I've thought long and hard about this important living virtue. I resisted it at first because thrift to me meant being stingy and cheap. I was wrong. As we'll discuss in the next few weeks, thriftiness is really about pruning the weeds that clutter your life so that you can get a handle on what you really want, need, and desire. Often, we don't even know what we want! If you've ever bought something, put it away, and then never used it, you know what I mean. Sometimes we buy so much stuff because we don't know what will make us happy. Thrift forces us to focus on our true desires, which means we must know ourselves well enough to know what we really want!

Thrift is about critical decision making and the pacing of purchases. Old-style thriftiness was about learning how to do without. My style of thriftiness is about moderation. I work too hard to forgo all the things I want or need, so I've learned the art of pacing myself. You don't have to do without everything you want, but you may have to learn to prioritize your wants and needs. Once you've prioritized your needs, cultivating patience helps you delay gratification and keep your monthly spending in check.

Every time I make a nonessential purchase these days, I search my feelings. If I just have to have an expensive designer jacket instead of the equally fabulous knockoff tagged at half the price, I ask myself why. Literally: I take a deep breath, exhale slowly, and say, "Terrie, can you give me a *real* reason why you need to have *this* jacket, at *this* price, right *now?*" Half the time I can't even come up with a *bad* reason; most of the rest of the time I come up with reasons that wouldn't convince a five-year-old. And that's why nine times out of ten I end up not buying the thing that, for thirty glorious seconds, had me believing it would heal all my ills. It's this ten-second act of self-interrogation that helps me remain conscious about my spending, and on my guard against overspending.

Thrifty people enjoy a level of freedom not experienced by those who are deeply in debt. When I was in debt, I was a slave to my creditors' monthly payment cycles. I dreaded seeing those envelopes arrive in my mailbox like clockwork. Today I am free because I can have both what I want and what I need. All I have to do is prioritize my wants and needs and pace my spending.

Over the next few weeks we'll look at wealth, financial freedom, and enjoying our money. Some people think that spending a lot of money on material goods is fun, but I've come to realize that it's more fun to be debt-free and in charge of my financial well-being. Delaying gratification and taking time to think about each and every purchase makes me question my true motives for spending. I find that with compulsive spending, once you've bought something, you no longer care about it. Remember when you were a child and you just had to have a certain toy? As soon as you got it, you lost interest. It's the same with our spending. Today I get the most enjoyment out of holding on to my money, saving and investing it, and watching it grow.

If money woes have been stressing you out, take heart. Over the next eight weeks, we're going to tame this monster. You'll learn how to incorporate thrift into every aspect of your financial life—spending, debt reduction, and wealth building. By understanding your real wants and needs, you'll no longer be a slave to the whims of the moment. Not only will you begin to enjoy your money today, but you'll invest in the future as well—for yourself, your family, and your community.

WEEK 15
Dollars, Cents, and Yourself

◩

Money . . . now plays an unprecedentedly
powerful role in our inner and outer lives . . .
any serious search for self-knowledge and self-
development requires that we study the meaning that money actually has for us.

JACOB NEEDLEMAN,
Money and the Meaning of Life

Recently I told some friends that I feel inadequate because I
haven't bought a home yet. They couldn't understand why I felt
that way, and I couldn't explain it. Many people don't own
homes, and they don't suffer from low self-esteem. Why did I?

Ever since I was a child, I've had a strong desire to own a
home. I used to fantasize about how I would decorate it, the family I would raise in it, and the parties I would throw there. It felt
like such a grown-up thing to do. Now, I'm not the richest person in the world, but I could buy a home easily. All it would take
is planning and budgeting, putting a few dollars away every
month. In a year or less I could have enough to get the brownstone of my dreams. So why haven't I done it?

Money experts always say that for most people, a home will be
their biggest purchase. While that's true, that's not what stops
me. After close examination I realized that just thinking about
buying a house brings up all kinds of feelings in me. I think
about planting deep roots, and there's a part of me that's not
ready to do that yet. It's a huge commitment, and I like my free-

dom. I want the property, but I don't necessarily want to be so tied down.

If you ever want to get to know yourself, follow your own money trail. Spend just one day tracking how much and on what you spend your money. The best way to keep track of your spending is to keep a written record. You can use your journal, money management software, or a simple ledger you can buy from an office supply store.

Reviewing your daily spending can be incredibly enlightening. I have a friend who eats out all the time. She totaled up her coffee shop and restaurant receipts for a couple of days and was shocked to discover that she spends thirty to fifty dollars a day on food! She asked herself what was going on and came to the very simple realization that although she likes to cook, she never seems to have the time. By the time she gets home from work, she's too tired to do anything but go out or order in. Now that she knows that she wants to get her finances back in balance, she's planning to increase her savings by cooking more—with the added bonus of reinvigorating her social life in the process. By having her friends over for dinner rather than always meeting in restaurants she can spend more quality time with them while saving money!

All too often our spending is done unconsciously. Wake up and watch yourself spending money. Pay attention to how you feel before and after a purchase, and you may discover that you're trying to medicate some part of your life that's not going quite right. Have you ever gone on a spending spree when you felt lonely? During my credit-card days, I would spend because I thought I deserved to "boost" my mood. Usually the good feelings were only temporary.

So what does all this emotional stuff have to do with thrift? Many times we want to be better money managers and enjoy our money more, but unconscious motivations and beliefs prevent us from doing so. If you've got unresolved issues around money, you can promise to budget and discipline yourself all you want, but you won't be able to stick to it if your soul has other plans.

To practice a lifestyle of thrift, first we must understand how money has the power to dredge up our deepest issues and conflicts. We cannot practice thrift if we still have issues undermining our desire to be debt-free and create wealth.

I have a friend who's a classic case of how old money feelings from childhood get in the way of adult plans. Imani grew up in a middle-class household. For the most part her childhood was a happy one—except during bill-paying time. Once a month Imani would watch her father sit at the kitchen table, pencil in hand, stacks of bills all around. When her father was writing checks, she was not allowed to speak to him or disturb him in any way. She and her sisters had to be very quiet. Usually a gentle, soft-spoken man, during bill-paying time he would snap at her for no reason, and he would drink too much.

Although her father was responsible about paying the bills on time, Imani's mother constantly complained about their debt. Because he was such a good credit risk, he often received new credit cards in the mail, and both parents would use them constantly.

"I learned two lessons from my folks—pay my bills on time and stay in debt," says Imani.

As an adult she tried to build a nice nest egg for her retirement, but her credit-card debt—more than fifty thousand dollars on her thirty-five-thousand-per-year salary was overwhelming. She was totally stressed out about it and feared that she might have to file for bankruptcy.

She finally sought the help of a financial counselor. It was very difficult, but thanks to the strong sense of responsibility her father taught her, she had the inner discipline to tough it out. Together, she and her counselor worked out a budget. He also helped her structure her debt so that the monthly payments were manageable. Imani's not out of the woods yet, but in two years, with all things being equal, she projects that she'll be completely debt-free. She couldn't have done it if she hadn't dealt with the mixed money messages she got from her parents.

Journal time

Money has to be the most emotionally loaded word in any language, and we've got to get a grip! We've got a lot to do in our journals this week.

- Let's explore how we feel about money. Do you see it as the "root of all evil," or is it a lifesaver? Write down words and phrases you use to describe money (say, *peanuts, filthy rich, dough*). Are you intimidated by money? Or is money your friend? Make two columns labeled "good money words" and "bad money words." See which one is longer. See what your lists tell you about your feelings.
- Write about your earliest impressions of money as a child. How did your parents deal with their money issues? Compare that to how you're managing your finances today. What are the similarities and differences? How did you earn your first dollar as a child? Did your parents teach you about money, or did you learn through osmosis? Did your parents fight about money? Was money invisible, and somehow the house just ran on its own? This exercise is critical in discovering our own emotions and practices around saving, investing, earning, and spending money.

WEEK 16
Understanding Needs, Wants, and Desires

🔲

It is thrifty to prepare today for the wants of tomorrow.

AESOP, circa 550 B.C.

What do you want?

What do you need?

What do you deeply desire?

These are three completely different questions, but we usually use the words *wants*, *needs*, and *desires* interchangeably. To begin to live a thrifty lifestyle, we must get some perspective on what we want, need, and desire. Why? Because these are our spending motivations, and they often operate at the unconscious level. We've got to raise them up to the level of awareness. We often confuse the three, and that's when our spending gets out of control. So let's define our terms.

Ironically, wants are the least important category for survival but the greatest motivator in our spending decisions. A purchase based on want usually makes us feel good, but doesn't meet our needs for survival. For instance, in New York you *need* a good coat to keep you warm in winter, but it doesn't need to cost five thousand dollars. Clearly a fur or cashmere coat is a want, not a need. After all, will the designer's label really keep you warmer?

Needs, on the other hand, are all about survival. We need to buy food for life. We need to pay the rent and utilities for shelter and heat. They are the basics that we need to function every day.

Desires blend needs with the feel-good of wants. You know that you're desiring something when your mouth begins to water or you feel a strong attraction. The result is an emotionally charged want. The motivation to spend because of a desire is probably the least understood and the most powerful. Desires feel like need, but frequently result in unnecessary consumption, like charging a two-hundred-dollar dinner when a home-cooked meal would have done just as well.

Desires and wants are seductive, but once you can separate them from needs, you can begin to understand and control how and when you spend money. You'll also begin to understand yourself better. What do your spending habits say about your desires? Do you buy more clothes than you can wear? If so, what's the underlying fear, emptiness, or yearning? By working with the deeper emotional layers, you may find that you're less likely to work it out on your credit card.

These questions are not about judging. Instead, I'm hoping to help you begin to understand the differences among your needs, wants, and desires. The more information you have about them and how they are tied to your spending habits, the sooner you can begin the road to financial health and freedom.

Journal time

In your journal this week, try to recall the purchases you made in the past few days. List them out with their dollar amounts. Beside them indicate whether they were a want, need, or desire. In particular, explore the motivations underlying the items bought because of want and desire. Try to really write about the feelings you had before and after your purchases. After you've tried this exercise one or a few times, try keeping a small notebook in your purse or pocket and write down your feelings *before* you make a want- or desire-based purchase. See if your desire to make the purchase remains the same.

WEEK 17
Get Out of Debt

🔲

Never spend your money before you have it.
THOMAS JEFFERSON

We all want to be contributing members of society, and in a way we are just by spending. The money we spend fuels our economy, and in turn our economy ensures the production of things we need and want. You could argue that our country's economic survival depends on us buying movie tickets, hair extensions, books, clothes, nail polish, food, wine, cars, gas, medicine, greeting cards, and a bunch of other stuff. The problem is, we're spending more than we're saving and investing, and sometimes even more than we're earning.

As a result, many of us are broke, and we're worrying ourselves to death over money. Credit cards, with their high interest rates, are a big part of the problem. The country is more than $360 billion in credit-card debt, and that number increases every year.

How is it that so many of us willingly got sucked into this debt slavery? We don't get a credit card with the idea that we'll be stuck with the same balance year after year. Often we think, *I'll just get this outfit and I'll pay it off in a couple of months.* Two months becomes four months, and in the meantime there's a pair of shoes and matching purse that you just have to have. Add on the cost of the oil change for your car, the restaurant bill, gas, medicine, and groceries and you've walked willingly onto the credit-card plantation.

One day you realize that you're in trouble. You can't pay all your bills on time. You start to juggle. You miss paying one bill this month to pay another bill that's past due. So now, in addition to the 22 percent interest rate (even though they initially sucked you in at 9 percent), you're paying late penalties. Your creditors, eager to collect high interest payments and late fees, eventually send bill collectors and threatening letters. You end up with a bad credit rating, low self-esteem, possibly even depression.

Debt is slavery, and there's a whole lot of us slaves living on the credit-card plantation. My credit-card problems started in college. I thought it was very grown up to have a credit card, so of course I couldn't wait to get one.

Credit-card companies market heavily to college students, which on the surface makes no sense considering the fact that they have next to no income. Year after year, thousands of college students get trapped into credit-card debt. It starts innocently enough. You're given a small limit of, say, five hundred dollars. Doesn't seem like a lot, but the cycle has begun. Five hundred dollars graduates to twenty-five hundred or more within a few short years.

For older folks it's the same game, just bigger dreams and higher credit limits. But if you are in debt, don't despair; there is hope. I know from personal experience that you can free yourself, build savings, and begin to really enjoy your money. These are four steps that really worked for me:

1. *Communicate.* Talk to someone who can help you free yourself from the cycle of debt. Financial counselors are a great resource. They can assist you in developing a plan, and some can even help you renegotiate the interest rates and terms of your debt. Work with your counselor to develop a budget that you can live with and then stick to it.

2. *Get used to spending cash.* Put the credit cards away. Give them to a friend you trust and don't take them back until they are all paid off. Better yet, cut them up. Keep one if you must, but always pay it off at the end of the month.

3. *Remember your income.* From this day forward, whenever you

consider making a purchase, think about your income first. What is your net income (after taxes) per month? If you buy this thing *in cash* will you be able to pay the rent and utilities, buy groceries, and so on? Your income is your reality. You haven't won the lottery, so you must discipline yourself to spend within your means. "Your means" is no fantasy number—it is your net income, plain and simple. Keep a running tab of every purchase you make for a month. Try to monitor your spending so you still have at least a small portion of your monthly income at the end of the month.

4. *Look for ways to save money.* Seems like there's a fee attached to everything nowadays. That's why I have never used ATM machines in my life. Once a week I withdraw the amount I'll need from the bank, and that's what I live on for the next seven days. If I run short, I'll go to the bank and write a check for cash. Here are a few more simple ways to pare down needless expenses:

- Avoid calling directory assistance.
- Make long-distance calls during off-peak hours.
- Don't let your checking or savings account dip below the amount designated by your bank.
- Some banks charge fees to deposit checks in person. Have your paycheck automatically deposited by your employer.
- Avoid late penalties by paying your credit cards on time.
- Use coupons when grocery shopping.
- Do you really need cable television? If not, cut it off.
- Turn off the lights and water when you're not using them.
- Call around to see if you can get a better rate on your auto insurance.
- Try to lower your credit-card interest rate by moving your business to another card. They'll often lower rates to get your business.

If you want to have a healthy, happy, and productive life, you must get out of debt. If you're sick and tired of being a slave on the credit-card plantation, cut up your cards and pay down those balances. If you want a financial legacy to pass on to your children, protect their investment by working toward debt freedom *today*.

As I write this I'm thinking about my car note. Many of us are paying off a car note, and that's not necessarily a bad thing. We have to get around, so for many of us, a car is a true necessity—but a "dream car" is not. I'm not telling you to get a junkyard special if you can comfortably afford a Rolls-Royce, but on the road to spending wisely I am encouraging you to set aside some of your automotive wants for now and think about what car will best meet your needs. If you're buying from a dealer, negotiate a good price for your dream car, but also negotiate good terms, because this is where dealerships often stick it to us. Shop around for low interest rates. Try to pay the car note down as quickly as possible. The sixty-month note has become standard in the industry, but if you can pay your car off in thirty-six months, do so, because the longer your note, the more you'll have to pay.

There are many techniques and services you can use, but they will only work if you work them. Today is the day to begin the process. The longer you wait, the more money you'll have to pay back. Which is more painful—giving up a few things *for the moment* or living the rest of your life as a slave? I've been a slave and I've been free, and freedom is better.

Getting out of debt is sometimes a painful step in practicing a thrifty lifestyle. My hope is that you will be patient, because after you heal your finances, the best part of thrift is yet to come.

Journal time

We've got a lot of journal work to do this week. Let's honestly assess our financial situations. Are you in debt? How do you feel about it? Do you know the total amount that you owe? Set goals for when and how you want to get out of debt. Try this:

- Take a clean sheet of paper, draw a line down the middle, label the left column "assets" and the right column "debts." Then put down everything that belongs in each column— *everything*, including the things you think are so small they "don't really count" (like your Exxon credit card . . .). This may sound hard, but just remind yourself that this is the time of reckoning, and it'll never be this hard again.

- Educate yourself. There are many excellent books that will help you understand as well as manage your assets and your debt. A few good ones are *Your Money or Your Life* by Joe Dominguez and Vicki Robin, *Making Peace with Money* by Jerrold Mundis, *Talking Dollars and Making Sense* by Brooke Stephens, *Debt Free by 30* by Jason Anthony and Karl Cluck, and any of Suze Orman's excellent books. Identify your problem areas and start following the advice offered. For instance, if you don't understand mutual funds, make an appointment with a reputable investment broker. Remember, the more you know, the better able you are to make decisions about your hard-earned money.

- Look up credit counselors and consumer education Web sites on the Internet and jot them down in your journal. Credit counselors can help you do many things. They'll look at your entire financial picture. They can help restructure your debt and even persuade creditors to lower your interest rates. Most important, they'll help you develop a reasonable budget and they'll check up on you periodically. Call the centers you've listed in your journal and find a counselor who is right for you.

WEEK 18
Buy Your Freedom

回

I freed thousands of slaves. I could have freed thousands more, if they had known they were slaves.

HARRIET TUBMAN

Recently I read about a woman whose idea of freedom was to own her own brownstone in New York City. Although her income was never very high, from the age of sixteen she began saving to buy her family a home. When she was tempted to buy something she didn't really need, she remembered her goal, and nothing seemed as important—and necessary—to her well-being as owning her own home. After years of saving and searching, she found the perfect house in Harlem, but the property was a mess. Because she had a clear vision of what she desired, however, she could see the possibilities, even in the ruins. With her savings, she bought and rehabbed the building, and now she and her family live in their own building. She's living life exactly the way she planned it.

I love this story because it proves that you don't have to be rich to be free, but you must believe that you will actually be free one day, and you have to be diligent about pursuing your freedom. When you have a burning desire to live life on your own terms, what you're really craving is freedom. Unfortunately, for too many of us in our society, freedom is only an abstract thought or cocktail conversation rather than a way of life.

African Americans have a lot to teach the world about the pursuit of freedom. Many of our enslaved ancestors were severely

beaten or killed because they kept trying to escape the plantation and harsh life under the whip. Despite laws against learning
how to read, they read in secret. The more they read, the more
they yearned to be free. As a sharecropper's daughter, my mother
can tell you all about the desire for freedom. She came north to
seek a better life. She and so many of her generation took the
words *life, liberty, and the pursuit of happiness* seriously, and they
pursued their freedom like an obsession. Folks like my mother
hate credit-card debt of any kind, because it's too much like slavery, but that's just one kind of debt—there are student loans,
small-business loans, second mortgages . . . They're all forms of
slavery, and we can't be free from them until we're free in body,
mind, soul, and pocketbook.

But let's also remember that freedom has a price. We pay taxes
to keep our freedom of speech, religion, and all the other sacred
liberties guaranteed us by the Constitution. I hate paying taxes,
but if it means that I get to write what I want, then it's worth the
money.

Many say they want to be free, but they don't act like it. When
you allow your credit-card balances to get higher and higher,
you're not pursuing freedom. When you stay stuck in a low-
paying dead-end job, you're not pursuing freedom. To live life on
your own terms means that you must kick your will into high
gear. You must be determined not to let anything get in your way.
This can be a challenge because it often means that you must
deny yourself instant gratification. Eventually you can have what
you want, but you may have to give it some time. If you feel your
will is underdeveloped, this week would be a good time to practice determination and perseverance around temptations in general. Turn down the shopping trip or offer to party when you
know you should be working. It may hurt at first, but keep doing
it and you'll develop strong "will muscles." And when you finally
do go shopping, you'll feel like you've really earned it. The quest
for freedom requires a strong will and backbone. Freedom is not
for sissies.

Freedom is intensely personal, and only we can decide for ourselves what it means to be free and how we want to be free. One thing's for sure, though—we all need money to be free. The question is, how much money do you need? Some people need a lot, while others need only a little. We are not encouraged to think about being free, and we surely aren't taught to plan for it. Think back over your many years in school. Were you ever taught how to be free? Probably not. Although we talk a lot about being free in this country, you'd never know it by the way we live. Indebtedness, poverty, addictions, poor health, and more rob us of our God-given right to be free.

One way to achieve your freedom is to develop a "freedom budget." That may mean planning for retirement—or it may mean having the freedom to enjoy a vacation or go to a spa every year. We all have dreams, but all too often they stay fuzzy and hopeful. This week we're at least going to begin realizing that we can have the type of lifestyle we desire.

To develop your freedom budget, try to project how much it would cost you on a daily, monthly, and annual basis to live the life you desire. Even though your desire may not be "practical" or "realistic," write down the numbers anyway. This is a very powerful exercise because you'll see, in dollars and cents, how much your freedom will cost. Once you know how much you'll need, you can begin to plan how much to save and invest *today*.

Working toward freedom is a goal powerful enough to discipline ourselves to practice a thrifty lifestyle. Ask yourself, *How will I begin to pursue my freedom?* Maybe the answer is finding a part-time job. Or maybe you'll keep your full-time job while starting a part-time business. Maybe you're making enough money and just need to manage it better.

Even if you never plan to go into business for yourself, an entrepreneurial mind-set can help you develop the skills you'll need to buy your freedom. For one thing, entrepreneurs are some of the thriftiest people I know. We have to be. Often we're trying to run the show on a shoestring budget, and there's no room for overspending—keeping a close eye on what you buy can often be a great antidote to frivolous "impulse" buys. We have to figure out creative ways to promote our products or services. We often work with other businesses to maximize our reach into a market or to pool our resources. If you approach your quest for freedom with the thrifty mind-set of the entrepreneur, it may take you a while to get there, but you will get to where you want to go.

Many folks have an IRA or have enrolled in their company's 401(k) plan, and they think they've done enough. This is a great first step, but then they forget about their investment and depend on money managers to take care of it. Entrepreneurs do not depend on others to handle their money, nor should you. Take the time on a weekly or monthly basis to check in with your fund manager to see how your money is performing, and don't hesitate to seek out advice. Your freedom is on the line!

Entrepreneurs are independent, creative thinkers. Especially when you're just getting your business started, you often stand alone. That's one of the costs of freedom, but absolutely worth the price given the potential benefits of financial prosperity and the rewards of independence, like being able to set your own hours.

Socially, it's difficult to stand alone. We've got this thing about keeping up with the Joneses, but the pursuit of freedom and a thrifty lifestyle may mean that you won't be able to keep up. Your neighbor may have just bought a beautiful new-model sports car, but curb your envy by reminding yourself that you've got the big picture in mind. A new car can wait.

Thrifty behavior means different sacrifices for different people. One couple's goal of financial freedom might mean that buying new furniture *right now* is not that important. They may shop at thrift shops or sit on pillows (which is actually kind of cool). When you become committed to this way of living, you realize that you don't have to follow the crowd. You can follow your own mind, no matter how strange you may appear to others.

Journal time

If you were totally free, how would you be living? This week, brainstorm your ideal lifestyle. Look in magazines for stories about folks who seem to be living the way you'd like to live and summarize these stories in your journal. Compare these lives to your own. What are they doing that impresses you, and how can you begin to incorporate their strategies into your own life? Cut out pictures that represent freedom to you and paste them in your journal. Burn these images into your mind until your idea of freedom becomes so real that you can smell, feel, hear, and taste it.

WEEK 19
Who Wants to Be a Hundred Thousandaire?

⊡

Today is the day I take control of my financial destiny.
> BLACK ENTERPRISE MAGAZINE'S
> DECLARATION OF FINANCIAL
> EMPOWERMENT

What are three words that profile the affluent? FRUGAL FRUGAL FRUGAL.
> THOMAS J. STANLEY and
> WILLIAM D. DANKO,
> *The Millionaire Next Door*

The hit television game show *Who Wants to Be a Millionaire?* teases us with the question that is often on our minds as we go to work, pay our bills, and spend our money. Who wants to be rich?

Except for a few monks and nuns who have taken a vow of poverty, most of us want to be wealthy. We dream of the day when we can provide for ourselves and our families in a comfortable or even lavish style. The real reason I wanted to make money was so that I could care for my parents and loved ones.

Over the years I was so focused on growing my company and putting out financial fires that saving and investing for the future had simmered on the back burner. Getting myself out of debt was good, but it was only the first step. At my age, having a retirement nest egg is essential to me. I don't want to depend on the government or my family for money when I get older. I don't want to have to worry about how I'm going to pay the bills in my golden years. Money is something I don't want to have to think about at all. To me, that's true wealth: having enough so that meeting basic survival needs, as well as a few nice wants, is not a problem. So I'm spending a lot of time learning about 401(k)s, IRAs, Social Security, money market funds, and other tools to build wealth for my retirement.

Women really need to focus on building wealth. If you're married, you're working on developing a nest egg with your mate (hopefully), but us single sistahs have no one to depend on but ourselves. Please understand that you're going to have to be able to rescue yourself. A prince may come one day, but don't depend on that. So God bless the sistah who's got her own. Not only can the independently wealthy woman take care of her own needs, but when the prince does come, she can choose not out of financial desperation but out of love and compatibility.

Do you want to be wealthy? If so, why? How much do you need to feel truly safe? Do you need millions, or might a few hundred thousand dollars do? Only you can decide how much you'll need, but I submit that you may not need as much as you think you do. The trick to becoming wealthy is thrift—intelligently managing your income and expenditures. Think of the tallest redwood tree in the forest and how its life began with one tiny seed. That tiny seed is the same as the few dollars every month you put away in a savings account, money market fund, CDs, or stocks and bonds. John H. Johnson, publisher of *Ebony* magazine, launched his publishing empire on a small five-hundred-dollar loan from his mother. A tiny seed.

Sometimes we're paralyzed by the fear that we don't make enough or we're too much in debt to begin planning for the future. Or maybe you regret that you didn't begin your wealth-building program when you were younger.

Whether or not you have debt, it's never too soon, or too late, to begin building wealth. Whether you earn a minimum-wage salary or much more, you can save and invest. Forget about Bill Gates and his billions of dollars! That's fantasy thinking, and we've got to deal with reality. In a workshop aired on PBS, Suze Orman advised a young man on a modest income to begin saving by simply by putting away the loose change he has in his wallet at the end of every day. That's money you won't even miss.

Self-education is critical to building wealth. Read the financial section in the newspaper to learn all you can about the money system and the many wealth-building tools out there. There are many good books and magazines that explore all aspects of debt management and building wealth.

Also, take an interest in the health of the economy. Knowledge is power. If you don't know what's happening with the economy, you won't know how to manage your money. The economy is holistic, and you're a part of it. Study the money system, and you'll discover ways to prosper in good times and bad.

Financial wealth is a blessing, and it's a goal worthy of our efforts. We lose perspective, however, when we make the struggle to accumulate cash all-consuming. Money is just money. It exists to serve us, not the other way around. If we didn't have a dime or own a thing, we could still have a happy life—if we had the right frame of mind. Material goods can make us feel good for a minute, but permanent joy comes from within and from the love we share with others. Don't get me wrong, I enjoy fancy things, like my Mercedes convertible, as much as the next person, but I know it can't heal my soul.

Pursuing wealth at any cost will result in imbalance, so let's make the *balanced* pursuit of financial wealth our strategy. In *The Millionaire Next Door* authors Thomas J. Stanley and William D. Danko found that rich people are often like you and me. They drive Toyotas and buy their clothes from Sears. They keep their money within the family. Many do not have advanced degrees, but they all know how to get along with people. They've got some perspective and balance about money.

Millionaires next door are a surprise because they seem so,

well, normal. Recently I attended my high school reunion, and while folks were interested in me because of the high-profile clients I serve, the really interesting person there was a former classmate who, over the years, amassed a fortune in real estate as a substance abuse counselor. This guy still saves money by living in his childhood home.

It's the wannabes who buy the expensive cars and wear designer clothes. Maybe we should follow the lead of the truly rich by keeping a low profile and being more discriminating about the things we buy. Maybe we should stop using money to work out our self-esteem issues and use it the way it's really intended: to help us meet our survival needs and to build wealth.

Journal time

Earlier I asked you how much money you needed to feel truly safe. This week in your journal, let's explore this issue. If you're feeling anxious about your money situation, write about that.

If you're single, how do you feel about the fact that you have to deal with money worries alone? Do you see this as a problem or an opportunity? If it's a problem, write about it. Now try to see the benefits in pursuing wealth alone.

If you're in a relationship, are you both feeling anxious about your current money situation? Do you make your children feel safe, or are they feeling just as scared as you are? How does your partner feel about building wealth together? If you're not particularly worried, what are you doing right and what could you do better?

Next, write down your wealth goals. How much do you need to feel safe? Without thinking too hard, write down a dollar amount. What if you were debt-free? How much would you need then? Write that down and compare the two numbers. If your first amount was a lot more than the second, you're probably worried about how you're going to keep the lights on and the refrigerator stocked. Get yourself out of the hole, but also, use your journal to begin strategizing on how you're going to develop your nest egg. In other words, what will you have to do, and over what period of time, to achieve your wealth goals? For example, if your company has a 401(k) or some other savings program, you may want to start allocating a percentage of your paycheck. Even a small amount will lay the foundation for future wealth.

Also, tried-and-true thrift tactics, such as couponing, will help you become wealthy. What are some other thrift ideas that can help you conserve money?

Finally, we usually define wealth in terms of money, but this week, write down other ways you can enjoy an abundant lifestyle. For me, good health and love are like money in the bank and way more valuable. Write down your thoughts about emotional, spiritual, physical, and social abundance.

WEEK 20
Ujima and Ujama
(or, The Art of Pooling Resources)

回

> If two of you on earth agree about anything you
> ask for, it will be done for you by my Father in
> heaven. For where two or three come together in
> my name, there am I with them.
>
> JESUS,
> Matthew 18:19–20

During the early years of the 1900s, Harlem was the Black Mecca, drawing folks from the South and, really, all over the world. People would make the pilgrimage there and do the most amazing things. Great music, literature, and works of art were born there. Everybody who was anybody lived, worked, and passed through there—James Baldwin, Lena Horne, Dizzy Gillespie, Zora Neale Hurston, and too many more to name. The Harlem Boys and Girls Choir, Dance Theatre of Harlem, and the Schomburg Center for Research in Black Culture set up shop there. Since racial segregation prevented Blacks from integrating with whites, rich and poor, middle and upper class, blue and white collar lived together as neighbors.

After many decades of struggling with decay and decline, Harlem is on the rise. It couldn't have happened without folks coming together to rebuild. When people work together (ujima) and pool their resources (ujama), anything can and will happen.

Ivan and Hans Nageman are wonderful examples of ujima and ujama. These two young brothers and *Essence* Award winners grew up in Harlem and attended the best private schools. Ivan did his undergraduate and graduate work in education at Harvard. Hans went to Princeton and Columbia Law School. Ivan went on to teach high school and serve as an administrator, while Hans worked as an attorney—as a narcotics prosecutor, chief council to a Senate subcommittee in Washington D.C., and chief council at the Neighborhood Defender's Service of Harlem. At one point Hans was getting six-figure job offers, but he just couldn't abandon Harlem.

I am so impressed with these young brothers. They both walked away from money, perks, security, and prestige. They hated what was happening to their community, so they decided to come back and do something about it. In 1992 they pooled their resources and cofounded the East Harlem School for children grades five through eight on a prayer and a shoestring budget. The school is based at Exodus House, the social services program their parents ran for years.

Before they could even get the school up and running, the brothers had to stand down the drug dealers on the block. At one point the police strongly suggested that they wear bulletproof vests. They still moved forward despite the death threats.

And it's been worth it. Four girls were in the first graduating class, and they each went on to attend boarding schools. Fundraising and dealing with the dangers in the community are obstacles that probably seem overwhelming at times, but the rewards are worth it.

Ujima means collective work and responsibility. Ujama means cooperative economics. We can do a lot alone, but when we pool our minds, creativity, energies, resources, and spirit, we're unstoppable.

I was happy to be involved in the birth of the country's largest Black-owned bookstore in the newly developed Harlem. Clara Villarosa, owner of the Hue-Man Experience bookstore in Denver, Colorado, came to Harlem, looking for an opportunity to expand her franchise. She told me what she wanted to do, and I introduced her to friends Rita Ewing and Celeste Johnson. Thanks to their partnership, Harlem now has a grand, new bookstore. Pooling our resources—our connections, money, and talents—made this bookstore happen. Even modest networking and goodwill can mean the difference between success and failure.

In any economy it's difficult to raise capital for new businesses or funding for nonprofit programs. But when people invest in one another, anything can happen. We have to want to make a commitment to each other as well as our communities to make this happen.

Immigrants come to America, often with only the clothes on their back, but they join family members and friends to share the costs of shelter and food so that they can save to buy property and start businesses. It's hard to trust that others will share our dreams and help us thrive, but I often find that folks who don't reach out can never achieve their dreams, while folks who do reach out often can and do.

Community doesn't just happen. It's built over time, and it's time for African Americans to reclaim and reinvest in our communities and our futures. As you think about this, organize a get-together for your building or block. Find out how many neighbors share your feelings. People often think networking is about business and power lunches, when really the most successful endeavors begin with the sharing of information and resources between two people who respect each other. Get to know and respect your neighbors and widen your circle of power.

Journal time

Is there something you want to do but just don't have enough money or support to get it done? Do you have a desire to own your own business or start a nonprofit organization? Have you thought about partnering with other kindred spirits? In your journal, describe your vision and write down the names of fiscally responsible people who share your vision. Write an outline detailing all the initial duties required to get the program up and running and how each person might contribute. When you've completed this, call these people and propose your plan. Listen to their feedback. No matter what happens, you'll find yourself farther along the path of self-discovery.

WEEK 21
When You Have Enough, Share (and You Have Enough)

🔲

I never had too much trouble being generous
with things, but I am trying my best these days to
be more generous with my heart.
MARIANNE WILLIAMSON,
O, the Oprah Magazine, December 2000

When I give, I give myself.
WALT WHITMAN

The late, wonderful, and inspiring Oseola McCarty was the
epitome of thrift and generosity. Miss McCarty had two skills:
washing clothes and ironing clothes. After diligently saving her
money over the many decades of her life, Miss McCarty donated
$150,000 to the University of Southern Mississippi. Her gener-
ous gift stunned the nation. She didn't earn a lot, but through the
disciplines of saving and thrift, she was able to amass quite a bit
of money. She taught us that everyone can make a contribution,
no matter how little or how much they have. Thanks to her lifelong frugality, she made a difference in the lives of young students. Her legacy inspired a community, and it lives on.

Whether you make a little or a lot, you can give. You have
enough.

There are times when it is appropriate to volunteer our time,
but there will be other times when nothing will do but to give
cash to an individual or a worthy cause. With government fund-

ing for social services programs drying up, there are many worthy organizations that need financial help. Pledging even a small amount will make a tremendous difference.

When you're suffering financially, it may feel like a hardship to give, but that's the time when you should really dig deep. The most powerful giving we'll ever do is when money is scarce. Ironically, that's when the blessings begin to flow. It's a faith thing. When you take a leap of faith and believe that all your needs will be met, no matter how empty your bank account may be, somehow the bills get paid. Giving money is an excellent spiritual discipline that develops faith.

Money is so important to us that giving it away, without any expected financial "return on investment," goes against the grain. Yet giving money because of someone else's need is an act of love that can develop us into more compassionate, loving people.

Selfishness is a real problem in our society, and giving is the cure. Selflessness is unpopular today; everywhere we're told to "get what's ours." But it's this very self-indulgence that is at the root of so much of the imbalance and stress that we suffer. A couple of hours of volunteering to a worthy cause could be just the thing to make your life seem more meaningful, which is so important to emotional health.

There are other ways to give, too. The beauty of thrift is that you have the resources to give back. Remember, practicing a thrifty lifestyle does not mean being cheap or stingy. You can give generously even when you're on a budget. In fact, I find that it's as much fun to give of my time and energy as it is to give money away. In my work with the kids at Kaplan House, my giving often involves listening and compassion. For folks who've never heard a kind word, this is a lot. Although I'm not looking for anything back, I always end up receiving just as much as (or more than) I give. But you *can* also give monetarily. Perhaps you have a favorite charity, or you match the amount your child saves every week, or you donate more at church. Whatever way you express your giving, it will leave you feeling the richer for having done it.

Journal time

Are you struggling financially right now? Well, ironically, giving reinforces your sense that you have enough. When you give, even a small amount, you'll find that you're still able to buy the things you want, need, and desire. When you give, you feel like you have more than you had to begin with. This week in your journal, look at your feelings around giving. Do you feel you have enough to give or not? Do you often spend a lot on restaurants and entertainment but have to think twice about donating similar amounts to charity?

Think about your family's history of giving. Did your parents tithe to the church? To a social or political organization? Did they ever talk to you about giving?

When you give, do you give freely, or do you bargain with God ("I'll put a dollar in the collection plate, Lord, if you just give me that job")?

WEEK 22
Enjoy Your Financial Freedom

"Money is not everything . . . but it's reasonably close to oxygen. And money will buy a lot of things:
a) House—but not a home
b) Bed—but not a good night's sleep
c) Companion—but not a friend
d) Good time—but not peace of mind

And I want all of those things—and they will only be achieved when you go through life righteously.

ZIG ZIGLAR

I want to be content with what I have. Because I used to be like that. I didn't care about fame or money. I lived in an apartment with roaches, rats and nine siblings. I didn't have nothing and was really happy, laughed every day and felt love. To return to that inner peace is the goal.

DAMON WAYANS,
Essence, October 2001

When I was a girl, my mother used to tell me that there was no worse slavery than the sharecropping system. Sharecropping worked like this: A landowner would buy the seeds (cotton, tobacco, and so on) and fertilizer that a farmer needed for planting. The farmer would plant the seeds in the spring, tend the fields in the summer, harvest and sell the crop in the fall. Whatever the farmer sold at market, *half* was owed to the landowner. Out of the remaining half, the farmer would have to pay back money owed for fertilizer, food, tools, and the like. As you can imagine, there wasn't much left after all the debts were paid. Most farmers became trapped in the system. It was designed to enslave, just like slavery, indentured servitude, and credit cards.

We want to be free, but when we're financially trapped all we can think of is what we want to be free *from*—uncertainty, fear, and bill collectors calling. That's how we tend to think when we're in crisis mode.

But this week let's also attempt to raise our thoughts to a higher level. In *The 9 Steps to Financial Freedom*, Suze Orman says, "The road to financial freedom begins not in a bank or even in a financial planner's office like mine, but in your head. It begins with your thoughts."

What would you like to be financially free *to do?* What does freedom mean to you and how much money do you need to be free? Some people need a lot, and some need very little.

Recently I read about a woman whose idea of freedom was to build a home on the beach. It didn't have to be a big home, just as long as it was by the water. For years she saved her meager income and looked for properties. After many years of searching and saving, she found the spot. It's as if it had been waiting there for her all along. It wasn't a big lot, but it was big enough to build a place she could call home.

A wonderful goal—and how gratifying it must have been to realize her dream. How many of us truly believe we could actually have a home on the ocean, or in the mountains, or wherever we chose? Before you're able to think like that, you have to know that you're free.

I know a woman who had always wanted to take piano lessons. She paid for lessons for her daughters, but never for herself. Now retired, for the first time she feels free to pursue this childhood dream. She isn't rich, but she has enough to take lessons. Now she's playing "Chopsticks"!

I know many sistahs who love to travel. There's a certain freedom in traveling far away from home. You can learn new things, meet new people. For just a little while, you can become a whole new person. There's freedom in that. You say you want to go to Kenya, Jackson Hole, Wyoming, or the Sonoma vineyards? All it takes is a little planning, some disciplined saving, and *voilà!* You're free to go!

"Look at all the different dreams of a rich life," says Stephen M. Pollan, author of *Live Rich,* "and you'll see every single one is based on having the freedom to do whatever you want to do. . . . To live rich is to be free, and to be free is to live rich."

Freedom is a mind-set. If you're free in your mind—if you know that you can do anything—you're free indeed. And when you're freed up mentally, you can start to have fun with your money.

My heart aches when I think about my slave ancestors who wanted to be free but by law were prohibited from enjoying the liberties promised by the Bill of Rights and the Constitution. Even when they finally acquired their freedom, they were still subject to the violent racism of Jim Crow segregation.

Today our country isn't perfect, but it's better than it was in that it allows us freedoms that many people around the world do not have. Just think—if your job doesn't pay enough or doesn't fulfill you, you can get another. If you have an idea for a service or product, you can form your own company.

So think about saving your money in light of the real power it can give you today. Unlike our ancestors, once we're free from debt we really are free to enjoy our money and pursue happiness on our own terms. Now that's freedom, and you owe it to yourself to enjoy it!

Journal time

Let's title your journal entry this week, "How I Want to Have Fun with My Money." First, take a look at your budget and determine how much money you have left over after bills are paid and you've put aside money for savings. Write that figure down. Even if it's a small amount, write down things you'd like to do with your money. Perhaps you'd like to hire a maid once a week. Go to the theater? Go out for dinner and dancing? Have a romantic weekend away?

If you know how you want to spend your money but you just don't have enough, don't despair. In your journal, work the figures. How many weeks or months would it take to save up the amount you need? Do you have a birthday coming up? (Ask for cash in lieu of gifts.) If you can delay gratification for a bit and save, the desired trip or object can be yours. It's important to realize that by being able to save, you have the power to give yourself what you want.

Enjoying your money is the reward you've earned for all your hard work and discipline. I don't know about you, but all work and no fun makes me pretty cranky. So remember to practice thrift while having a good time. What's the point of saving if you can't have fun?

Living Virtue 4

Love

Perhaps love is the process of me leading you
gently back to yourself.
ANTOINE DE SAINT-EXUPÉRY

Growing up I always had real conventional ideas about love. I saw a lot of movies, watched some television, did plenty of day-dreaming, and figured when the real thing came along I'd know it 'cause I'd start hearing some angels sing. Dating would be all hearts and flowers and going out to dinner every night. Then we'd get married and I'd wind up with a family just like the one I grew up in: two parents, two kids, and a nice little house in the 'burbs.

As I got older, my notions of love and family loosened up a little bit, but not all that much. Even as I was busy building my business and giving back to the community, in the back of my head I was hanging on to that idea of someday getting married and settling down. When it became pretty clear that wasn't going to happen, I just kind of assumed things like a partner and a child would have to be for everyone else. I had different goals, goals that put serious demands on my time, goals that required sacrifices. For me, love would just have to come from close friends and relations. I can't say I was happy with that decision, but I didn't see that I had any other choice. Then Rocky and Xavier showed up in my life, and everything changed. Together those two young men broke through all those fears and doubts I'd been holding so tight for so many years. They taught me the most important lesson in the world: Love can come to you from the most unconventional places. But until you allow it into your life, you will never feel truly fulfilled.

It's been a year and a half since that fateful day when Xavier sat beside me in a dark movie theater and massaged my shoulders, which were tight from years of stress and anxiety. A true healer, he absorbed my pain; we shared it, and that changed my life. Usually folks come to you for what they can get, not for what they can give to you. I had never known caring like Xavier's before. I didn't even know how to accept such an amazing gift, but it made me sit up and pay attention.

Xavier's friendship opened my heart, and I was terrified to see the emptiness inside. For years I'd buried my needs in my work because I was afraid that if I reached out, I would be rejected. My desire may have been buried, but it wasn't dead. I still dreamed about sharing my life with a kindred spirit who understood me. Marriage was not a necessity, and with Rocky around, I wasn't looking to have a baby anymore. I have a lot of work to accomplish before I leave the planet, and I wanted a partner whose life mission complemented mine. It was a lot to ask for, especially considering the fact that I still saw family as something requiring Bill Cosby handing out wisdom from a big armchair. I'd pretty much given up hope.

So when Xavier came along, I didn't fully grasp that in our friendship my prayer had been answered. All I knew was that this brother had invaded my space and it felt uncomfortable and nice at the same time. I thought that a friendship with him could meet my needs. In fact, for the first few months, I watched him with suspicion. It wasn't that he was a saint—he's got his faults like the rest of us. But his good points were so good that he just couldn't have been real.

Brothers, whenever a sistah you like tests you, hang in there. Chances are she's trying to deal with some past pain. She wants to trust, but it's hard. That's exactly what I was going through. Xavier probably thought I was nuts, but he just kept on being himself, and he hung in with me while I exorcised my fears. From day one, he has treated me with nothing but honesty, respect, and love. I thought I wanted to find a soul mate because that meant I'd never need anyone else. But instead, sharing my life's work with Xavier has helped me open up, relax, and start trusting people more. Because of his loving friendship, all of my relationships have changed.

One of the greatest lessons I've learned about love is that you never know where you're going to find it, so you've got to keep yourself open to it at all times. Turns out that for me, love came wrapped in a kind of unconventional package. As soon as I was willing to let go of those narrow old ideas, there it was. Suddenly I felt liberated. I looked around me and realized there was all kinds of loving going on that I'd been missing out on. I've deepened my relationships to family, friends, and neighbors. I've even found the grace to extend compassion to those I used to call my enemies. Truth is, I'm more full of love than I've ever been in my life. I was afraid creating a family would drain me, but now I realize that the real drain comes from being alone. When I think about all the Friday evenings that I'd spent solo, with no one to talk to and share ideas with, it makes me want to cry. Love's the fuel that feeds the fire, the greatest force on the planet. People need each other—there's no big mystery in that.

Of course, no one person can solve all my problems. Asking for that is just putting too much pressure on any relationship. Life is hard and I still get depressed, but even at the lowest points I know I am blessed. And I believe that the miracle of Xavier's and Rocky's love has come to me because, as I began working the virtues, I freed up a lot of the worries and doubts I had about my own self-worth. I finally opened myself up to love.

Over the next few weeks, we are going to work on creating positive conditions in our lives so that our love for ourselves and others can grow. We'll also learn to push aside our preconceived ideas to give the real thing room to breathe, and to give ourselves the chance to become better human beings. We're going to stop questioning and doubting ourselves, and start rejoicing in those gifts love delivers to us every day.

If you're alone and looking for love, or if you're in a relationship with some serious problems, I invite you to really work on understanding the ideas that we'll cover in the next few weeks. Take time with them, do the journal exercises, and allow the thoughts and feelings they bring forth to truly sink in. I want to encourage you to stop despairing and start believing right now. Because if working the virtues helped me open my life up to love, there's no reason on God's earth it can't do the same for you. Let's try to understand this powerful soul force together. It's a big world out there, packed with love enough to fill every living soul. All we've got to do is open the door.

Week 23
What Is Love?

Love is patient and kind; it is not jealous or conceited or proud; love is not ill-mannered or selfish or irritable; love does not keep a record of wrongs; love is not happy with evil, but is happy with the truth. Love never gives up; and its faith, hope, and patience never fail. Love is eternal.

1 Corinthians 13:4–8

What is love? Ask six billion people that question and you'll get six billion answers. But to me, the quote above from Corinthians says it best. We often think of love as some sappy feeling that robs us of our common sense, but that's not true. Love actually makes us smarter. It makes us strong. It develops character. We're not talking some Hollywood version that begins and ends quicker than you can change your stockings. We're talking about a force that has the power to mature us. Such love is hard work, but the rewards are huge.

Read the quote from Corinthians carefully and think about the role love plays in your life. How close do your most important relationships come to fitting this definition? Chances are you still have work to do, both with yourself and with others, but the coming weeks will give us some space to think. What does love mean? Where should we go looking for it? And how do we know when we've found the real thing?

Here are just a few thoughts to start us off:

• Love is patient and kind. Love requires being patient with yourself and with others. It's tough when you love someone so much that you want—and expect—them to fill your every need. But it's unfair to ask for that from any relationship. We're all beautifully and messily human, so don't expect perfection. Stay open and willing to grow. A big part of our work in the coming weeks will involve reaching a place where we can welcome love into our lives without all those expectations about what it's "supposed" to be.

We spend so much time these days rushing around, scratching things off lists, and making it to the dry cleaners before they close. But love doesn't move at our modern pace. You can't squeeze it between meetings or into a few quick minutes before bed. Love takes time. My friend Crystal, who's raising four-year-old twins, makes it a weekly job for the three of them to go to the grocery store together. The errand takes about ten times longer than it would if she left the kids with her husband and went on her own, but this way she and her children know they'll be spending a serious chunk of time together every Saturday afternoon. They sing songs in the car and unpack the grocery bags one apple at a time. Seems to me that's just about the right pace for getting love to grow.

• It is not jealous or conceited or proud. This may sound pretty basic, but an important part of love is making it a shared experience. It's not about one person's needs being more or less worthwhile than the other's. It's not about ego, but about communion. If you're worrying about who's doing what or when or how, you're probably draining the relationship of more important things, like loyalty and trust. Have faith in your partner. Resist the temptation to "keep score."

When my friend Raymond met his first wife, it was love at first
sight. They dated hot and heavy for about a year, and you
couldn't talk to him for five minutes without hearing how kind
and loving and generous Lisa was. Now, Raymond's a good-
looking brother and he'd had some wild times in the past, but
once Lisa came along all that was over. He loved her with every
cell of his being. Trouble was, Lisa couldn't seem to believe she
deserved someone as good as Raymond. She couldn't get past
worrying he'd take off the second she turned around. She'd get
jealous when he talked to other women. She'd question him
whenever he was late getting home. After they got married,
things only got worse. Instead of putting down a foundation of
trust, their relationship got stuck in a mess of jealousy and suspicion. Try as he might, Raymond couldn't convince Lisa that he
was there to stay, and eventually it got so bad he wound up leaving. Negative feelings like pride and envy only wind up destroying love.

Think some about the role trust plays in your relationships
with the people you love most. Are you impatient with your children? When your spouse or lover goes to lunch with someone
else, do you get jealous? Have you ever lied to a loved one? Do
you suspect your mate of lying to you? If you answered yes to any
of the above, think about this dynamic in the coming weeks.
What are you afraid of? Often our difficulties in trusting others
stem from lack of trust in ourselves.

• Love is not ill-mannered or selfish or irritable. Mentally or
physically abusive relationships are the opposite of love. They
shut people down instead of opening them up. If you're involved
in such a relationship, even with yourself, know that it's not helping your health or your spirit any to stay. Love means being ap-
preciated for who you are, while at the same time finding enough
support and encouragement to grow.

• Love does not keep a record of wrongs. During arguments
with loved ones, do you throw their past mistakes in their face?
Loving means forgiving. It means getting humble. We've all

done things we aren't proud of, but it's no good holding them against each other. Even if you're harboring some real anger toward another person, do your best to practice compassion. Most people act because they think what they're doing is right. Love means opening your mind, practicing a little care and understanding.

My Kaplan House kids are always teaching me about forgiveness. A few years ago I took a boy named Brian under my wing. Brian had spent most of his life in and out of foster homes and never knew what it meant to have a steady, caring presence around. Sometimes when I saw him he'd greet me with a huge hug, but just as often he'd spot me and act like he couldn't care less. I kept trying to get through to him any way I knew how. I'd invite him to come along to parties or just stay quiet and listen when he needed an ear. But no matter how often I assured him I wasn't going anywhere, Brian still made it a point to regularly reject me. We'd arrange to meet and he wouldn't show up. I'd send him cards with messages like "stay strong" or "hang in there," and he'd ignore them. He was dealing with some serious hurt, and he never could get himself to trust me. Though I felt for Brian, I never held those rejections against him. I just did my best to give him what he needed: unconditional love.

Gradually, over time, Brian started to open up to me. He made me a birthday card. He'd call me when he was having troubles. When he was thinking about dropping out of his GED classes, he came to me and we talked it through and got him back on track. I like to think my presence made a real difference in his life. By making the choice not to focus on what wasn't working, I gave our relationship the space it needed to grow.

• Love is not happy with evil, but is happy with the truth. You're not helping anyone if you avoid looking closely at your relationships. If there's something you refuse to address, it could be because you know things are going down wrong. Sometimes we even need to take our cues from those around us. Are all your friends telling you your mate doesn't treat you right? Are you avoiding talking to your mother because you don't want to deal with her always finding fault? I spent a lot of years just keeping silent when I had a problem with another person. But silence is just another way of lying. Real love does its best to tell the truth.

Many years ago I lived next door to an older couple, Roy and Evelyn. They were a sight to behold, holding hands and heading off to church together every Sunday. But two or three times a week I used to hear them having screaming fights through the walls. For over a year I kept expecting to hear the news that Roy and Evelyn had decided to call it quits. I just couldn't believe all this battling was part of a happy marriage. Then one day I met them in the street and they told me they were about to celebrate their fiftieth wedding anniversary. Roy filled me in on all they'd lived through together: the depression, the Second World War, the death of their son, Evelyn's bout with breast cancer. He finished with a big old grin on his face and told me his wife was still as lovely as the day he first set eyes on her. So I asked them about the secret to a happy marriage. It was Evelyn who answered.

"We don't hold back," she told me. "If we've got a problem, we deal with it. We yell and scream if we have to, but we work it out. If you keep your troubles bottled up, you'll just wind up suffocating all that love."

• Love never gives up; and its faith, hope, and patience never fail. Part of strengthening a bond of love is working through the rough patches. Going the distance. There will be times when your love is tested, when those you care about frustrate you or even make you want to throw the remote control across the room. The people closest to you can get under your skin. When this happens, remember what you love about them. Be patient with them. Take the time to look at what they're going through. Communicate and be open, as open with each other as you can.

From the moment we're born until the day we die, it's our job to learn about giving and receiving love. Our experience of love shapes our personalities and determines how we approach the world. When we don't feel love, or when we act out of fear or anger, we're out of harmony. Love brings us back, every time.

• Love is eternal. No explanation needed—if you follow the paths laid out above, eternal love will be yours.

Journal time

This week, meditate on the page about your own personal description of love. Where do you get your ideas about love? A mate? A best friend? A child? How do your loved ones express their feelings? What have you learned from each person? How many of your ideas about love come from other sources, like books and movies? Jot down anything you can think of: memories, images, even tastes and smells. Love follows no formula, so don't worry if your thoughts feel wild or silly or different. Just trust in your own experiences and put them down on the page.

Read back over what you've written. Think about which aspects are the most important. Now try writing just a two- or three-line definition of what love means to you. Once you've come up with your definition, stick it away someplace where you won't be tempted to go back and adjust it. But be sure to keep the paper handy. We're going to pull it out again in seven weeks and see if anything has changed.

WEEK 24
Getting to the Roots: Family Love

It's easier to build strong children than to repair broken adults.

FREDERICK DOUGLASS

The first place we learn about love is from our families: our mothers and fathers, aunts, uncles, grandparents, siblings, whoever had a place in the family home. They supply our earliest model for what it means to feel and express love for another human being.

Families can be one of our greatest gifts, and they often provide our strongest support systems. What we learn from them, we eventually take with us out into the world. If our family was full of love, then we probably are, too. But if family members had conflicts about how to love themselves and each other, many of those conflicts might have been passed on to us as well. So if we're going to start exploring the good and not-so-good ways we're working love into our lives, the first step is taking a close look at the past.

Start thinking about your personal history with love. How did your mother and father act together? Were they romantic? Did they fight a lot? Did they never fight at all? My friend Simone had parents who felt they should never disagree in front of the kids. If they had a conflict, they waited to settle it in private, after the kids had gone to bed. Sometimes Simone would sit up late at night and listen to her parents arguing in whispers downstairs. She always figured fighting in a relationship was something shameful, that it should be hidden and avoided at all costs.

As she got older, Simone felt like every fight she had with a loved one was a signal that the relationship had failed. When she had a problem with a lover or a friend, she'd squash it down for as long as she could, assuming something was wrong with her for finding fault. She figured a truly successful relationship was one where no one disagreed at all. It wasn't until she met her husband, a guy who likes to confront a problem as soon as he sees it, that she started to realize that conflict is actually a natural and healthy part of a loving relationship. Those lessons we pick up in childhood are powerful teachers. It's important that we take the time to look at how they've shaped our ideas about love.

The example offered by our parents not only colors our future romantic relationships, but also has a strong effect on how we'll later behave with the children in our lives. Were your parents overly lax or strict? Were they judgmental or impatient? Did they encourage you to form your own opinions? Did they interfere too much in your life? Or did they not take enough interest at all? Start thinking about how their attitudes have shaped your own family. Often we repeat the patterns of our childhood without even realizing it. I bet we've all had the experience of opening our mouths and hearing our mothers' voices come out. Try to remember what you did and didn't admire about your parents, and pay attention to how their behaviors could be resurfacing with your own kids.

Of course, even once we're grown up and out on our own, loving family can be one of our biggest challenges. Unlike friends and romantic partners, we didn't choose our families. Sometimes it turns out we don't even have a lot in common with them. Maintaining family relations as an adult is tough. Many conflicts date back to childhood, and over time, as patterns sink in and are cemented, those disagreements grow harder and harder to resolve. But now that you're focused on getting a better understanding about what role your family played in developing your feelings about love, it's a good time to try settling whatever still gets you riled. Sometimes this step will involve resolution, but sometimes it just involves letting go.

I'm sure plenty of us can relate to having mother problems. Though I consider myself close to my own mother—one of the strongest and most generous women I know—she's still capable of getting under my skin faster than anyone on this earth. When those old issues rise up, I get to feeling like I'm ten years old all over again, about ready to burst into tears.

One of the keys to finding love for your family is making an effort at open communication. If you've got an old grief you never discuss, now's the time to get it out there. Practice patience and respect. Remember what you love about your family members, and all the good they've done for you over the years. But also remember that you've got to take care of your own needs—and sometimes doing both isn't possible. If you have to cut things off, that's okay too. It may be painful, but you need to do what's best for you to heal. Last of all, try to remember that behind all the dysfunction, if you keep looking for the love you'll probably find it.

Journal time

This week, meditate on the page about how your family has influenced your ideas about love. What kind of love did your parents share? Was it a peaceful home? Chaotic? Did they stay together? If not, how did their separating color your ideas about long-term relationships? Take a close look at how their ways of loving are reflected in your own relationships: with your romantic partner, with your children, with your community. Are there things you value from your past that are missing in your present life? Are there patterns you didn't want to repeat but are? If you're single and want to be together, or are feeling stuck in an unhappy relationship, pay special attention to how your family dynamics might be affecting your current attempts at love.

Also this week, take a look at where your family relationships stand today. Are they healthy? Or are there old conflicts that still bother you? Often these ways of being have been going on for so long that we forget it's possible to change. But changing our lives is what working the virtues is all about. What do you need to do to make peace with your family? Do you need to make compromises? Voice your feelings? Cut your ties? Whatever you need to do, now's the time to take action. It's called making room for love in your life.

WEEK 25
Love Yourself

The key to cherishing yourself is recognizing that you are valuable, lovable and definitely worth being cherished. Once you are ready to make this decision for yourself, you will discover an inner confidence that was trapped just behind your fears.

MICHELLE MORRIS-SPIEKER,
The Cherished Self

Scripture says that before we can love our neighbor, we must first learn to love ourselves. It's a basic lesson, but many of us find self-love one of our greatest challenges. As a society, we started talking about loving ourselves back in the 1960s. For decades we've been talking up a storm, but have we gotten to the point where it's really happening?

Do you love yourself?

I'm pretty good at loving other people, but cherishing myself is still tough. When you're stressed, depressed, or full of anxiety, it's hard to love yourself. Even as I write these words, I'm having to work at jump-starting my self-esteem every single day.

Too many of us always want to judge ourselves harshly. We blame ourselves for every little thing that goes wrong in our lives. We feel guilty for things we didn't even do. When we're constantly condemning ourselves for being too heavy, too skinny, too broke, too whatever, we resist love's healing presence and there's nowhere for it to go. Whatever mistakes you've made in the past, it's time to start forgiving yourself, and learn to let go.

Being kind to yourself can be tough, especially if you've gone through some hard times. Someone hurting or deserting you has a way of making you feel like you're no good. Not too long ago my friend Pearl was left by a man she'd been seeing for two years. He just took off one day without even telling her good-bye. Now, Pearl had been feeling extremely confident since she got with that man. She was looking good, she got a new promotion at work, she even redid the kitchen in her apartment. But as soon as her guy walked out the door, the poor girl crumbled. She didn't even want to get out of bed. Of course, some grieving was in order, but getting your self-worth all wrapped up in whether another person loves you always leads to no good.

After her guy left, Pearl—same woman who'd had it all together just a few months before—started slamming herself every chance she got. Suddenly you couldn't talk to her two minutes before she was telling you she was too fat and lazy for anyone to love. It hurt to see this together woman breaking to pieces just because of what was going on in her own mind. And before long, her attitude started rubbing off on her life. All that complaining meant people didn't want to be around her. She got back to dating some, but the brothers never stayed long, not with Pearl going on and on about how little there was to stick around for. She had all her self-esteem wrapped up in whether someone else loved her. Once her man split, it was as if Pearl had split, too.

The only solution to getting out of a state like Pearl's is to begin loving yourself. It's not easy. It takes more than a hot bath or treating yourself to a facial to pick your self-esteem up off the floor (though those things don't hurt!). It takes having a real honest look at what you have to give. Stop comparing yourself to others; it's a game that's impossible to win. Besides, if you're always worrying about trying to be as good as someone else, you'll never discover your potential to be even better. Focus on the person you were last year, last month, even last week, and make sure that person continues to grow.

Let's start simply, with self-acceptance. There's been a lot of talk about reinventing ourselves—new bodies, careers, and homes. Some even go under the knife to change their face and body parts. And while there's nothing wrong with trying to improve ourselves, there is a problem with trying to change the essence of who we are. We can change the conditions in our lives, but still, we must face the same person in the mirror every day. When we face ourselves, there can be no game playing. We must take off our masks and be real.

When you find yourself cutting yourself down, just stop. Freeze your brain. Ask yourself what you're really trying to say. Are you calling yourself fat because you're scared of owning your own body? Are you dissing your accomplishments because feeling good about yourself means you'll get out there in the world and start taking risks? It's time to stop denying that you have something worth offering. I love this quote from Marianne Williamson's "A Return to Love" (which Nelson Mandela also included in his 1994 inaugural speech):

Our deepest fear is not that we are inadequate.
Our deepest fear is that we are powerful beyond measure.
It's our Light, not our Darkness, that frightens us.
We ask ourselves, who am I to be brilliant, gorgeous,
    talented, fabulous?
Actually, who are you NOT to be?

What are you afraid will happen if you start accepting yourself for who you are? Are you afraid that if you put yourself out there you won't be loved? By tearing yourself down first, are you making sure no one else does it for you? Girl, you've just got to take the chance. I know that fear because I lived it for over forty years. But let me tell you, it ain't worth it. Now, I've still got a lot of work to do in this area. I still like to beat myself up for every little thing. I still worry that my business, my body, my mind won't be good enough. But by working the virtues, I'm really learning that you can't take care of the world until you take care of what's going on at home.

Try telling yourself every day, "I love me." It might feel weird or corny for a while, but keep at it. Soon enough, it'll get easier. You'll begin to believe it, and when you do, watch out! That love you start feeling for yourself is going to spill out onto others and make its way all over the world.

*J*ournal time

If you're anything like me, there's so much you could write about this week that you might need to get another notebook. Go ahead and let her rip. Fill the pages with thoughts about yourself. Tell the truth. Do you love yourself? If not, why not? What do you think is wrong with you? Go ahead and pour your heart out on the page. Now take a careful look at what you've listed. Can you change any of those things you hate? If not, you're gonna have to learn to live with them. Focus on the positive. This may sound like a cliché, but it's true: Until you love yourself, it's gonna be tough to find someone else to love you.

Once you've made it through everything you don't like about yourself, turn the paper over and try making a list of all the things you do like. It can be anything. Maybe it's the way you're so good with kids. Or you can throw down in the kitchen. You might have a knack for making people laugh, or wake up with a smile on your face. Not everyone does that. Whatever it is that's great and wonderful about you, celebrate it.

As you're working on loving yourself, try to come up with some things you can do to feel better about those parts of yourself that give you trouble. If you don't think you make enough money, find some ways to splurge that don't take a lot of cash—

like going on a picnic or playing hooky one afternoon and going to the movies. If you think you're too quiet and boring, try spending time with friends who make you feel fun and alive. Sometimes all we have to do is start looking at our lives from a different angle to realize there's a whole lot there to love.

WEEK 26
Committed Love: Finding the Romance

🔲

> Love doesn't just sit there like a stone; it has to be made, like bread, remade all the time, made new.
>
> URSULA K. LeGUIN

The way I figure it, romance works kind of like a drug in our culture. You know the stuff I'm talking about—hearts and flowers, honeymoons, getting swept off our feet. We get bombarded with images from television and the movies, until we start believing that real love means two skinny people spotting each other across a crowded room, followed by lots of hot sex and a big expensive wedding. What most of us end up with is years of feeling inadequate because our own love experiences don't measure up. There's a reason all those fairy tales end as soon as the prince and princess hook up. Long-term loving is a lot of hard work, and that's just not much fun to read about!

The truth is, relying too much on romance to get you through a relationship can be dangerous. Because though romance may be a part of love, it sure isn't the whole thing. In my experience, confusing the two only leads to trouble.

My friend Janet has always had a hard time telling the difference between love and romance. If the guy sends an expensive present or brings a dozen roses on the first date, she falls for him every time. She never bothers to check for the deeper things—like caring and commitment— that make a relationship last. All he has to do is pull up in a stretch limousine to take her out to dinner and she's his for life. Of course, eventually all those flashy guys disappoint. Janet's heart is broken about as often as it's put back together again. Truth is, she can't distinguish the high of romance from the depth of love.

Now, don't get me wrong, I'm not dissing romance here. Romance can be great. In fact, it's an important part of a committed relationship. Romance—stuff like flowers, surprises, real tender sex—is an expression of love. It tells us that we're special. But notice I said "part" of a committed relationship. Too many sistahs approach romance like an all-or-nothing deal. They're all over it when they're looking for a mate, then as soon as they get settled in a long-term relationship, they let the silly, sappy part of loving slide. But letting the romance go can be just as dangerous as letting it take over. The trick here is the same as it is in every other part of your life. You've got to achieve a balance. Romance keeps passion and caring alive in a relationship. Without it, the two of you'd just be real close friends. But a strong, healthy relationship has to be grounded in something more.

As I've grown up and shed some of my old beliefs about romance, I've learned a lot about what it really means to share your life with someone. The biggest adjustment for me has been letting go of that high-drama model and realizing that committed love means being ordinary together, just experiencing simple daily communion. Fighting and making up. Being there when the person you love is sick, loses a job, can't understand you, or even lets you down. It's about trusting someone enough to expose your hopes and fears. And it's about sharing real things, things that last, like dreams and wisdom, companionship and a sense of humor.

The truth is, committed love is a whole lot more work than romance because you've got to stick around even in the not-so-exciting times. But by now you've been working the virtues long enough to know that the more you put into your life, the higher the payoff is going to be. When you're half of a genuine, meaningful relationship, you're less easily hurt because you go home to someone who cares about you. Love like that boosts your immune system. You feel more generous with the world around you because suddenly you've got love to spare.

Sometimes I think those of us like Janet just go for the romance because we're afraid to travel deeper into a relationship. True intimacy is definitely something I continue to struggle with. We know that the more we invest, the more it hurts if things don't work out. Sometimes it just seems wiser to put those feelings on hold. I've known sistahs who have sworn off love entirely in favor of just having a good time. Are they happy? I don't think so. I think they just try to keep moving fast enough that they'll never have time to notice what's not there. We all know about the pain of heartache, but bad as it hurts, it's better than the pain of not loving at all. Part of commitment is taking the risks. We're stronger than we think we are. We get hurt. We recover. We move on. We even grow.

As you're working the love virtue this week, start paying attention to what you're looking for in a relationship, or what you value in the one you've got. Are you making things like good looks and a fat wallet your top priority? I've got a friend who used to date a real slickster like that, and we all started calling him her "New Year's Eve Man." He was real good at showing up for special occasions, but when it came down to real life—I'm talking feeding her chicken soup when she was sick and hitting the store for tampons—he was nowhere to be found. When you just fall for money, looks, or attitude, you're falling for a thing instead of a person. Now, if those things just happen to come along with the smart, funny, loyal, and compassionate package, I say all the better. But if the slick stuff is all there is, chances are you'll wind up disappointed. Real loving calls for something more.

Journal time

This week, spend some time thinking about your feelings on love and romance. What do you want out of a committed relationship? Are your desires realistic? Think about the qualities you value in your mate, or imagine for a potential mate. Are they things that will stand the test of time?

If you're single and having trouble finding someone to love, make a list of the qualities you look for in a good relationship. Are they all romantic things like getting gifts and being taken out? Is there a chance you've just been going for romance instead of something deeper? This doesn't mean you won't find someone good looking and rich, or that there's anything wrong with that. Just make sure you're also searching for something more.

If you're already in a committed relationship, think about what role romance plays in your life. Is it everything? Or has it disappeared entirely? What might you do to achieve a better balance in your life?

WEEK 27
Let's Get Physical: Showing Your Love

If we want a love message to be heard, it has to be sent out. To keep a lamp burning, we have to keep putting oil in it.

MOTHER TERESA

Physical intimacy is tough for me. I know it's a real important part of relationships, and I'm not just talking about with a lover. I mean with friends, family, anyone who's important in your life. Touch is the easiest way to send the message that you care. A hug, a kiss, a cuddle, or even just your hand on someone's arm transmits the warmth of your feelings right away. There have even been studies showing that physical touch boosts your immune system. When premature babies have to spend weeks hooked up to machines, family and hospital volunteers come in for hours just to hold and rock them. Those babies need physical contact as much as they need food and air. Human touch is necessary for them to thrive.

Even if you know all this, you may still find touch difficult. It can make you feel awkward or vulnerable or self-conscious about your body. You may be afraid that you're sending messages you don't mean to send. What if some guy friend thinks you're coming on to him? What if you wind up offending someone who feels you're being inappropriate? It can just seem safer to keep your hands to yourself.

A few years ago I discovered a friend who was just as iffy about reaching out and touching people as I was. Though she was as warm as could be to talk to, I noticed that whenever anyone hugged her or kissed her on the cheek, she'd stiffen up like a board. Eventually I called her on it. We talked over our mutual discomfort and decided to do some hugging practice one-on-one just to test things out. At first it was kind of stiff and funny feeling, but gradually we started to relax and even laugh. To this day, every time I see her, we greet each other with open arms. I have to admit, those regular hugs have made me feel much closer to her. And our successful experiment has made me braver when it comes to reaching out to other people in my life—especially my Kaplan kids.

Talking about getting physical is a tricky area. We've got an idea in this culture of ours that as soon as we're getting into touching, it means we're getting into sex. But there are all kinds of nonsexual, yet still very physical ways of expressing our love. In many countries physical intimacy is a part of even the most casual friendships. Go to France or Italy or Egypt and you'll see friends, both male and female, kissing or walking down the street with their arms around one another. Touch like that is so valuable. It's literally passing the warmth. It boosts your energy level, and your self-confidence, to have loving contact with another human being.

Being physical was probably a big part of our close relationships in childhood. I definitely remember pinching and squirming, holding hands and piling on top of my best friends. But as we get older, we tend to isolate. We figure touch is only for sex, so we train ourselves to go without. For many of us, it's going to be hard getting reacquainted with the idea of sharing our bodies. It might seem awkward. It might take some work to get to a point where we feel we really want to get close to the people we love in a physical way. But if you're having trouble, just stick with it. Start small, with patting a friend on the hand or touching her on the shoulder, then work your way up to a kiss or a hug. My friend Mike is real conflicted about hugging—says it makes him squirm but he still wants to be able to express his feelings of affection. So he's let us all know that hugs from him will be forthcoming, but only after long absences and on special occasions. Over the years I've noticed him getting more comfortable with sharing himself. The absences don't need to be quite so long or the occasions quite so special for him to give his friends a hug.

Of course, when it comes to your romantic partner, there will be plenty of times when touching is about sex. And a good sex life is important to keeping the spark alive. It can bring trust, pleasure, excitement, and a bunch of other good stuff to the table. But I don't care how hot and steamy things are in the bedroom, you can only be having sex so much of the time. The truth is, sometimes we want to get close to our partner but we don't feel like "getting some." We just want to be with the person. That's okay, too.

Don't feel like you're strange or deficient just because you'd rather cuddle on the couch while you watch a movie or hold hands under the dinner table. Those are very important ways of expressing your love. It's not so much what you're doing as what you're bringing to it. We've all had the experience of getting under the covers with someone who's there but not really there. Just as sex can be casual, casual touch can be fully charged. So stop worrying about how things look, and start focusing on what you're feeling. It's healthy to want to reach out.

Begin by doing what you think you can handle and know that it gets easier. No one's gonna care if you start out a little awkwardly. (They probably won't even notice.) No matter how hard or silly it seems at first, it's worth the investment of time and the weathering of a few rough spots. Human beings need warmth, intimacy, loving, holding, and caring. Being together physically says something more than we can express with just words.

Journal time

This week, take the time to be really conscious of physically expressing your love to those around you. This can include anything from being especially tender with a lover to hugging a close friend to taking time to cuddle with your kids. Also, imagine what it would be like to touch someone you would like be closer to. How might it make the relationship stronger? If you feel up to it, try hugging the person or just putting your hand on an arm. Write about how the experience made you feel.

WEEK 28
Taking the High Road:
Love Your Enemies

Love your enemies and pray for those who per-
secute you.

> JESUS,
> Matthew 5:44

Nonviolence is the answer to the crucial political
and moral questions of our time: the need for
man to overcome oppression and violence without resorting to oppression and violence. Man
must evolve for all human conflict a method
which rejects revenge, aggression and retaliation.
The foundation of such a method is love.

> MARTIN LUTHER KING JR.

Recently, the daughter of a friend of mine was being bullied by
one of her classmates. As my friend tried to help her through the
problem, she remembered the "love your enemy" scripture in
the Bible and read it out loud. The girl stared at her mother in
total disbelief. "We're supposed to love our enemies?" she said.
"Why are we supposed to do that?"

My friend said, "It's easy to love people who are nice to you,
and it's easy to hate people who pick on you. When it comes to
dealing with bullies, we're not supposed to take the easy way out
or else we'll be as bad as they are." Her daughter was honest and
said that she didn't know if she could love her classmate, but I

give my friend a lot of credit for planting such a powerful seed. That day a little girl learned that you don't have to respond to evil with evil. By taking the high road, we can learn more creative solutions to conflict.

The first step to loving our enemies is making an effort to understand what's going on from their point of view. You may not be privy to the details, but everybody has a story. Begin by thinking about the people in your own life who cause you difficulty. Did an ex-boyfriend leave you in a bad way? Is one of your colleagues trying to undermine your ideas at work? Did a trusted friend betray you? Take some time to think about why they might have acted the way they did. Sometimes people are insecure about their own abilities. Sometimes they're responding to past hurts. You can't control other people's motivations and behaviors, but you can control how their actions affect your own life. Instead of sitting there and letting that anger boil inside you, take steps to move on. Confront them about their behavior if you need to. Then, whether or not that other person decides to hold on to a grudge, do the good thing, the loving thing, the healthy thing. Let it go.

Loving your enemies doesn't mean making excuses when people treat you badly. And it doesn't mean turning into a wimp or a doormat. It means taking the high road, even if that means accepting some of the blame yourself. Almost five years ago my friend Marion had a falling-out with one of her close friends, Sam. Sam had been drinking a lot and he was getting mean and ugly. He'd turn on Marion when she tried to help him, and he stopped returning her calls or showing up when they'd planned to meet. The final straw came late one night when he came to her apartment drunk and started cursing her out for not lending him some money. She kicked him out and told him not to come back until he'd cleaned up his act. The two of them didn't speak again for years.

Then a few months ago, totally out of the blue, Marion got a call from Sam, who's now living across the country in California.

He said that ever since they'd split, he'd been thinking about Marion and regretting that his ugly behavior ended what he considered a real precious friendship. He'd cleaned up his act and joined an AA program, which included a step of working toward forgiveness. So he was calling to apologize for the way he'd treated Marion all those years before. Well, Marion was blown away by his reaching out to her like that. She says her only regret was that they hadn't gone back for the love in their relationship sooner, that they'd both wasted all those years hanging on to bitterness and grief instead. In fact, his call made Marion think about other people in her life it was time she forgave. She made a few calls, and rebuilt a few bridges of her own. Love begets love. It stops the cycle of damage. The truth is we're never going to feel at peace with ourselves until we make our peace with the world.

Once you've looked at what you can do to resolve conflicts with those around you, start thinking a little broader. There will always be people in this world whose beliefs and practices make us angry or who make the decision to hate us without even knowing who we are. In *A Course in Miracles*, a spiritual self-study guide, Marianne Williamson tells us that the opposite of love is not hate but fear. Racism, sexism, and all the other *isms* are usually built on fear of differences. Your reaction to these "enemies" can defuse such fears, or it can make things worse. If someone believes something about you just because you're Black or female or old or young, don't wind up proving her right by screaming or cursing or starting a fight. Again, take the high road. Understanding and tolerance lay a foundation upon which love can grow. When up against people with such narrow kinds of beliefs, it's easy to just get pissed off. But being a loving person often means opting not to make the easy choice. It means resisting the urge to head down to someone else's level, and instead doing your best to raise her up to yours.

The most powerful tool we have to fight injustices of all kinds is our compassion. Love is stronger than hate. It lives longer and grows faster. At the end of the day, love is what every single one of us is on this earth to find.

*J*ournal time

This week, meditate on the page about a personal conflict. Write about your feelings toward the other person involved, no matter how ugly those feelings might be. Then spend some time thinking about why you're hanging on to your negative feelings and how you might deal with this anger in a more constructive way. Are you benefiting in some way by staying hostile? How is your hatred holding you back in the rest of your life? How might you go about resolving this conflict? Is it possible to confront the person in a respectful yet direct way? Remember, this isn't about making excuses for someone else's behavior, but about making peace with yourself. What would it take to forgive an enemy, and even eventually love her? How would your life improve if you could move on?

Also spend some time thinking about other people whose beliefs or behaviors make you consider them "your enemies." What is the best way to deal with such people? How can you follow in the footsteps of Martin Luther King Jr. and others who preach nonviolence? Do you believe in his way? Why or why not?

WEEK 29
Completing the Circle: Learning to Accept Love in Your Life

回

> I can't be who I'm supposed to be until you be-
> come who you're supposed to be.
>
> XAVIER ARTIS

Up until now we've spent a lot of time focusing on how to give love—to yourself, to your mate, even to your enemies. But this last week we're going to take the time to remember that love is a circle. In order to stay balanced, we have to give but we also have to receive. Accepting the love others offer us is just as important as sending it out to them. And for some of us, this accepting is the hardest part.

A couple of years ago my single but looking-for-love friend Shellie started dating Chris, a smart and sweet young doctor who wound up falling for her in a big way. From the outside, things looked to be getting real serious real fast, but Shellie never seemed to want to admit how close she and Chris were getting. Every time she'd talk about how incredible that man was, she'd also have to go and explain what was going wrong. It was like she just couldn't take the idea of someone wanting her so much.

Their jobs kept them living four hours apart, but almost every weekend Chris came up for a visit. During the week, he called and sent flowers just to make sure Shellie knew how much he was thinking about her. But instead of reveling in all that affection, Shellie did her best to push Chris away. When he said he missed her, she'd tell him he was getting too clingy. When he

scheduled a visit, she'd make plans to make sure they weren't together all the time. Thing was, she was never happier than when
she was with him. She was just having real trouble believing she
deserved someone who loved her as much as he did.

Lucky for Shellie, Chris was an understanding and patient
kind of a guy. When he saw Shellie needed some space, he did
his best to back off. Meanwhile, all of us friends started laying
into Shellie about why she wanted to go and screw up such a
good thing. We kept pointing out how much Chris cared for her
and how gone she obviously was on him. We rode that girl so hard
that finally she promised to take an honest look at how she was
behaving. And once she did that, she had to admit that she wasn't
unhappy with Chris. She was just scared. She was worried that
she wouldn't live up to all those expectations he had about her.
So she and Chris sat down and had a real heart-to-heart about
what Shellie was feeling. He promised to move more slowly and
she promised to do her best not to turn him away.

It took some time, but understanding her own fears about
being loved so much helped Shellie get comfortable with accepting Chris's affection. A year later, when he asked her to
marry him, she said yes. These days they're a real healthy and
happy couple, with both of them feeling free to contribute to that
circle of love.

Like Shellie, plenty of us find that it's a whole lot easier to
give love than to receive it. Accepting love from a friend or mate
can make us feel vulnerable and uncomfortable about what the
person will want in return. Often our own low self-esteem gets in
the way. We might think we just aren't good enough to be the object of someone's affection.

If you find accepting love difficult, take some time this week
to ask yourself why. Are you afraid of not measuring up to expectations? Go back and think about all the work we did on self-
love a few weeks ago. Get out that list of things you value in
yourself and read it over. Chances are, other people have noticed
the same things. Of course we all have faults and we all make

mistakes, but that doesn't mean people will stop loving us when they discover we're not perfect. After all, our flaws are what make us human.

My friend Lanie has always had real trouble believing anyone can love her just for herself. She's always buying her friends expensive presents or taking them to lunch, figuring she'd better shell out good if she wants them to stick around. Whenever someone does something nice for her, she instantly gets to worrying about how she can pay the person back. She just can't seem to believe that love isn't some kind of transaction—you do one thing for me, I do one thing for you. The sad part is, Lanie's convinced herself that the only way people can love her is with all those strings attached. She gets so caught up in keeping track of who's done what, she winds up missing out on the whole experience of just being cared about.

It can be easy to get stuck in the same trap Lanie did and start mistaking love for a prize, something we've got to work hard to win. We might even feel like we have to buy love in other ways. Maybe we think that we owe it to our friends to be accomplished or entertaining or exciting. When things aren't going well, we might turn them away, figuring they'll get tired of us in our less-than-perfect form—I know I'm guilty of this. But when you're experiencing tough times, when you feel dull or boring or stupid, that's just when your cheering section wants to be there for you the most. The people who love you don't do it because of your job or your bank account, your fancy house or cool connections. They love you, the person, no matter what you're going through.

The truth is, we all deserve to be loved. So if someone's offering, you owe it to the person, and to yourself, to let down your guard and accept those feelings being extended. It may feel very risky at first, but the alternative of a life without love is far, far worse. Try looking at it from the other direction. Have you ever extended your love to someone and been rejected? It hurts. It's not fair or generous, or loving, to treat others that way.

When it comes to love, if someone in your life takes the first step, I encourage you to be brave enough to follow. Try to move past old issues like anger, jealousy, or insecurity. Love won't always arrive in the forms we expect or even want it to. It's up to us to learn to be flexible and forgiving. Whether it's an old friend reappearing just when your life's full enough to burst or a lover singing your praises when you're feeling down, part of loving is learning to take the time, feel the feelings, and hear the message. Accept what's being handed to you. Do your part to see that this circle stays complete.

Journal time

This week, take some time to think about the different ways in which you receive and accept love in your life. Are there times when you don't welcome the love others extend to you? Why not? What kind of message does this send? Is it what you really want to say?

If you're involved in a relationship in which you have trouble accepting love, try taking a closer look at what's going on. What's standing in your way? Are you worried about what she expects of you? Concerned about letting him down? What sorts of changes do you need to make to open yourself up to this other person? Maybe it's a question of taking the time to spend with a friend or relative. Maybe it's giving yourself permission to feel worthy of praise. Come up with one thing you can do right now in order to free up room inside you for that loving gesture.

Also this week, go back in your journal and find that definition of love you came up with seven weeks ago. Take it out and read it over. Now that you've been working the love virtue, do you still agree with what you said? If not, how have your beliefs changed? Think about how can you apply this new definition to your life as you strive to give and receive love each day.

Living Virtue 5

Community

We have all known the long loneliness and we have learned that the only solution is love and that love comes with community.

DOROTHY DAY

Despite everything that Harlem did to our generation, I think it gave something to a few. It gave them a strength that couldn't be obtained anywhere else.

CLAUDE BROWN,
1965

Right up there with our physical need for food and oxygen is the need to belong and be loved. If we don't connect to others, we feel lost and alone. Alienation is a big problem in our society today—too many of us are like lonely flowers, growing in our own solitary gardens, barely connecting with others. We pride ourselves on not needing anyone, but the price we pay for this arrogance is high: depression, imbalance, and loneliness.

Barbra Streisand sang about people needing people being the luckiest people in the world. I would say, people who *know* they need others are the lucky ones. They know that they were not put on this earth to live alone. They're the ones who choose their friends and loved ones wisely and consciously—instead of letting folks drift in and out of their lives. Those of us who think we can make it on our own often end up in relationships that don't even begin to touch our souls.

I have a tendency to be a loner, so I have to constantly guard against withdrawing into my shell. I always say that I studied social work and psychology because I wanted to help people. While that's true, I also wanted to understand myself better, especially in the intimacy arena. Being intimate with others scares me. Revealing myself to someone else takes me out of my comfort zone.

Let me clarify. When I say intimate, I don't mean sex necessarily (although that could certainly be an important part of an intimate relationship). By intimate, I mean that deep sharing of thoughts and feelings with someone really special whom you trust. That could be a spouse, a child, or a good friend.

We all have inner conflicts that we must balance, and this is mine: the need to balance solitude with togetherness. Relationships are very important to me, but I'm conflicted. Part of me wants to enjoy the companionship of others, while another part wants to be left alone.

I began to realize the need to work through this challenge when I left home for college. When you move out of your parents' house and you're on your own, you no longer have a readymade family, friends, and community. For many of us, it's hard to forge community. We find ourselves feeling lonely, but we don't know what to do about it.

I'm not a "joiner," in the traditional sense—I don't belong to clubs or sororities, for example—it is up to me to create community for myself. The easiest way for me to make friends is to get involved—mentoring young people, working in shelters, raising awareness for worthy causes, attending political events. Usually these events are tied to my work.

A few years ago I began to yearn for a kind of connection I wasn't sure existed. It wasn't a yearning for romance or even conventional friendship; I was longing to share my experiences and my time with someone young. In truth I think it was my biological clock finally going off. I wasn't close to having a child, yet I very much wanted a connection that allowed me to express my maternal instincts.

Around that time, I also began my work at Kaplan House. David was a young man with a mother and grandmother addicted to crack. He was a survivor, and I was so moved by his story that I wrote to him and sent him a book. David called me, and I invited him to a Knicks game. George Daniels, Kaplan's program director, asked me to come to speak to all the residents. From that humble beginning my relationship with David, the other residents, and staff at Kaplan House began and continues to this day.

The relationships I have at Kaplan House changed my life. The kids and I love each other, which is beautiful, sometimes painful, and always healing. I hope my kids get as much out of our relationship as I do. They are my teachers in the hugs and kisses department. When I walk in the door, I'm always greeted with hugs. I've also learned about intimacy from the kids who find the hugging ritual difficult. I know what it's like to need affection but not know how to ask for it, and some of these kids are truly starved. Some of them don't even know how to hug at first.

Every time I come away from one of those prolonged hugs, where we're just standing there, wordless, arms around each other, I am reminded that when you do things for others, you get the gift. As I risk opening my heart to these special people, the warmth carries over into other areas of my life and I experience more healing and love. When I'm getting caught up in self-imposed work-related stress and not handling it properly, one of them will remind me to breathe, smile, and stop acting like a crazy lady. After a visit with them, I can see how I've been acting. They help me to be a little less serious. Somehow—I don't know how or when it happened—all the kids at Kaplan became *my* kids.

When I met Rocky, I realized that all my experiences in life had been preparing me for this wonderful young man. I first set eyes on sixteen-year-old Rocky when I put together a mentoring project for young Black men that was tied in to the *Essence* Awards. My goal was to assign them older, more experienced mentors. Rocky had such a strong, positive presence that we clicked immediately. He was a fighter and a survivor. There was no question—I would be his mentor. I took him under my wing.

Meeting Rocky took me out of my comfort zone and even deeper into intimacy. No way could I maintain a safe distance from him—nor did I want to. The more time I spent with Rocky and got to know him, the more I admired him. I found that when I wasn't with him, I'd think about him, wondering if he was all right. I'd worry that he wasn't getting enough to eat. I'd wonder if he'd done well on a test that he was studying for. When I went to the grocery store, I'd buy two of everything—one for me and one for him.

My feelings for Rocky were growing and there was nothing I could do about it. This was the relationship I had wanted all my life. I had always longed for children, but as time went on I knew I'd never have them. The desire to mother a young person never left me, but I never dreamed that I would actually get to experience a relationship that could fulfill me in this way. I not only felt like his mother and was acting like his mother, but I truly *was* his mother. I'd gone from mentor and teacher to mother. Now, when had that happened? I wondered, but I didn't care. I'd never had a child before, but I knew instinctively this was exactly how being a mother felt.

In my relationship with Rocky, suddenly family and community truly became one. It was scary loving someone so much, but my relationship with him literally forced me to become involved with every ounce of my being. There was no safe harbor for my emotions. I had to experience each and every one, from love to anger. There could be no emotional flatlining around Rocky.

I quickly discovered that living with a person can test even the greatest love. I invited Rocky to move in with me so that he could have a decent place to stay. He was trying so hard to survive, like an adult, it touched me. I wanted to make sure that he was well fed and clothed. I gave him his own bedroom and bath, and his own phone. All my attempts at dividing my space didn't mean a thing. We were still living together, which meant that I had to give up my precious privacy. I couldn't walk around the house naked anymore. I couldn't just go in and out without talking to him first. I had to say "good morning" when I really didn't feel like talking. Basically, I had to learn how to live with another human being.

Living alone for so many years, I had gotten pretty stuck in my ways. With my new roommate, I had to learn the art of compromise and negotiation. We had to develop a new rhythm together. We had to remember to call each other if we'd be late getting home. We had to share chores. I had to get used to his ways, and he had to get used to mine. There was so much to learn about creating a home together.

Although there were some trying times, I never once regretted my decision to have him move in. Neither of us had to do this. We had nothing holding us together beyond our mutual desire to explore and celebrate the connection we miraculously found.

Not only did my capacity for intimacy grow leaps and bounds, but I learned an important lesson: The potential for creating family—and belonging—is everywhere. All you have to do is be willing to receive love and when it comes, open your heart. When I hear people say that they can't find love and that they're lonely, I understand because I there, too. There was a time when most of my relationships were so tied in to getting work done that they weren't really satisfying. But when you open your heart to intimacy, it's like the sun begins to shine for the first time, lighting up all the other beautiful flowers in a great big garden. You're not the only one out there! All it takes is desire and the willingness to step out of your safe space and meet new people!

Yes, I love Rocky, with all my heart. In my darkest days I thought I'd never have a child. I ached at the thought because family is the foundation of our lives. I wanted my life to continue on in my children. The problem was, I had taken a very narrow, biological view of family. Marriage licenses and birth certificates don't make family. It's all about the love you share. When Rocky came into my life, I finally got it. You don't have to give birth to be a mother, and you don't have to be related to be a family. Rocky is my son and there is no two ways about it.

I've watched him go from challenged adolescent to high school graduate to confident college student. Now he is a strong, wise, and gentle man. I'm so proud of him. He's still trying to figure out what he wants to do with his life, but whatever he does, he'll be good at it. He will make quite an impact on this world.

And we continue to deepen our special bond. The other day I was talking to him about my concerns for the agency. He told me that he, too, had been thinking about the "family" business and had some ideas. Hearing that made me cry—since I had no kids, I'd never looked at the agency as a family business. Now, I don't expect Rocky to follow in my footsteps, but his interest in the business touched me.

People may think our relationship different, but in many cultures around the world there is no dividing line between family and community. I mentioned this to my friend Alan Gansberg, and he told me that in his readings, he came across an African precedent to my relationship with Rocky. The Samburu tribe of Kenya raises all children communally. But sometimes a natural bond develops between an adult and a child to whom the adult is not biologically related. When that happens, the child is considered the offspring of that adult and treated by all accordingly, even if the child's natural parents are both still living. And no one thinks this odd or strange.

It doesn't matter that I didn't carry Rocky physically. I'm his mother, he's my son, and we are family. Through Rocky, community and family are one for me.

A focus on community as a living virtue brings us back into balance. I define *community* as a place and a verb. Community can be where you live, worship, work, and play. It can also be your active and emotional involvement with others around common interests. As creators of family and community, we seek kindred souls who can give us the love and friendship that we need. This involvement leads to a wonderful, fulfilling sense of belonging.

This section is about understanding the impact of community on our lives and strengthening bonds. The human need to belong is powerful, and I see it in its raw, undiluted form at Kaplan House. We are all needy, whether we want to admit it or not. Community provides many opportunities for relationship and intimacy—and it is one of the few things that can meaningfully meet our needs. Each week will help you sustain, nurture, and enhance community.

Over the next few weeks, we're going to look at how we're shaped by those relationships. We'll look at how our family and community origins influence and continue to develop us. We'll talk about the fact that many of our communities are out of control. We no longer feel safe in them or feel a sense of ownership—in real estate or responsibility. With so many of our communities in turmoil, it is important to celebrate successes whenever they occur, so we'll also look at how family and community traditions empower us.

To paraphrase the old saying, no woman is an island. If you have been afraid to experience the joys (and challenges) of communal intimacy, then together, let's get in our boats and row to shore. There's a big continent of kindred spirits awaiting our arrival. They've been there all along.

WEEK 30
Origins

In every conceivable manner, the family is link to
our past, bridge to our future.

ALEX HALEY

My family is getting older. Aunt Helen and Aunt Mary recently
passed away and even though we weren't that close, I was rocked
by their deaths. They were a foundation of the family. Throughout my whole life, my aunts were a strong presence. On some
level, I see their deaths as preparing me for the inevitable passing of my mother and father. It is very unsettling.

So I am now on a quest to find out as much about my origins
(and myself) as I can. The older I get, the more I realize how important our original families are. I used to be too busy to listen,
but I'm paying attention to the old stories now. Origins shape our
attitudes, values, priorities, needs, desires, and emotional capacity. As I talk to my relatives, I'm discovering how I learned to relate to others and why I am the way I am.

Whenever I'm going through a challenging time, I remember
my grandmothers and how hard it must have been to raise many
children alone. My mother says that her mother had a strong faith
in God, and that's what got her through. There were times when
there was no food on the table, but my grandmother would pray
and by the end of the day, there would be enough to feed all the
children. You have to be strong to get through poverty, hunger,
and abandonment. It helps me to know that the strength of my
grandmothers runs through my veins. Their faith has become

my faith. My mantra is, "If they could get through it, I can get through it."

What about your first family? What was it like living with your parents and siblings (if you had any)? How are you like your parents and even grandparents? What were the strengths they gave you?

We are all born into families—biological, adopted, or many other varieties. This is where it all begins. In *Roots*, Alex Haley showed us how family origins, community, and history work together to shape our personalities and values, as well as our deepest dysfunctions. Family life is like a classroom. In it you learn the lessons that you'll carry into adulthood.

In a *Publishers Weekly* interview, author Gary Paulsen talked about his tough childhood. He said, "Both my parents were drunks and just hated each other. They fought and screamed and never should have been married. . . . So to me childhood was mainly something to get through alive." He said that his childhood taught him "tenacity and independence and the willingness to fight." Despite his difficult past—or maybe because of it—Paulsen became a successful author. He often draws on his childhood experiences to give life to the scenes and characters in his books.

Was your family life like Paulsen's or the Huxtables'? Can you even remember, or do you leave that chapter in your life buried in the past? Unresolved issues from family often cause problems in adulthood. That's certainly the case in my life. Wonder why relationships never seem to work out or why you're always broke, despite your best efforts? No doubt it's got to do with issues that you're still carrying around from childhood. *Everything* goes back to that.

Understanding our origins is extremely important. You can't know who you are and where you're going unless you know where you came from. That's been the problem with Black folks for so long. We can only go back into our history just so far, and then the lights go out. We know dimly that our ancestors came from Africa, but we don't know much more than that. Having been robbed of that knowledge keeps us in the dark in many ways. What are the strengths—and weaknesses—that flow through our veins? Knowing your origins can answer those questions and more.

Journal time

Even though many of us cannot trace our lineage back more than two or three generations, we can still learn much about our origins and ourselves just by talking to family members. Record your talks in your journal, or get a video or tape recorder with lots of batteries and cassette tapes.

This week, make a list of all the grandparents, parents, aunts, uncles, and cousins you need to talk to. Get telephone numbers and addresses (there's usually one person in the family who knows where everybody lives and their phone numbers). If you were adopted or spent a lot of time in foster care, you might have to contact an agency or group home. Don't give up! There are resources out there to help you find your biological family.

Talk to the elders to get the big picture of family history. We want to know who they were, what they did, and how they contributed to the community. Some of us have bank presidents and college professors in our families, but we know nothing about them. Some of us have grands and great-grands who picked cotton down south. Have they ever told you what it's like to pick cotton? This week we're going to find out about our people.

Ask to see artifacts. Dig through photo albums and old newspaper clippings. You'll begin to see your own face in every picture.

Go visiting. Take a drive and visit the old neighborhood, church, school—even graveyard (which is a very peaceful place). Eat and listen. Some of the best conversations take place in the kitchen. Make a meal together from scratch. As you listen to the old stories, take note of how they're affecting you. See how these stories can help you develop new relationships beyond our first family. What kind of community do you want to be a part of? We don't get to choose our families, but we do get to choose who we commune with.

WEEK 31
Family Is Where You Find It

Call it a clan, call it a network, call it a tribe, call it a family. Whatever you call it, whoever you are, you need one.

JANE HOWARD

The bond that links your true family is not one of blood, but of respect and joy in each other's life. Rarely do members of one family grow up under the same roof.

RICHARD BACH,
Illusions

When I think of family, I am reminded of geese. When a goose gets sick, wounded, or shot down, two geese drop out of formation and follow it down to help protect it. They stay with it until it dies or is able to fly again. Then they launch out with another formation or catch up with the flock. The best families are like flocks of geese. They stand by one another during sunny and cloudy days.

For many of us, our family of origin prepares us to stretch out into new relationships and beyond the life we knew as children and into relationships we've felt deep inside all along. Your people are out there, your "real" family, soul mates, kindred spirits, and best friends. We may be forever rooted in our biological clan, but from there we journey out into the world, finding kin and friendly neighbors of all different shapes, colors, and backgrounds.

We live in such a transient society today. We move around so much that we're likely to move away from our communities of origin—which means we need to spend extra time thinking about ways to stay connected to our families back home even as we forge our own families. I have a good friend who gives prepaid phone cards at Christmas with the understanding that they can be used only to call family members. It's a fun and simple way to help your loved ones stay in touch.

But what if your original birth family was so unhealthy that you're just thankful to have been able to get away in one piece? Growing up gives us an opportunity to heal these wounds. Sometimes finding love and acceptance and creating family for yourself can give you the distance and strength you need to forgive your own parents. Although forgiveness is not always an option, some of the healthiest people I know are the ones who've found a way to let go of childhood pain and trauma. One of my cousin's best friends had a very traumatic childhood filled with sexual and physical abuse. Her twenties were a tough time as she struggled with the legacy of that abuse. But she was a survivor, and with the help of survivor groups and a good therapist she really began to reclaim her life. When she hit thirty she met a very caring man who gave her much of the love she didn't get in childhood. After her first child was born she really felt she had her own family— and a wonderful thing happened. The childhood rage and sorrow that had been trapped in her for so long finally surfaced and diminished. She'll never be fully reconciled with her parents, but she no longer feels haunted by her childhood. She's even managed to restore a relationship with an aunt who now functions as her child's grandmother. So although a dysfunctional family can leave a hard legacy, forging new family can create a space of healing and love.

Whether your family is by blood or choice it should be the place you feel safe, restored, and whole. When life overwhelms you, think about taking a vacation into your family. Sometimes a little bit of family time can do wonders for lagging spirits or deflated self-confidence. Think about things you love about your family, and it'll soon dawn on you that you're also talking about things you love about yourself.

---

*J*ournal time

Whether you are blessed to be in a good relationship with your family of origin or have created an entirely new family, or both, it's important to maintain those relationships. Taking folks for granted will slowly but surely kill the best of relationships. We must tend those fragile and lovely gardens.

In your journal this week, meditate on the page about the special, intimate relationships you maintain outside of your family of origin. How do these "family" relationships differ from your original ones? How do they help you, and how do you support them? What do you feel was missing in your family of origin that you receive from your "collected" family?

You might also want to think about dedicating one hour a week to "family time." Perhaps it's every Saturday at ten or one evening a week. Then spend some time reflecting on what came up during this time. You might even want to journal about it or keep a log. It's a great way to check in with everybody and address small issues before they get bigger.

WEEK 32
Discovering Community
(I Am Because We Are)

回

My friends are mirrors and crystal balls: they reflect the good in me, and they assure me that my future is as bright as I want it to be.

VERONICA CHAMBERS,
author

There is a commodity in human experience. If it has happened to one person, it has happened to thousands.

OPRAH WINFREY

We are each other's harvest; we are each other's business; we are each other's magnitude and bond.

GWENDOLYN BROOKS

The African saying, "I am because we are" (also translated "I am We"), goes against the grain of our society's inbred individualism. But I believe that we need that strong sense of being connected with each other to change from a society of special interests into one human community. Individualism taken to the extreme is the source of a lot of our psychological problems. It's one of the reasons we feel lonely and isolated from one another. But one of the best cures for that sense of isolation is learning to build community around you.

When you're in true community, you share yourself with folks. The mask comes off and you risk revealing (and exposing) the real you. Sometimes even now I'm afraid to say I'm in pain because I'm not certain I'll be accepted. When I'm facilitating a workshop or keynoting an event, I attempt to create "instant community" by telling my audience who I really am, pain and all; by not pretending to know more than I do or to be somehow perfect. By taking the risk first, I create a safety zone, and all the war stories proceed to pour out of troubled souls. We vent, we cry, we laugh, we may even heal some, and in the process, if only for an hour or two, we don't feel alone, we forge a sense of community.

Our lives in the new millennium are very complicated, so finding community can require an extra amount of willpower. The best way to create community is to find a group of people who share your interests. If you live in a large anonymous city like New York, you may feel as if community building is impossible, but it's not; you just have to be creative. One of my interns is a big movie fan, and she found her community online. Every week she would log on to her favorite movie chat room and meet lots of people who shared her interests. But those relationships didn't end in cyberspace—two of the women she met online live in New York. They made a plan to get together, and now they see each other regularly for movie night. I have another woman friend who bought a bicycle and started riding to work. She liked riding so much that she joined a weekend riding group and now counts several of the people in the group among her closest friends.

There are tons of ways to forge community these days. Think interests, not geography. Many women I know met their dearest friends through reading groups or by attending church functions or singing in church choir. The key is identifying your hobbies and interests. Just reflect on what you like—skiing, knitting, swimming, fishing, ceramics, needlepoint, music, tennis, in-line skating, running—and find a group of people who share your enthusiasm. Community doesn't spring up overnight, but with a little work (finding what you love to do and finding people who share your love of doing it) you will slowly build a supportive and caring community based on who you truly are.

As I write these words, hoping that this book will help you create the life you've always wanted, you and I have created community that is beyond time and space. Just by reading these words you and I have shared something. After all, discovering and sharing the things we have in common increases our sense of belonging—and that's what community is all about.

Journal time

This week let's look at those communities you participate in that help you grow and help make your life enjoyable. Do you have communities of interest now? If not, think about ways that you can create community around your interests. Write down all the things you're interested in and why. Read over your annotated list and decide which one you're most passionate about. Go online, or to the library and look for groups focused on your interest. When you've found one, attend a few meetings or events and write about the experience. You may have to try a few different things to find a fit for you, but don't give up. Keep journaling about your feelings and experiences until you find the right place to share your interests and yourself.

WEEK 33
Honoring Our Differences

What we have to do . . . is to find a way to celebrate our diversity and debate our differences without fracturing our communities.

HILLARY RODHAM CLINTON

There is nowhere you can go and only be with people who are like you. Give it up.

BERNICE JOHNSON REAGON

My friend Tony was raised in an all-Black community in Detroit, Michigan. Except for what he saw on TV, he grew up not knowing anything about white folks.

Tony left school in the eighth grade because he had a son and wanted to support him. Many years later, he decided to leave the world he had known all his life for the unknown in Los Angeles. He had never been on his own, never even had a job. Because of his openness to new experiences, he met his first true friend of another race.

Rullo was the owner of a construction company. When he met Tony, he saw a young man who was trying to better himself, so he hired him. Tony started out in an entry-level labor position. Over the years, he was promoted to operating engineer and then field supervisor.

When Tony's family became too large for his little one-bedroom apartment, it was Rullo who saw to it that his loan for a new house got approved. Although he was Tony's boss, they were good friends, and they're friends to this day.

Prejudice is limiting. Dissing a whole group of people because of the color of their skin is insane. Some of my greatest blessings have come from people who don't look like me. Unlike Tony, I was exposed to other races and developed friendships with many different types of people early in childhood. This openness has allowed me to receive many blessings. Trust me, we're all the same.

For example, there is a white woman, Jan, who lives down the hall—she's also in public relations. One day she saw me on the elevator, struggling with too many bags to carry, and she helped me carry them to my apartment. At the time the Prozac just wasn't working and I was going to ask my therapist to adjust the dosage. But—and this is why you have to be open to relating to anyone, regardless of differences—my new friend and I started talking, and she told me about a healer client of hers, David Grand. Well, Let me tell you, he did more for me in an hour than I had received in years of therapy. He helped me realize that medication was limited, that there were other things that would help me. So often I see people (Black, White, Muslim, Christian, Jewish, Gay, Straight) who lead diminished lives because they are either too afraid or too prejudiced to relate to folks who look or act differently than they do. This attitude prevents the creation of personally meaningful and expansive community.

You can't feel connected to your community if it's exclusionary. And if you've forged an exclusionary community, you're not a part of the larger American community. Diversity is one of our greatest strengths, but honestly, most of us still don't see it that way. Groups are still targeted for hate crimes. Blacks are still racially profiled. Women still make less than men in the workplace. Pick any group in this country, and you'll find an object of bigotry.

We all have prejudices, and we all need to get over them. It's hard because some of our feelings about other groups were created in childhood. We may feel irrational hatred or disgust for a group and not even know why.

The basic tenet of tolerance is respect. My friend Bob Law, entrepreneur and veteran radio broadcaster, would always tell listeners that he respected them no matter what their viewpoint. Over time he began to notice that his callers were responding in kind. The respect he showed his callers really let them open up and talk candidly with him and his community of listeners. Let's resolve to stop name calling or saying cutting and hurtful things to people who don't share our viewpoint. Without openness and freedom of expression, all our lives would be diminished. Loving tolerance is a way of saying, "I accept that you have as much right to your space on the planet as I do."

Bigotry and prejudice are caused by folks who don't love themselves. We've heard it many times, and it'll always be true: You can't love another until you love yourself. This holds for communities, too. Your community will never become tolerant until you move beyond bigotry in your own heart. Compassion and acceptance of yourself and others are the true cornerstones of humanity and community. We can never become who we're supposed to be until our community becomes what it's supposed to be.

Journal time

First, let's become aware of our feelings. If you've been harboring prejudice against another group, shine a light on it and be honest with yourself. Ask yourself why you feel the way you do. Have you been manipulated by media images? Or did something happen once to you or a friend, and as a result you've generalized the bad feelings to the entire group?

In your journal this week, imagine what it would be like to be a member of a group that you have some prejudicial feelings toward. Put yourself in their shoes. Imagine what their days are like for them.

Also, explore the diversity of your own relationships. Do you just hang with members of the group you most readily identify with, or are you open to new experiences? What feelings come up when you interact with folks from different groups? Sometimes the thing limiting us the most is fear. Work with your fear and see if your feelings don't change over time.

WEEK 34
Take Back Your Community

⊡

In every community, there is work to be done. In
every nation, there are wounds to heal. In every
heart, there is the power to do it.

MARIANNE WILLIAMSON,
A Return to Love

See those fine women on billboards, liquor store
posters, and point-of-purchase advertising? The
little brothers are sure checking them out. You
can't walk through the hood without seeing
women selling alcohol, beer, and malt liquor.
Sometimes you'll find these and other ads close
to schools—right where children can get a good
look at them.

ALFRED "COACH" POWELL,
Message 'N A Bottle: The 40oz Scandal

Our neighborhoods are going through a transition. For many
years they were held hostage by the forces of destruction, but I
have hope today. As I crisscross the country, I'm seeing glimmers
of revival. There are still abandoned buildings, vacant lots, crime
sprees, poor education, poor health care, and unemployment, but
I think we're beginning to see these things as opportunities to
build and help one another.

The bad guys won't win if we don't let them. Yes, the media
feeds us stories about horrible murders, rapes, and drug busts.
Children addicted to drugs and alcohol at an early age and the in-

nocent victims of abuse. I'm not so rosy-eyed that I'll walk the streets alone at night. But I'm not giving up. I love my community, and I'm not going to let evil have its way.

Whether you live in a large city or a small rural town, no corner of our society has been spared from violence and crime. Even areas that were once thought of as safe have felt the impact. Columbine taught us that. Since we cannot run away from the problems, it's up to us to do something about them.

Must movin' on up mean moving away? By reclaiming our communities, we increase our group self-esteem and make sure we have a place to come home to.

I was inspired by a *New York Times* article, "Joined at the Stoop," about Black neighbors in North Philadelphia who have refused to give up their community without a fight. They didn't move, even though, like so many working-class communities, North Philly is plagued by drugs, crime, and violence.

Many of the residents are older. They work as domestics and factory workers. Some live on Social Security and modest pensions—and they practice community as a living virtue. They meet to discuss community issues, conduct voter registration drives, and plant gardens. They help their older neighbors cook, clean, drive, and grocery shop. A simple "Are you okay?" lets a neighbor know that someone cares. In a society that throws away its old folks, North Philly can teach us a valuable lesson in honoring and caring for elders.

As eighty-year-old Dorsha Mason says, "This is not a ghetto. This is a place where people worked hard to build a community."

There are communities in every city that are having problems. Even if we don't live there, we should see what we can do to help. My friend Susan Taylor and her husband, Khephra, once got a group of us together on New Year's Eve Day to deliver and serve meals to the sick and shut-in through the Meals on Wheels program. It was one of the best ways I've ever celebrated the hope and promise of a new year. We all began the year feeling like we were doing something that mattered, and it bolstered our commitment to helping others in the months that followed.

Some folks sit around and complain about the decline in their communities, and others do something about it. That's what I call taking back your community. We're not going to just give up our communities to the evil elements of the world. We're supposed to fight to make our communities livable, beautiful, and safe for ourselves and our kids.

Malaak Compton-Rock is another well-known person (she's the wife of comedian Chris Rock) who is committed to helping, by taking back the community in a very unique way. She helps individuals who are making the transition from public assistance to the workplace feel better about themselves.

Malaak began her career in public relations and special events at the agency. She once told me that when she was growing up, she was never allowed to say "I." She had to say "we" and share everything. When she worked at the agency, she was always helping someone. Later she worked at the U.S. Committee for UNICEF but still desired to help folks in a deeper way.

Malaak left her UNICEF job to give more time to her marriage. She was also on a quest to find her life mission. One of the things she did during this period was work at the Gay Men's Health Crisis Center.

During this time, major changes were being made in the welfare system. Millions of families across the country were being released from generations of dependency on the government. When you've lived your entire life being dependent on another for money, food, and shelter, becoming independent is a major challenge. Job training can help, but the problem is much deeper than learning how to type or fix computers. Change must involve pulling out from the root all the old ideas about being dependent and unempowered and instead planting the knowledge of inner power, resourcefulness, and the ability to take care of self.

It dawned on Malaak that her love of fashion and beauty could be used to help people, especially women, develop self-esteem and confidence. She incorporated styleWORKS, a Brooklyn-based nonprofit organization that provides free grooming consultations, makeovers, and comprehensive job training to individuals entering the workforce, many for the first time. She brings former welfare recipients together with image professionals (hairstylists, makeup artists, manicurists, and so one).

"Going from welfare to work is really difficult, and more so when you don't even know how you're supposed to present yourself," says Malaak. "We help women look better and feel better about themselves, and ultimately that will help them succeed."

And don't even think that because you're not married to a rich and famous person, you have no power to take back your community. You have the power. And when you come together with others, that power is multiplied.

In church there's a strong sense of community. Every Sunday the minister reads the names of members who are sick or bereaved. The minister and church members visit the "sick and shut-in" in hospitals, nursing homes, and their homes. They call them on the phone, and they send cards and flowers. They pray with them and for them. That's community.

Journal time

This week let's try to identify how some of the problems in your community are affecting you personally. This exercise is important because all too often we simply cope. We forget that we can actually do something about the problems. But first, we have to bring to our conscious awareness what they are.

What is your community like? Do you feel nervous or anxious there? Do you fear for your children? Do they have to avoid certain routes in the neighborhood because of gang warfare? Are your neighbors apathetic? Do you even know who your neighbors are?

Making community a living virtue means that you can't just sit
on the sidelines. This week, let's really get involved in our many
communities. Here are some ideas:

- Attend a block club or building association meeting. If your
  community doesn't have such an organization, start one. Get
  to know your neighbors—especially the kids. Become aware
  of your environment. Potholes in the street and a leaky roof
  in your apartment are unacceptable. We must stop coping
  and do what we can to change our lives for the better. Together, write letters to local government representatives (the
  ones who are accountable to you). Confront your landlord together. You'll be surprised at the difference a unified front
  makes.
- Volunteer to help with a church project. Religious institutions are godsends in our communities. Government can't
  solve all our problems, but the church, mosque, or temple
  can surely step in to help. Volunteer to coordinate a fund-
  raiser or work in the soup kitchen.
- At the very least, pay your PTA dues. Best bet, volunteer
  and support your local PTA's many activities.

WEEK 35
Own Your Community

🔲

The vacant lots and boarded-up houses—these
may be eyesores, but they also may be your opportunities.

FLOYD FLAKE,
The Way of the Bootstrapper

In *The Way of the Bootstrapper,* Floyd Flake, author and pastor of
Allen A.M.E. Church in St. Albans, New York, tells the story of
Charles Jenkins, a retired social worker and church elder, who
decided to do something about the decay in his community. In
his neighborhood was a vacant lot that was filled with garbage—
probably a hangout spot for folks who weren't doing anything uplifting. The sight of the lot was so offensive to Jenkins that he
decided to do something about it. He had the bright idea of turning it into a garden. What was once an eyesore became Jenkins's
opportunity to own a piece of his community. Flake says, "In the
fall, he plants tulips to bloom in the spring. Once the tulips begin
to fade, he then plants vegetables, which are enjoyed by other
members of the neighborhood."

I love that story because it shows how just one person can
make a difference. From Charles Jenkins's strong sense of responsibility for his community, it was no great leap to owning a
problem and then doing something about it.

A friend once told me that after renting for many years, she finally bought her own home. But it would be five more years before she would even paint a wall. Why? Because even though she
owned her home on paper, she didn't own it in her heart. She was

responsible enough to pay the mortgage every month, but until she became infused with "it's mine!" her house still looked like it belonged to the prior owners.

Owning your community means that when there's something to be done, you don't wait on someone else to do it. If there's litter in the street, you pick it up because it's your street. If there's an abandoned building on the block, instead of letting it degenerate into a crack house, you pool financial and other resources to buy the building, rehab it, rent it, and share the income.

Author Monique Greenwood and her husband own the Aquaba Mansion, a wonderful bed-and-breakfast in Brooklyn and now a second in Cape May, New Jersey. This dream of Monique's came to fruition because of the community's strong investment in the project.

John Bryant founded the nonprofit Los Angeles-based Operation Hope with the vision of empowering folks to be self-sufficient in inner-city communities. His organization partners with government agencies and community-based organizations to help folks take responsibility for their financial lives and ownership of their communities. The goal is to convert us from check cashers to savers, renters to homeowners, dreamers to small-business owners, and minimum-wage to living-wage workers.

Before any of these self-starters decided that they were going to assume responsibility for their community, they first had to decide what ownership meant to them—and so do we. Owning means a complete investment. What are you willing to invest your time, money, and energy in?

Owning is a commitment. What project in your community could you own and commit to? What will you take responsibility for developing and completing? Do you have a vision for how your community could be but are afraid that you'll get no support? Are you afraid that you'll be turned down? Owning also involves some risk taking. How much do you love your community? Are you willing to risk all to see your community change?

You will have nothing in life unless you take a risk. If you don't wake up every morning without a knot or butterflies in your stomach, it means you're playing it safe. Every day I'm scared because I know that I've got to take risks to keep things moving.

Owning your community also means sharing a stake in an enterprise with other folks. Each person makes a financial investment to bring a vision to reality.

Every day, a person or a group decides that enough is enough and they are not going to let their communities decline anymore. Whether it's a government program, a local cooperative project, or a single person going for it, it all begins with a mind-set of ownership. It's a great journey from slavery to self-sufficiency, but it's one worth pursuing because the rewards can be tremendous.

Journal time

This week let's think of two ways you can take ownership of your community. The first project can be one that you do yourself, such as homeownership or buying a rental property. The other project is one that you can do with others. In your journal, brainstorm ways to get started. How will you raise money, meet the right people? If you're in a project with others, how can you manage your resources so that money earmarked for the project is actually used for it? Who will you talk to? Who would you want to work with? Use this week to actually plan your projects and take your first steps.

WEEK 36
Celebrations and Traditions

回

When you tell a story you automatically talk
about traditions, but they're never separate from
the people, the human implications. You're talking about your connections as a human being.

GAYL JONES

Every day of the year is an opportunity to celebrate family and
community. I don't wait for holidays to give presents. I give all
year long. During the past several years, family reunions have become major annual events. Some families are so large and organized they have Web sites and newsletters.

There was a time when I didn't make participating in family
get-togethers a priority. There was always some meeting or business function to attend. The deaths of my aunt Willa Mae and
aunt Helen changed all that. I now make it a point to be present
and embrace family events, and that is bringing more balance
into my life.

I have another reason for my renewed focus on family: Rocky.
I don't have just myself to think about. Rocky needs my people
too, because my people are now his people.

During Christmas 2000, my mother, Rocky, and I had brunch
together. My mother gave each of us an envelope. I held it up
and said, "How come Rocky's is bigger than mine?" And my
mother said something that nearly brought tears to my eyes. She
said, "Because I've never had a grandson to give a Christmas card
to before." Although I usually try to get together with my folks
during the holidays, I decided then and there that there would

be no more trying. Family celebrations were worth making the commitment to.

My aunts' deaths helped me realize just how precious my relatives are. We need to cling to each other a little more, and celebrations are an excellent way to do that. Sometimes we don't see each other until a funeral or a family crisis. Celebrate family while we're still alive and well. I learn from my cousin Pat, who is amazing at working hard to keep family ties solid. She always calls to say happy birthday, and she'll drive long distances to attend celebrations. She goes out of her way to keep us all together.

Get together on birthdays, Thanksgiving, Christmas, Kwanzaa—or make up your own family holidays. Every year Larry and Faith, Carol and I throw *the* party event of the summer. Larry and Faith provide the big house, food, and drink. Carol coordinates the catering, decorating, and music, and I develop the guest list.

It's important to take time out to celebrate family and community. So much of our time is spent on the struggle that it's good to relax with the people we care about. The traditional holidays, from New Year's to Christmas, provide many opportunities to get together. But don't forget special cultural ones. Just because I'm Black doesn't mean I can't appreciate Cinco de Mayo or St. Patrick's Day. Let's all celebrate the first fruits of our communities and the spirit of Kwanzaa. And by all means, be creative. Organize a block party and donate the money you raise to the local after-school program. Or initiate a street fair where kids can learn to sell crafts and local vendors can display their goods while getting to know the people who buy from them.

Celebrations reaffirm our connection to community, and they reunite us with the folks we love and share friendship with. They also allow us to catch up with folks we haven't seen in a while. Let's take time out to honor our commitment to each other.

Celebrations are our reward for the hard work that goes into building and sustaining our families and communities. They also reaffirm our cultural bonds. When we celebrate with one another, we're honoring the experiences of our shared past and the vision of the future.

Journal time

The following are some ways to celebrate community. If you're interested in getting involved in a celebration, use your journal for planning. Do a budget, schedule meetings, what have you. Here are some things folks are doing across the country. Take your pick and get involved!

- Cultural celebrations. June 19 (Juneteenth) is a sacred day for Black folks. The Civil War ended in April 1865, but it was on June 19 that the last slaves in Texas found out they were free. And that's only one cultural holiday. There are so many other holidays that reflect the diversity of cultures and faiths that if you wanted to, you could have a party every day!
- Family reunions. They can be as big as you want them to be, or as simple as my own family's Albany or Mount Vernon get-togethers. The point is to get together. Don't let another year slip by without hanging out with the folks.
- Parades. This is a great way to get out of the house and have some fun with friends, neighbors, and families in the community. The Bud Billikin Parade in Chicago, the second largest in the country, promotes Black unity *and* diversity, as does the West Indian parade in Brooklyn.
- Surprise and celebrate someone in your family or office just for being her wonderful self. I've wanted to do this for a long time, and as they say, there's no time like the present!

Living Virtue 6

Spirituality

There is never a time in the future in which we
will work out our salvation. The challenge is in
the moment; the time is always now.

JAMES BALDWIN,
1961

My introduction to religion was probably no different from that
of millions of Black children. I grew up going to the Macedonia
Baptist Church in Mount Vernon, New York. My parents, sister,
and I went to church every Sunday until I left home for college,
and my sister and I attended Sunday school as well. While some
folks seemed to be spending all day in the house of God, my parents were pretty balanced about attendance. We did our Sunday
thing because they thought it was important that we have a
strong religious foundation, just like it was important that we be
exposed to museums and Black culture. They also made sure

that we were practicing the lessons that had been preached on Sunday morning all throughout the week.

Over the years after I left home, as I graduated from college and moved out into the world, my religious identity turned more than a little muddy. Sure, I'd go to church when I had time but it was more to put in an appearance than because it gave me any real spiritual sustenance. I got caught up in work and relationships and all that other big-city-living stuff. Basically, I made the choice to just let my spiritual self slide.

Like I've said, my life had its ups and downs, but as I got older I was feeling like the downs were coming around a whole lot more often than the ups. Even after I made the choice to start living my life according to the seven virtues, when it came to spirituality, I had to admit I was feeling lost. There was a very large hole in the place where I was supposed to be finding my self. But that commitment I made to work the virtues challenged me to finally look down the hole instead of just keep stepping around it. I realized I had to find some way to deepen my faith.

At first I tried returning to those old familiar habits from childhood. I started going to church every Sunday, and tried reading the Bible every night. But something important was still missing. The virtues got me thinking about spirituality and how discovering it takes something more than just going through the religious motions. They forced me to ask some serious questions. How do I feel about spirituality? What do I mean by faith? What do I want to take from the Christianity I grew up with? How do I form my own belief system?

I did my best to keep working on these questions, but I've got to admit I hit a real spiritual roadblock. Depression continued to haunt me. I didn't know where to turn.

Around that time my friends Charlie and Tonja invited me to attend a Christian retreat sponsored by the Christian Athletes United for Spiritual Empowerment. I decided to accept. That sentence makes the decision sound easy, but it wasn't. To be honest, I really didn't want to go. They had invited me to join them before, and I'd always turned them down. But this year things were different. I'd committed myself to those seven virtues and was truly blocked on the spirituality thing. This year I wanted to live my life by opening doors, not closing them. Though I was scared to death, I kept telling myself not to rule anything out. I was really nervous—there were so many unknowns. But part of me, the part committed to charting my spiritual path no matter what the cost, knew that it was something I needed to try.

So I got on a plane and flew out west, to a hotel located in the beautiful Cheyenne Mountains. When I got there, all I wanted to do was get right on another plane and go back home. What the heck was I doing with these real Christians? Who were these people? What kind of faith did they practice? Would they try to force me to swallow something I didn't believe in? I felt so uncomfortable and out of place, as if all the attendees were more spiritually evolved than I was. I was single, they were married with families. I felt inadequate from the very start.

I also felt like I had been stripped totally naked. Now, I meet strangers in unfamiliar circumstances all the time. I even pride myself on being able to finesse all kinds of crazy situations. But that's always work-related, places where I can hide behind my PR game face. Here, I had none of my old crutches to rely on. I had no choice but to focus on myself.

You know how at church sometimes, the preacher goes into a zone and is really moved by the Spirit? That's what happened the first night of the retreat. He spoke for a long time and touched on a lot of the things I'd been struggling with, like what to do when we lose that love for ourselves and how to know where to find faith. I expected his words to be more about God and religion and all that other "Christian" stuff, but instead he spoke about how to deal with real feelings and experiences. It was like he was giving us a tool kit for keeping ourselves whole. All around me, folks were shouting, and I suddenly realized I had tears rolling down my face. It was painful facing up to my unhappiness like that. Part of me still just wanted to leave, but I didn't. I stayed because of what the preacher was saying and what I was just starting to feel, but most of all I stayed because of what I was sensing in the people surrounding me.

It was scary to find myself so vulnerable in front of all those strangers (who of course knew each other and started hugging and chatting and praising the Lord the second we arrived!). But there was so much love in the room that first night—and the rest of our time there together—that before long those strangers felt like my best friends. Those same people came up to me all weekend long, holding me, hugging me, offering words of encouragement. I felt like they knew exactly what I was going through—could provide strength enough to help me on my way. As they shouted and chanted, praised and worshipped God, I was blown away by how comfortable they seemed in themselves. They'd found what I'd been searching for: a way to make their faith a constant and fulfilling part of their lives. It felt like they'd all planted a central pillar of joy inside themselves, and it just kept sending out ray after ray after ray. For a woman who'd been living nowhere but down for far too long, the experience moved me more than I can say.

As my mother always used to tell me, you don't learn anything meaningful by playing it safe. I'm so glad I stuck it out at the retreat. It literally changed my life. What did I find there? I discovered the roots of my true spiritual being. I discovered that spirituality means figuring out how to locate the abundance of the universe somewhere deep inside yourself. For me, it took reconnecting with God and others who worship Him to wake up that sense of being both grounded and full of hope. That weekend also showed me that if I'm going to be spiritually healthy, I have to take time out of my life to tend to my faith. It takes work, but there's no question in my mind that it's worth it. Do you ever have one of those mornings where you hop out of bed knowing that no matter what obstacles you face, you're going to soar right over them 'cause you just feel too good to let anything bring you down? Spirituality means aiming to live your entire life that way, infused with compassion and a real sense of optimism toward the world.

Over that weekend in the Cheyenne Mountains I realized that a lot of my depression and inability to get motivated was based in my lack of faith. I didn't believe in my own inherent goodness or the goodness of the world around me. But seeing all those other people who'd found their inner strength and joy through God's love made me realize that, with a little effort, I was capable of doing the same. I resolved to take the time to pray and worship and take part in my church community. I resolved to look first to God instead of food or my career to heal any pain I was feeling. Only spirituality can recharge your battery, and spirituality comes from within.

Of course, I also realize that spirituality isn't something you lose and then find again like some favorite pair of earrings. It's an ongoing process. I certainly know I've got a long way to go. But I've made a conscious decision to do what I need to do to stay on that spiritual path. I go to church every Sunday, even those Sundays when my brain's telling me God really wouldn't be offended if just this once I slept in. I read my Bible. And when I'm feeling real low down, I just keep reminding myself to respect my own journey. Loving myself is the first step toward loving the world.

This section on spirituality is extraordinarily important. When all else fails us, it's spirituality that can create balance in our lives. It can give us both power and peace. So begin to ask yourself some of those important questions. What do you have faith in? What does spirituality mean to you? Where are you in terms of developing your spiritual self?

Over the next few weeks, we're going to spend some time strengthening our spiritual muscle. Let's not wait for a crisis to develop faith, love, patience, and compassion. Let's begin to meditate on these things right now. And let me be real clear here: I honor your spiritual journey, wherever it may take you. Although I'm Christian, I see the beauty in all religions, faiths, and spiritual beliefs. Christianity is my home, but you should feel the freedom to live anywhere. As long as you make sure you're alive.

WEEK 37
Religion versus Spirituality: Looking Beyond the Rules

▣

Every day, people are straying away from the
church and going back to God.

LENNY BRUCE

Soul is like electricity—we don't know what it is,
but it's a force that can light a room.

RAY CHARLES

There are a lot of people out there who are just religious. They
go to church or temple every week. They read the Book and follow instructions about what to eat or say or do. They repeat their
prayers. They spend year after year going through all the motions
of a religious life, yet they never once communicate with their
spiritual selves. Now, I'm not saying there's anything wrong with
plain religious practice. But if you're really set on working the
virtues, you're going to have to dig a little deeper to get in touch
with your true spiritual core.

I never thought a whole lot about the difference between religion and spirituality until I tried going back to those old religious
habits of childhood in the search for my spiritual self. The truth
is, all that praying and churchgoing and hymn singing was pretty
empty without having done any of the spiritual work. Religion
can lay down a lot of "shoulds" and "shouldn'ts." If you're
Catholic, it tells you to eat fish on Friday, confess your sins, and
say your rosaries. If you're Jewish, it tells you to attend temple

and observe the Sabbath. If you're Baptist, it tells you not to swear or dance or drink. But rules like that can carry you only so far. If religion is a kite, then spirituality is the wind. Without spirituality blowing inside it, you can read every Good Book in existence or sit and meditate until your eyes cross, but there's no one way that kite's ever going to get itself up off the ground and fly.

In my mind, the problem with plain old religion is that it just doesn't go deep enough. It gives you a lot of rules to follow, but not enough questions to ask. When you don't question the deeper meaning of your faith, you wind up with a sort of spiritual quick fix. And like any quick fix, be it food or drugs or wild spending, it leaves you unchanged. There's no way around it. You gotta do the work.

Religion is real good at handing out rules. But without the heart and love behind them, those rules mean nothing. At best, they make you feel safe 'cause someone else is telling you what to do. At worst, society goes and uses those rules as an excuse to hold other people down. A lot of bad stuff has been done in the name of religion over the course of history. In the 1690s in Salem, Massachusetts, Puritan ministers convicted nineteen people of being witches and—beginning with a West Indian slave girl— had them hanged or even pressed to death. Back in slavery times, many slaveowners called themselves God-fearing Christians, and then used their religion to justify keeping other human beings in bondage. Through much of the last century, the Ku Klux Klan used religion as a basis for beating and lynching many southern Blacks as well as Jews and Roman Catholics.

Religion can help provide us with an ethical code. When you don't know how to act in a given situation, look to the Book (the Bible, Koran, Torah, and so on). It'll set you straight. Spirituality, on the other hand, forces us to go beyond our surface behaviors into the emotions and reasons of *why* we do what we do. We're empowered only when we start to explore the truth about ourselves and come to terms with both our strengths and weaknesses. While religion focuses on laws and regulations, spirituality is about the love we share with God, the universe, and each other.

The words of the Bible can be just words. Or they can res- onate spiritually. We can apply them to our own lives. We all know about the Ten Commandments; they are laws handed down from God. From a religious perspective, we're supposed to obey them—or pay the price. From a spiritual perspective, though, we're empowered by God's laws only when we try to un- derstand and live according to their deeper meanings. It's pretty simple to master "thou shalt not kill" (people, that is). But once we've absorbed the basic instructions, we have to probe further for a deeper meaning. We have to look at other ways we might be killing—killing the spirit of a young person with harsh words. Killing an idea when we're overly critical. Killing our bodies with cigarettes, drugs, overeating, and sedentary lifestyles. Killing our emotions with low self-esteem. When we stop committing such crimes, we begin to seek the beauty and power that life has in store for us. We begin to grow.

Of course, religion itself can contain many good things. These rules and practices can help us focus our spiritual selves. Churches, synagogues, monasteries, and other religious gather- ing places help us form bonds and communities with those who share similar ideas and beliefs. Some people get in touch with their spirituality by digging deeper into the religious practices they once worked with only on the surface. That's the experi- ence I had with Christianity. Other people go a different route. My friend Carla grew up in a Southern Baptist family and put in a whole lot of time praying and singing and visiting revivals, but it never really spoke to her. As an adult, she realized that her true spiritual self was moved by something different. She'd always been attracted to nature and the elements, and so she sought out a spiritual practice that was highly in tune with those things. These days she's a peaceful, powerful, self-loving Buddhist.

Whatever road you choose to follow, chances are you'll dis- cover that developing your spirituality is much more challenging than just sticking to religious regulations. The path is not always clear. Sometimes it can be downright confusing.

When I'm being gentle with myself, I realize that I'm only human, and anyone's bound to do some slipping around when she's trying to walk and question at the same time. As with any real meaningful journey, getting in touch with our spiritual selves involves negotiating a lot of twists and turns and rough patches. But I know that if I want to become empowered, if I want to get my life in balance and make it through the anxiety and depression, I have to reach beyond the rules in search of the spiritual elements. I have to actively seek out the good in the universe instead of waiting around for it to come to me. Spirituality requires constantly engaging yourself. It requires thinking through difficult questions or simply sitting still with yourself long enough to locate that love and grace lodged inside. You can't just go through the motions.

Spirituality will not force itself on us. We have to make the investment required to invite it into our daily lives. When it comes down to it, each and every one of us has to do the work if we're going to reap the rewards. Just showing up isn't enough. We've got to dig deep and get dirty.

Journal time

In this week's journal exercise we're going to revisit Exodus 20:3–17, the Ten Commandments, and meditate on their spiritual meanings. The Commandments are listed below. As you read them, try to go beyond their surface meanings. Think about how they can empower you in your relationships, money matters, health issues—every aspect of your life.

1. Thou shalt have no other gods before me. What are you worshipping? Cars, clothes, a love object, your addictions? Do

you worship material gods? Think deeply about what you spend your time and money on. Have consumer items taken the place of God in your life?

2. Thou shalt not make unto thee any graven image, or any likeness of any thing that is in heaven above, or that is in the earth beneath, or that is in the water under the earth. What's your idea of God? Is He an old white man (or woman) sitting on the throne? A white boy with shoulder-length hair and blue eyes dressed in a long, gauzy robe? Could your image of God be diminishing your self-esteem? Is it limiting your relationship to God instead of allowing it to grow?

3. Thou shalt not take the name of the Lord thy God in vain. When you get angry, do you curse or use the Lord's name in vain? How does this color your relationship with God or any other powerful spiritual figure? What is the purpose behind showing respect in your religious and spiritual beliefs?

4. Remember the Sabbath day, and to keep it holy. Why is it important to observe a day of rest? In addition to physical rest, do you rest from negative thoughts and bad habits? Do you devote specific time in your life, a day or regular time of day, to developing your spirituality?

5. Honor thy father and thy mother. Even though you're grown, do you speak to your parents with respect? How do you treat the elders in your family and community? How do you demonstrate a respect for others' experience?

6. Thou shalt not kill. What are you killing in your body, mind, soul, and relationships? What ideas have you killed lately with self-doubt and self-judgment?

7. Thou shalt not commit adultery. Have you been or are you being disloyal in any of your relationships? Have you been sneaking around in order to associate with people, places, and things that are not good for you?

8. Thou shalt not steal. Did you take an idea from someone on the job and not give credit where credit is due? Did you steal a

child's ability to think or do for herself? Did you steal from yourself by not pursuing your dreams?

9. Thou shalt not bear false witness against thy neighbor. Have you lied to yourself lately? Do you have any blind spots that you're not seeing? Ask a friend, because sometimes we just can't see ourselves. Are you in denial about anything in your life? Are your actions true to the person you want to be?

10. Thou shalt not covet thy neighbor's house; thou shalt not covet thy neighbor's wife, nor his manservant, nor his maidservant, nor his ox, nor his ass, nor any thing that is thy neighbor's. Have you been spending beyond your means or reordering your life to keep up with the Joneses? Are you jealous of your friends or neighbors? Why? What is it that you really want out of life that you think they already possess? What do such feelings of envy say about your own self-esteem?

WEEK 38
Seek and Ye Shall Find:
Defining Your Spirituality

回

Our body is nothing more than a launching pad
for the soul and spirit to continue on its life
journey.

SIR SHADOW,
artist

God is voluptuous and delicious.

MEISTER ECKEHART,
theologian

For me, one of the toughest parts of working the spirituality
virtue has been deciding just what spirituality means. Spirituality is a great mystery. We can't see, touch, hear, feel, or taste it.
There's no prize we get when we've found it, no certificate that
we can stuff into a drawer and pull out again when we're feeling
uncertain. How do we even know what spirituality feels like?
How can we tell when we've gotten in touch with our spiritual
selves?

After spending some serious time with the virtue—and asking
a lot of tough questions—I think I've finally got a good sense of
what spirituality means to me. For Terrie Williams, spirituality is
about creating a world filled with joy and compassion. It's about
learning to accept and love myself without condemnation or
apology, and letting go of expectations about who I'm supposed
to be. It's about forgiving myself for my mistakes and staying

humble about my successes, because I know the world is a whole lot bigger than just me. It's about finding balance in my life, a sense of wholeness and togetherness, so I feel like I'm standing in the center of my being. Now, I won't pretend I'm always at this place of peace and power, but when things are going well, and I'm working the virtue like I want to be, I get all those things from my relationship with God.

Wow! I know, that's some heavy stuff. I bet you're asking how I have time to eat and sleep while I'm dealing with all that, let alone run my own business and run the Stay Strong Foundation. But that's the beauty of finding your spirituality. Once you've figured out what it means to you, you realize that you can work the virtue all the time, no matter how busy you are leading the rest of your life. When I spend time with the young men at Kaplan House and am really able to give of myself because I feel good about who I am, that's a spiritual act. When I'm able to let go of some conflict at the office because I know that in the greater picture it's really not that important, that's a spiritual act. Once you understand how it makes you think and feel, you'll find that spirituality is with you no matter where you are.

In order to figure out just what fuels our spiritual selves, most of us need to start by going back to our roots. For me, reaching a definition of spirituality has been a complicated process. Some of it ties back to how I grew up in Mount Vernon. Though I worship at Community Baptist Church in New Jersey now, it was the Macedonia Baptist Church where I first formed a relationship to God and where I go back periodically to keep close to Him. It's important to me that my spiritual practice includes visiting church regularly, praying, and reading the Bible. Those things keep me in touch with that sense of love and compassion. They keep me true to my spiritual self.

Another woman at my church, Martha, comes from a Catholic family. She too loved God and felt that regular worship was an important part of nourishing her spirituality. But there were things about her past beliefs that made her uncomfortable. She didn't agree with all the rules and laws of the Catholic Church, and she felt that she wanted a more loving, interactive religious community than the one she grew up in. When it came down to it, that belief system just didn't feed her faith. She believed she was a Christian—she loved God and drew strength from the Bible—but not a Catholic. After considering what she needed in her spiritual relationship with God, she went out and kind of tested other Christian faiths until she found one that filled her like she wanted to be filled.

This week, spend some time thinking about your own interpretation of spirituality. How does it make you feel? When is it most present in your life? If you're feeling a little lost spiritually, think over what you believe right now, at this moment. What's working for you? Where are the holes? How might you be able to fill them?

Also start thinking about where and when you feel the most spiritually at peace. Is it inside a church or other religious building? A private area in your home? Someplace out of doors? Who are the people in your life who help feed your spiritual self? Who's more of a spiritual drain?

The answers to these questions are going to be different for everybody. I'm a social person. When things are going well and I'm healthy and full of love, I like to be around other people. It's only when I'm feeling lost and depressed—when I can't find that spiritual peace—that I tend to hole up and prefer to be alone. At that conference out west, surrounded by all those Christian folks who were creating all that joy, I realized that a big part of my own spirituality is celebrating it with others who share my faith. I love going to church, praying together, just being together. But for other people, the spiritual journey might be more of a solitary process. They might like to meditate by themselves, or slip into a back pew and stay quiet. They might like to keep their relationship with God real personal. That's okay, too.

Seeking your own version of spirituality will take courage. You'll probably find yourself going down a path that has never been mapped out before. Trust your heart. Let it guide you. In the end you may find your religious practice reenergized—or you may choose another. But no matter what choices you make, know that getting comfortable with your spiritual self touches every aspect of your life—your health, finances, relationships, destiny—everything. Being at peace with ourselves is the most profound choice we can all make as human beings.

Journal time

This week, consider your religious upbringing. Even if your family didn't worship together, you probably had some thoughts and feelings about spiritual beliefs. Do any of these old habits still fill you with a sense of spirituality? Why? If not, what is it that's missing? What elements of your past do you want to carry into your present definition of spirituality? What will you leave behind?

Also, spend some time thinking about a place that makes you feel spiritual. It could be a particular church or other house of worship. It could be a designated place in your own home. Or perhaps some spot in nature, a mountaintop or garden or open field. If possible, spend some time in that place. If not, visualize how it looks and feels to be there. What does your spiritual place awaken in you? How does it make you feel empowered? How might you carry some of those feelings into your everyday life?

WEEK 39
Contradictions in Faith: Tackling Tough Spiritual Questions

回

> Sometimes I've believed as many as six impossible things before breakfast.
>
> LEWIS CARROLL

In the Jewish religion, there is a tradition that involves debating issues contained in their Good Book, the Torah. Learned scholars spend hours reading and discussing questions raised in the text, often arguing about the true meaning of the word. In Jewish communities, having a family member become such a scholar is considered a great honor. Even after thousands of years, they believe the Torah still contains many questions that haven't been answered. Such debate is a deeply valued component of their religion.

No matter what religion you practice, it's good to remember that spirituality is not just about the feel-good stuff. For most of us, getting close to our spiritual selves will involve dealing with some questions and some doubts. When we are born, we are "baptized"—through teaching, rituals, and osmosis—into the faith of our parents. As children, most of us accept our teachings as "gospel." As we grow up, though, inevitably we start to question their faith and our own. We begin to wonder about God, death, and the afterlife. For many of us, making the choice to get in touch with our spirituality as adults means digging deeper into many of the articles of our faith. Spirituality isn't like a math quiz, where there's always a right and wrong answer. It's full of contradictions, and that's even before we bring in all our own personal insecurities.

Sometimes it's easy to feel jealous of those people who never seem to have any spiritual questions at all. On the outside, they may seem "more spiritual" because they don't struggle like the rest of us do. But look more closely and you'll notice that it's not so much that such people don't have questions, but that they've just chosen to ignore them. The church is filled with folks acting in ways that contradict their professed beliefs. They gossip, lie, and sleep around—even though they know they're not supposed to. At an even deeper level, they say they have faith, but they fear that they won't be able to pay the rent. They say they believe that God is love, but they really believe that God is a vengeful man who will send them to hell for any little reason. They know that putting money in the plate is the right thing to do, but they're often giving because they feel they should, not because they want to. They believe in peace, but they pick fights with those they love. They want to be free to worship God in their own way, but they follow leaders who tell them what they should and shouldn't tolerate.

Anyone who's actively striving to understand spirituality will come up against some contradictions, and if you're really working the virtues, you probably won't be able to just let them slide. And you shouldn't. Blind faith may be attractive, but it isn't a good thing. It just means you're allowing others to do your thinking for you. Having questions is healthy. And these questions probably won't be limited to the laws of the church. Many of them will come up internally, as you work to find your own definition of faith.

My friend Melody is a born-again Christian. It's very important to her spiritual practice that she follow the Bible word for word. When it says "Thou shalt not lie," that means she doesn't. Not on her income tax returns, not to make someone feel better, not when she's making excuses for being late to a meeting. Never. But her church also preaches having and expressing compassion for those around you. And there are times when the compassionate thing to do is clearly to lie. What is Melody supposed to say when a close friend asks whether Melody likes her husband and the truth is, Melody doesn't like him at all? How can she answer a business colleague who wants to know whether she sees them doing extensive business together in the future when in truth Melody hopes to sever the relationship as soon as possible? This may seem like a simplistic example compared to the questions some people grapple with—like, does God really exist?—but for Melody it's a daily struggle.

"I think it's good to not always know the answers," she says. "It's God's way of making me stay focused in my faith. If this were easy, I wouldn't spend so much time and energy coming to peace with my beliefs." Our spiritual contradictions play an important role in expanding and enriching our faith. They force us to spend quality time with our spiritual selves.

One of the greatest spiritual contradictions I deal with is how there can be so much destruction and suffering in this world when I believe that God is a good and benevolent force. Like most spiritual questions, this one doesn't have a straightforward answer. I'm constantly searching for ways to be at peace with the ugliness in the world. I've come to believe that those who suffer on this earth go to a better place when they die. And I consider it the responsibility of those of us who are in touch with our spiritual selves to spread our love and sense of empowerment as far and wide as we can; in a way we are the messengers of God. But those resolutions still aren't always enough. Part of me knows to leave it to faith, and to believe that God knows what He's doing.

It takes courage to honestly question your spiritual beliefs. It can feel like a very lonely process. But posing such questions is one of the best things any of us can do in order to strengthen our faith. So if you're feeling confused or unresolved, don't be shy about it. Don't feel ashamed. Ask questions of your preacher or your fellow worshipers, your friends or family. They may be able to help you work your way through some of these contradictions, or at least offer support and guidance as you navigate the path. You have every right to own all aspects of your spirituality, even those you haven't yet come to terms with. Feeling uncertain doesn't make you less spiritual—it makes you more so. It means you've made a serious commitment to developing your relationship to your faith.

Journal time

Let's use our journal time this week to raise our level of self-awareness about our beliefs. What are some of the contradictions of your faith? We often gloss over the things that bother us the most. Are there ways in which you have been hypocritical? Are there long-standing questions you still can't resolve? If there are too many contradictions, maybe that's a signal that you're in the wrong faith. Also, think about how you've dealt with spiritual contradictions in the past. Have your methods been productive? Is it possible there's a better way?

Now spend some time meditating on the page about some of your own internal contradictions. Think about the definition of spirituality you came up with last week. Are there elements in there that you're unsure about? Do you seek to come to peace with the world at the same time you seek to change it? Do you want to worship as part of a congregation but have trouble finding a church that preaches everything you believe? Sometimes negotiating your spiritual path may call for compromises. What kinds of compromises would you be willing to make? How can you reconcile these conflicting personal needs?

WEEK 40
Dealing with Everyday Life: Spirituality in the Material World

⬚

We can be the curates or curators of our own
souls, an idea that implies an inner priesthood
and a personal religion. To undertake this restora-
tion of soul means we have to make spirituality a
more serious part of everyday life.

THOMAS MOORE,
Care of the Soul

Sometimes I think those early Christians had it pretty easy.
After all, how hard can it be to stay true to your spiritual self
when you're spending all day hanging in the desert with no dis-
tractions to speak of? What would they have done if they were
surrounded by shopping malls and MTV like we are today?
Sometimes it seems practically impossible to hold on to spiritual
integrity and still be part of the modern world. How are we supposed to live among so many temptations while still remaining
spiritually whole? It's not easy.

For many people today, material quick fixes have taken the
place of genuine spirituality. Instead of buckling down and doing
the more difficult spiritual work, they take the easy path lined
with things like food, drugs, alcohol, and consumerism. Though
these people may seem satisfied with life on the surface, deep
down I suspect many of them are unhappy. It seems clear to me
that they've made the wrong choice. But what is the right choice?
After all, the truth is that we do live in the modern world. And

unless we plan to join some religious sect that isolates itself from the rest of society, we're going to be dealing with plenty of non-spiritual wants and needs. How do we go about it?

Working the virtues is teaching me a lot about what it means to be spiritual in a material world. I've discovered that one of the most important steps is to stop taking the path of least resistance. It's okay to want things; after all, there are very few saints out there, and you're probably not one of them. But do your best to recognize when you're reaching for something physical and immediate to fill what's really a deeper, spiritual need.

The Old Testament story about the children of Israel wandering in the wilderness has always interested me. God could have just sent the Israelites straight to the Promised Land, but instead He kept them wandering around in the wilderness for forty years. Why?

Without working with God for those forty years to dismantle their slave mentality—one filled with things like jealousy, dishonesty, and ingratitude—the Israelites probably wouldn't have been ready for the Promised Land. They might have trashed it as soon as they got there. I think this biblical story is a good metaphor for dealing with modern, material life. For many of us who feel lost or unfulfilled, the process of strengthening our spiritual identities can seem like a similar journey through a similar wilderness. Our "slave mentality" might yearn for material goods instead of tackling the real issues, like loving ourselves and seeking balance in our lives.

When you find yourself hungering for those old quick fixes, stop and think about why. Many of us have spent a long time nursing certain kinds of dreams. We want the car, house, and mate. We want to make a lot of money. It can seem like these are the things that would truly make us happy. But are they? If that were true, then wouldn't all those celebrities and CEOs out there be the most fulfilled people around? Plenty of people who appear to have everything are still miserable. Peace of mind takes something more than hard cash.

It's okay to have material wants, as long as you aren't using them to fill your spiritual needs. For the most part, it's a question of remembering your values and your priorities. Whenever possible, I try to make sure tending to my spirituality comes first. For instance, it's real important to my spiritual health that I go to church every Sunday. But the realities of my business can make this difficult at times. I have to make choices about what's truly important to me. Once upon a time, business would've always won out. But since I've been working the virtues, my priorities have changed. These days, if there's a business conflict on a Sunday morning. I just explain to the client that I have a previous commitment to God. Though I've come across some king-sized egos in my time, most people are willing to wait for the Lord. If I'm traveling, I find out where I can attend a service near my hotel. If I'm feeling sick or tired or depressed, I haul my butt out of bed anyway 'cause I know it's something I need to do. I've shifted my material world to make room for my spiritual needs.

I know I've said this before, but it bears repeating. This getting in touch with your spirituality is an ongoing process. I certainly still have my moments of weakness. And in those low points when I find myself reaching for the ice cream spoon because it's easier than reaching for God, I do my best to cut myself some slack. I practice the very spiritual act of forgiveness. We're all going to fall off the path at one time or another. The only thing that really matters is that we pick ourselves up and get back on.

*J*ournal time

Spend some time this week thinking about the material things you enjoy the most. Write down your biggest "weaknesses." Is it chocolate, lottery tickets, designer clothes? What role do these things play in your life? Do you ever use these material wants to fill your spiritual needs? Do they work? Why or why not?

Also this week, make a list of ten things you want the most in your life. Don't chastise yourself over what they are, just list. Now go back and look over that list. How many of those things are material desires, things like a new house, a new car, or a sexy boyfriend? How many of them are more spiritual, such as self-love, compassion, and integrity? Being as honest as you can, rate the things on your list from 1 to 10, with 1 the thing that's most important to you and 10 the thing that's the least. How do the material and the spiritual measure up? If you list the material things first, why is this? What do you think those things will bring you? How might you work to make your spiritual goals a more important priority in your life?

WEEK 41
The Power of the Practice: Prayer, Meditation, Ritual

When we first started meditating during stretching before practice, I thought it was crazy. I'm
closing one eye and keeping the other eye open
to see what other fool is doing this besides me.
Eventually I became more accepting. . . .
> MICHAEL JORDAN,
> *For the Love of the Game*

As a child, I said the Lord's Prayer pretty regularly. "Our Father,
who art in heaven. . . ." In our house we recited this prayer as a
daily ritual, in the morning and evening. We also said the "God
is great, God is good" prayer as grace before every meal. But as I
got older, I got lazier about my praying and giving thanks. When
I first became a PR professional, I was afraid to say grace at
power lunches. You just don't do that when you're networking or
trying to close a deal.

Since I've been working the virtues, I've learned that you
can't ever be ashamed to give God thanks. You don't have to
stand up and shout in the restaurant, but just taking a brief moment to remember God before you eat is a good spiritual practice. Praying before meals seems like such a simple thing to do,
but it helps you to remember how blessed you are to have food
to eat. I'm discovering that it's these small moments of remembering and appreciating the grace of God that truly cement our
faith.

Of course, these days my spiritual practice consists of a lot more than just saying grace before meals. In fact, regular prayer and other rituals have become a vital part of my spiritual life. I used to feel funny about praying or talking to God anywhere but in secret. I was worried about all those stereotypes some people have going on about "Christians." I was unsure of my faith and commitment to God and it was showing in my very flaky spiritual practice. It was also showing in how miserable I was. But now that my spiritual practice is deepening, I've stopped acting like I've got something to hide. I'm proud of my relationship with God. I'm proud of the love He's filled me with, and of the love I've been able to pass on to others since I've been feeling more spiritually whole. Praying regularly, saying grace, listening to inspirational tapes, reading the Bible—all these things have become the foundation of my spiritual self. They keep my body, mind, and soul in balance.

Prayer, rituals, and meditation are all different ways of doing the same thing—taking time to truly focus on and contemplate our relationships with our spiritual selves and with God. They offer us a chance to give thanks, work through problems, or just settle all the craziness going on in our heads. They help us listen to our guiding spirit, whether we believe that spirit resides without or within.

For many Christians, prayer is a major part of our spiritual practice. Praying together bonds us and reminds us of the mutual love we've got for each other and the universe. Praying on our own develops our personal relationship to the Lord. Ultimately, it doesn't matter what words you use. What counts is the faith behind your request. God will take it from there.

For other people, spiritual exploration takes the form of meditation, setting aside time to empty your mind of all your worldly worries and just be with the universe—kind of a regular tune-up for your spiritual self. It can be done in a church, a monastery or other gathering place, or in some quiet spot all alone.

Rituals can include anything you do on a regular basis to bring yourself closer to your spirituality—things like saying grace, reading verses, bowing down in respect. In her book *Black-Eyed Peas for the Soul*, Iyanla Vanzant describes it like this:

> Secret, sacred words uttered in secret, sacred places teach you to honor yourself. . . . Doing it the same way, at the same time, in the same place, even when you cannot see and do not know what will come of it, teaches you to honor and trust your divinity. That is what I call a ritual.

For me, taking time to pray and practice other rituals surrounding my faith allows me to listen to the Still Small Voice within. That voice is the one telling me I'm full of love and so is the universe. It's telling me that I'm strong and God is even stronger. That voice helps me stay true to my spiritual self. I know it's always speaking to me, but sometimes it talks so quietly I can't hear through all the chaos of my life. I've got to take some private time, every day, to be still and listen to what it has to say.

You can't be lazy about praying, or whatever form your spiritual practice takes. If you're not present, you ain't doing the job. We may wear our game face with the entire world, but when we get quiet with God, we have to get real. In fact, you might even start to notice that people who've truly developed that sense of faith and compassion, who've found a way to get real and stay real with God, don't even need a game face anymore. They're at peace with their true selves. Of course, getting to that place requires some real hard-core spiritual work. I'd be the first to admit I haven't arrived yet. But I'd sure like to. Having God in your life makes you feel better about yourself. Praying or doing some spiritual practice on a regular basis gets you grateful, thinking on all the blessings you've received.

Some people feel uncomfortable or silly about conducting a regular spiritual practice. They don't know how to talk to God or just be with themselves. They're not sure what to say. If you're feeling like this, don't sweat it. You've got plenty of company. Lots of major sports teams say a prayer before taking to the court or the field, and I've heard about more than a few real smooth guys who couldn't put two words together when asked to speak to God in front of the team. But praying shouldn't stress you out; it should bring you peace. You don't need a lot of flowery words. Keep it simple. God isn't interested in the packaging, only in the love inside. And don't fret over whether God hears you. He hears. And He answers you, too. If you don't think He does, just try looking a little closer. When I started working the virtues, I prayed to God for guidance in rediscovering my spirituality. Now, I sure as heck didn't expect Him to send me packing off to some Christian athletic conference in the middle of the mountains, but He knew better. I asked and God provided. It doesn't get much simpler than that.

When you go to church, mosque, or temple, prayer and meditation tend to be very formal, but your daily spiritual rituals don't have to be. You can take some quiet time during a long commute to work, before going to bed, or upon waking up in the morning. First thing every morning, I pray silently and give thanks to God. Then I turn on the TV and watch Joyce Meyer's show, *Life in the Word*. This little ritual means that before I even go out into the world, I've found that sense of balance needed to get me through the day. It reminds me of my unshakable love of God and self. And in the end, that's what truly turns the world.

*J*ournal time

This week, set aside a time for spiritual practice every day, even if it's just a few minutes in the morning. The practice can take whatever form you're most comfortable with: prayer, meditation, or just silent contemplation. Write about what comes up. How do you communicate with God? Do you ask for things? Count your blessings? Does this regular spiritual practice make you feel more in touch with yourself and what's going on in your life? How so?

Often when praying and meditating, a million things tend to flood into our minds. If you're finding yourself getting distracted, try this simple exercise to gently ease your focus back to your conversation with God. Visualize something calm and soothing. Some people like to use a beach or a clear sky. Others like to focus on the face of a loved one, or just take ten long deep breaths. Experiment and see what works for you. Then, every time you find your mind wandering, just keep returning to that image. Don't worry if you're having trouble getting focused. Praying is another one of those spiritual muscles. If you haven't worked it in a while, it may take a little time to get it back in shape.

WEEK 42
Testing Your Faith:
Staying Real with God

You gain strength, courage and confidence by
every experience in which you really stop to look
fear in the face . . . you must do the thing you
think you cannot do.

ELEANOR ROOSEVELT

The Parkinson's showed me I wasn't invincible.
But at the same time, this disease taught me that
my faith is strong; taught me to appreciate life
more, to appreciate music a lot more.

MAURICE WHITE,
founder of Earth, Wind & Fire,
Savoy, February 2001

Most people, even those who don't know squat about the rest
of the Bible, have heard about the story of Job. They know that
God rained down troubles on him nonstop, destroyed his home
and his family, made him tired and hungry and weak, basically
tested him in every possible way. I think we all know about this
story because we all can relate to it. Everybody goes through real
tough times, times when it might be easy to lose sight of God and
all the good in the universe. Such circumstances test our faith.
They show us our weak points and hopefully make them strong.

Remember my friend Melody from a few weeks back, the
born-again Christian woman who struggles with how to make not

lying and always loving a regular part of her spiritual life? Well, a couple of years ago that woman was tested like I don't think anyone's been tested since Job. Things had started out good for her that fall. She'd been seeing a real special man, someone loving and giving and creative and funny, and they got married in October. Then, just two days before Christmas, Melody got a phone call. Her mother, brother, and sister had all been in a horrible car accident down in the Dominican Republic. Her mother and brother were killed; her sister was hanging on by a thread. Well, Melody flew out right away to be with her sister. And she prayed to God for guidance and the strength to get her through it all. She spent months nursing her sister, who lost a leg but survived. And instead of blaming or questioning God, Melody did her best to stay true to her faith. She thanked Him for sparing her sister. She told Him to take care of the rest of her family. She prayed a lot and tried to be grateful for her blessings, especially her husband, Robert, who was her pillar of strength through it all.

About a month after Melody came back home, Robert went off on a boating trip. In some kind of freak accident in the shallow water, he hit his head on a rock and drowned. Melody was devastated, and I don't use that word lightly. The first thing her broken heart wanted to do was blame God. After all, she'd been doing her best to be a good person, to live her life according to God's rules, and spread love and compassion to all those around her. Was this the reward she got for keeping the faith? Why did God choose to test her, Melody, when there were so many other people out there who needed His lessons more, who hadn't committed themselves to their spirituality the way Melody had?

"I wish I could say my faith never wavered," Melody told me. "But that wouldn't be the truth. After Robert died I spent a lot of time feeling sorry for myself and asking, why me? There were moments when I stopped believing God was even there."

Her trials forced her to face some of her greatest fears, about being alone and knowing she can rely on herself, and she's stronger for having stood up to those fears. Though I wouldn't wish Melody's experiences on anyone, she'd be the first to admit she's a stronger, better person for having come through them. Bad things are going to happen, and it's in those times when your faith is being tested the most that you'll need that faith the most.

It took a lot of work for Melody to come back to peace with God, but she did it. A few years later she even married again, to someone she deeply cares for and who deeply cares for her. Most important of all, she knows her belief in God can get her through anything.

The way I see it, sometimes God moves too quickly for us to take in His messages right away. His wisdom can come down like a rainstorm, leaving behind giant puddles that take a while to soak in. It's exactly at such times, when we're feeling lost and confused and alone, that our spiritual presence is strongest. That's when God's showing us the direction we've got to take in order to grow. We all know how the saying goes: "What doesn't kill you makes you stronger." And strength is what gets us through this world.

Journal time

This week, meditate on the page about a person or situation that's testing your faith. Are there things going on in your life right now that seem overwhelmingly difficult? Is it possible those things are coming down for a reason—to teach you something about yourself or about the world? Work and family relationships can provide us with some of our most challenging—and rewarding—learning opportunities. Write about how you're coping with the situation. Are you making choices that will allow you to grow? What might be the lesson God's sending you?

Also this week, meditate on a time in your life, now or in the recent past, when you've done something you weren't proud of. What did you do? Treat a friend or loved one with disrespect? Lie about a work or personal matter? Often such behavior stems from situations that have in some way tested our faith. Why did you do what you did? Were you acting out of fear? Anger? Denial? What might you have done differently had you been in a more spiritually balanced place?

WEEK 43
Spread the Love:
Creating a Spiritual World

I live in the space of thankfulness—and I have
been rewarded a million times over for it.
OPRAH WINFREY

Up to now we've been doing a lot of work on finding our spiritual selves and keeping the faith with those around us. But when it comes to working this virtue, that's just the tip of the iceberg. Once you get in touch with your own spirituality and establish a healthy relationship with God, you will start feeling powerful enough to spread His influence everywhere. You start to see the whole world as a spiritual place, and you start looking at what role you play in that world. I talked a little way back about how people in the past have used religion to do harm. Now let's spend some time celebrating how we can use our spiritual health to make the world a better place.

One of the most important lessons God teaches us is tolerance and forgiveness. He loves everyone equally—man, woman, Black, white, smart, slow, good, evil. All of us are His children. It's our spiritual responsibility to follow in His path and treat the human soul like the precious thing it is, no matter what sort of package it comes in. Now, to many of us tolerance might not sound like such a hard thing; after all, we love our brothers and sistahs. But it's not always as easy as it sounds. I learned a real lesson about tolerating and forgiving other folks from my friend Sean.

Sean is someone I know through church, and a few Sundays ago we got to talking. Eventually it came out in conversation that his apartment had been robbed two weeks before. Someone broke through the front door and took his computer (with all his work on it!), his stereo, his TV, and even some jewelry he'd inherited from his grandmother. Sean called the police, got a new lock, and tried to get on with his life. Then, a week later, the same thing happened again. Only this time there was nothing to steal, so whoever broke in vandalized the whole apartment, ripping up Sean's clothes and setting fire to his front door. Now I know I've got some problems with anger one-on-one, but if any folks stomped all over my things like that I'd be about ready to shove their heads into a brick wall. Not Sean. He calmly went about the task of restoring his home.

When I asked him why he wasn't more pissed off, he said that he was just taking his cue from God. What those burglars had done wasn't about him, it was about their own journey. Sean figured God has some bigger picture in mind, and Sean's role was to help the less fortunate (in this case the punks who took his stuff). Their wrongdoing was just as much a part of the universe as his good, and all of it was heading toward a purpose far greater than his own. He forgave them because forgiveness was part of his spiritual path—to love and nurture, not to judge. Now, Sean's one brother who's seriously in touch with his spirituality. With God's love, he's become generous enough to realize that other people's actions aren't about him. He refuses to see the world as anything but a loving place.

Another real important spiritual concept is respect. Every human being on this earth has earned the right to be treated with respect and decency. In the movie *Dead Man Walking*, based on a real-life story, a nun befriends a man on death row and takes it upon herself to try to get him saved. When the man asked her why she was doing it when she didn't even know him, she told him that it was out of respect for another human life. Her words touched that man deeply. Just when he was feeling like the universe had forgotten about him, someone stepped up to say she cared. Your respect and love for those around you can have the same kind of power.

Many of us tend to rush through our lives and get caught up thinking only about ourselves and our needs. But being that way doesn't serve the world. Tending to your spirit means taking the time required to treat others well. If you see a homeless person on the street, don't just go walking over her like she isn't even there. Smile, say hello, offer to buy her a cup of coffee. When a waiter serves you, go to the trouble to say thank you. If someone's got you angry, swallow your emotions long enough to keep cool and work toward a solution. A few years ago I made a friend who gets real offended by profanity. Now, I've got a mouth on me when I want to use it (which can be pretty often), but because this woman was uncomfortable, I try hard put a lid on it whenever we spend time together. She noticed my effort right away, and our friendship deepened because of it. When I occasionally slip now, she laughs and tells me she wouldn't have me any other way.

You owe it to everyone out there to value how they choose to lead their lives, even if you don't agree. Give God's love back to the world in every way you can. As soon as you start treating other people with respect, you'll start feeling better about yourself.

---

*J*ournal time

This week, let's meditate on the page on some of the ways in which we can spread our spiritual strength into the world by practicing things like tolerance and respect. Think about how tolerant you are of others who have different ideas, beliefs, or opportunities than you do. Are there certain "sorts" of people you treat badly? Are you judging them instead of keeping an open mind? There's room for all kinds on this earth. Try to use God's love as an example when you deal with those who are different, and perhaps less fortunate, than you are.

Also this week, take the time every day to commit an act of respect. Hold the door for a stranger, thank your colleagues and loved ones for their support, buy lunch for someone, have a conversation with the kid or the old woman down the block. How does it feel to pause long enough to truly consider others? Does sending respect out into the world make you feel differently? Do others treat you with more respect as well?

WEEK 44
Redefining Miracles: How Spirituality Can Change Our Lives

▣

Manifestation has much more to do with . . . shaping ourselves and our world—than with acquisition. . . . Manifestation is an act of trust. It is the soul pouring itself out into its world.

DAVID SPANGLER,
Everyday Miracles

When most of us think about miracles, we consider only the really big stuff. We expect trumpets sounding and angels singing, followed by spontaneous healings, winning the lottery, or coming back from the dead. Though I do believe those things can happen, it's rare that such momentous acts of God will touch any of our lives. So these days I'm leaning toward a slightly different definition of miracles, one that shows they can come in all sizes. Miracles are what come to pass when we start using our spirituality to create fresh possibilities in our lives.

A spiritual presence is there with us always. It makes sure we wake up each morning. It keeps our bodies working and the sun shining and the ground firm beneath our feet. But by working the virtues and tapping the good in ourselves and the world, we turn our spirituality into something far more powerful. And we start experiencing a whole lot of things we just might miss for the miracles they are.

One of my favorite stories about my grandmother is the one she used to tell about the day my grandfather walked out on her and their nine children. The morning he left, my grandmother had cooked the last meal in the house. There was no more food, no more money, and ten hungry mouths to fill. As the story goes, she got to praying. By and by, a neighbor came knocking, and then another, and then another, each of them leaving a little something behind. By the end of the day, there was food enough to feed them all. Now my grandmother used to say what happened was a miracle of prayer, but I see it as evidence of God's love working through her. My grandmother had spent her whole life being a generous person, helping out others even when she didn't have two dimes to spend on herself. Her neighbors knew her as a good, hardworking, spiritual woman and they respected the way she'd handled hardship with her head held high. If my grandmother hadn't been working her spirituality every day of her life, I don't think those neighbors would've been so ready to come knocking on her door with food they really couldn't spare. That miracle grew directly out of the seed my grandmother planted with her love for others and her faith in God.

In the Bible, Jesus says that our own faith can heal us. I think that's true. I believe that taking full responsibility for our spiritual health makes us more powerful than we could ever imagine. My friend Kim, a real spiritual woman, refers to laying the groundwork for such miracles of faith as "putting something out into the universe." If she's feeling confused about her work, she puts the question out into the universe. If she feels like a relationship is missing in her life, she puts it out into the universe. She works hard to be as loving and generous as possible, and places the rest of her troubles in God's hands. The thing is, the universe almost always responds.

In the past Kim had been working on some trust issues, but last year she got to the point in her spiritual journey where she finally felt ready for love. So she decided to put it out into the universe that she was hungering for a long-term mate. Well, two days later a new neighbor moved in down the hall. Kim spotted him on the stairs and thought he looked pretty fine. So that evening she knocked on his door, just to welcome him to the neighborhood. Turns out she'd found herself a sweet, caring, single man (and we all know there aren't too many of those around!). The two of them have been together ever since.

Now, someone could look at what came down there and call it blind luck, Mr. Right arriving like that at Kim's front door. But I see Kim's success in finding love as something she created herself, with the help of her faith in God. She had the strength to keep working on herself until she felt ready to give enough to take part in a healthy relationship, and she had the courage to go knock on that man's door. Everyday miracles like Kim's are jump-started by our faith and spiritual work. When we take the leap, that's when the magic happens.

Working toward what we want for ourselves in this life can be a spiritual act, provided we do it with grace and love and trust in God. I'm not talking about those games we play with ourselves, the ones where no matter how much we achieve, earn, or do, it never seems to be enough. That's our way, not God's. I'm talking about working our spirituality the way Kim worked hers, by focusing on love for those around us and gratitude for the blessings we receive.

Often, recognizing a miracle is all in your attitude. They're happening all the time, only sometimes we're just not in the right state of mind to see them for what they are. If you're being guided by your fears instead of your strength and compassion, an opportunity can start looking like a burden. A while back a couple of friends of mine, John and Natalie, were both laid off from the same company around the same time. But talking to the two of them, you'd never have guessed they were going through the same thing. Natalie saw losing her job as all suffering, and she kept on moaning over how miserably the world was treating her. John was excited about his prospects. He viewed what had happened as an opportunity to move on to something different and more fulfilling. Do I even need to mention that John wound up taking a great new job working for a civil rights organization?

He'd always dreamed about holding down a job like that, and now every time I talk to him he's telling me how finding it was his own little miracle. A year later, Natalie is still unemployed. My neighbor, who grew up a sharecropper during the 1920s, always loves to tell me, "There t'ain't much difference between a blessing and a curse." It's all how you choose to approach the world.

Spirituality is far more than just a practice or a set of values, it's a way of interacting with the universe. No matter what's going on in your life, whether times are tough or you're spilling over with good fortune, being spiritual means always returning to those same building blocks. Love yourself, respect others, believe in the good of humanity, and draw strength from divine guidance. Do that and I promise you, the miracles will come.

Journal time

This week, meditate on the page about how you might open your life up to everyday miracles. Make a list of a few things that aren't working for you just now. Is there a relationship that's suffering? Job problems? Think back on what you've learned about spirituality and how you've grown in the past eight weeks. How can you apply some of these lessons to those problem areas? Do you need to exercise more tolerance and patience with a friend? Are you acting, or not acting, because you're afraid of what might happen? What would it mean to put yourself in God's hands?

Many people think creating miracles is the process of them asking and God answering. But in truth, miracles stem from the groundwork we lay ourselves. Think about the one thing you most want to change in your life. Do you want a new house? A different job? A more loving relationship? How can you lay the groundwork for such a "miracle" to occur?

Living Virtue 7

Creativity

In the beginning, when God created the universe, the earth was formless and desolate.
GENESIS 1:1–2

Joy is but the sign that creative emotion is fulfilling its purpose.
CHARLES DU BOS,
What Is Literature?

The way I see it, I did you a favor and saved the best for last.
Creativity is the result of all the work we've been putting in for
the past forty-four weeks. And though every single one of them
is important, I think creativity is the most powerful and rewarding virtue of them all. Think about it. Our creativity is the ultimate expression of who we are. It recharges our batteries, and
gives us a sense of power and accomplishment. When we're cre-

ative, we find joy in what we do, whether it's knitting or making a collage or writing a story. Creativity means creation, giving birth to some new piece of ourselves. It's regeneration. It's life.

For a long time I didn't think I was creative. I thought creativity meant writing poetry or dancing or painting in oil—and trust me, I can't do any of these things! Such a narrow definition prevented me from seeing my own creative spark. There is an inner artist in everyone, but it took me a while to catch on to mine. Ironically, my journey to self-awareness and self-expression began with my appreciation of the works of other creative souls.

I thank my parents for planting the seeds of creative appreciation when I was a kid. The cultural events, museums, and concerts they took us to opened my eyes to a different way of perceiving my surroundings. I didn't always understand art, but all of it—the music, the plays, the paintings and sculptures—made me realize the world was a much bigger place than what I experienced day to day.

Later, when I grew up and was out on my own, I took art for granted—until I was in desperate need of its power to heal. My love of art resurfaced during my social worker days. I was so miserable at the hospital that I needed an outlet to get my mind off my troubles. I started hanging with a graduate school classmate of mine, Lynne Edwards. She was laid back and artsy, the perfect companion for exploring all New York had to offer. We went to every cultural event we could find—poetry readings, art and photography exhibits, jazz concerts. This was back in the 1970s, the days of the Black Arts Movement, and those brothers and sistahs were challenging everything, from the way we talked to the way we thought about our place in society. The Frederick Douglass Creative Workshop in New York used to host poetry readings, and we went to them all. We met and hung out with poet Quincy Troupe and South African jazz trumpeter Hugh Masekela.

What I watched and learned during those days developed a new dimension in me. I became much more aware, and appreciative, of the beauty of our African heritage. That was a tremendous gift because for way too long Black folks had been told that we weren't smart or worthwhile. Well, those Black artists started talking back, saying, "Hell no." They gave us a huge dose of collective self-esteem. My exposure to Black culture helped shape my thinking about the world, my work, and my philosophy of life. It taught me about the power of creativity. Looking at those canvases, listening to that music and poetry, I learned how creating something beautiful can help form our identity and give a sense of pride, purpose, and history. It was a lesson I carry with me to this day.

Though I loved the entire scene, the art galleries spoke to me most of all. I'm a very visual person, and just looking at the images, whether of Black life or abstract, colorful paintings, gave me so much pleasure that I knew I wanted to collect. The problem was price. All the collectors I'd ever heard of were rich folks, and with good reason. Most of the photographs and paintings I loved were way out of my price range.

Then a few years later, I was invited to an event that would start me on the road to finding my own personal creativity. An organization co-founded by Marquita Poole called the Nzingha Society sponsored an annual auction of the works of major Black artists. The auctions were small, intimate gatherings that were fun and casual and not intimidating at all. I decided to bid on an Ed Clark lithograph, an abstract painting in pastel colors. Not only did I buy the piece, but I was so excited to have something of his that when I got it home, I immediately hung it on my wall and stared at it for hours.

That auction lit a spark. Today every inch of my home is covered with works of art, and I never tire of looking at my collection. One of my favorites shows a baptism in the South. Four older women sit side by side with their church hats on, just looking so blessed and wise. I also love the portrait of two kids sitting next to each other on porch steps on a beautiful summer day. It reminds me of my own childhood. I get great pleasure from being surrounded by the colors, textures, styles, and stories. Every time I look at these pictures they inspire me.

But even as I began to form a collection I was proud of, it never occurred to me that what I was doing was creative. After all, how much inspiration does it take to spend money on art? I didn't realize until I started placing these treasures in my home that hanging art is a very creative activity in itself. Shapes, colors, styles, and size all determine where I place a piece, but mostly I just follow my instincts about what makes the room feel good. For example, there are some pieces that seem just right for the long wall that goes from my living room to my bedroom. Others that touch me personally, like photos of myself when I was a little girl, I put in my bedroom.

As my inner interior decorator started to wake up, I got braver and braver about following my own vision. I added other things to my walls, like fabric, scarves, necklaces, even objects as unlikely as a beautiful cell phone case made of papier-mâché. The walls in my home have become my canvases, and I use the works of other artists to design the space. Sometimes I walk around my home just looking at the images. Every one of them represents some phase of my life. I can look at each one and not only meditate on the story or image, but also remember what I was going through at the time I acquired it. So my pictures are more than just a source of pleasure and creativity. They are my history.

The realization that I'm creating even as a collector was real liberating for me. It opened up my understanding of what an artist is and helped me to free my creative self. I love decorating my home, hanging things in different ways. I love that I can support the community of African American artists and at the same time fulfill my vision for the space around me. And I realized that I have many other creative outlets as well. In fact anything I do just for me, for the joy of enriching my life and my spirit, is a creative act. Writing in my journal is creative. I get to pour myself out onto that page in a way that has nothing to do with business or making contacts or worrying about other people's eyes. I can just scribble down whatever I feel like—a poem, a sketch, thoughts on the day, whatever helps me develop as a person. Even smaller things, like preparing a simple meal or picking out an especially stylish outfit, can make me feel creative. They are an expression of the unique individual me. They make me happy.

I have been blessed to know many artists and musicians as friends, and to see the richness that creative expression has brought to their lives. My dear friend Sir Shadow is a street artist, and his art is created specifically for the people he meets in his travels. He does amazing one-line renderings of dancers, singers, musicians, and lovers. I met Shadow a couple of years ago at a theater festival, and we've been inseparable ever since. Although he does get paid for his work, his focus isn't really on making money. He believes that the purpose of his art is to communicate powerful and uplifting messages to people. He calls us, all of us, his patients, and his art is his medicine. His life may not look too glamorous from the outside, but he's chosen to follow his own path and be true to himself. He's one of the most balanced and joyful people I've ever known.

When I look around at sistahs I know, the happiest are the ones who have something of their own. It doesn't have to be anything fancy; any hobby works fine as long as it brings you pleasure. You can try quilting, taking cooking classes, dancing, joining a choir, whatever speaks to you. The point is to become aware of your own creative spark. Over the next several weeks, we'll search for ways to express creativity every day. Have you heard of writer's block? Well, that doesn't just happen to writers. We can all get blocked sometimes, so we'll explore ways to unblock and release our creativity, creativity that can be carried into all aspects of our lives.

Creativity plays an especially important role in the lives of Black women. So much of what we've produced historically has been lost. And so much of our energy these days is directed toward tending to other people's needs. We've got to learn that digging into our creative souls isn't about being selfish or indulgent. It's about taking responsibility. A good creative flow is a signal of a healthy culture. It's a sign things are thriving. Creativity is essential to well-being. It's about the deepest self-expression. It's been a long hard road for our people. It's about time every single one of us started rediscovering our creative impulses and rejoicing in who we are.

WEEK 45
Unblocking Your Creativity: Getting Over the Fear of Failure

🔲

> If you are unhappy with anything . . . whatever is bringing you down, get rid of it. Because you'll find that when you're free, your true creativity, your true self comes out.
>
> TINA TURNER,
> *I, Tina*

I bet there are plenty of you out there who feel just the way I used to feel. In fact, you were tempted to skip right over this chapter because you're "not creative." You don't paint or write or design your own clothes. Well, sistah, keep reading. The idea that some people are creative and some people aren't is just a big old myth. As we'll learn in the coming weeks, creativity is all about giving yourself pleasure, and anyone can do that.

The truth is, we're all artists. It's just that some of us need to take the time to explore what's standing between us and that creative spark. Chances are you're already creative in everyday ways, ways you may not even notice. It's in how you dress, how you decorate your home, how you do your hair. We're not talking Art with a capital A here; we're talking expression. It's all about taking the time to discover who you are.

If you're having trouble making a connection to your creativity, just know that you're in good company. Some of the most famous writers and actors and painters in the world get blocked and have to spend years working their way through (don't worry, it won't take you that long!).

One of the biggest reasons we shy away from finding our creativity is our fear of getting it wrong. We start asking ourselves questions like: *What if my painting looks stupid? What if I sing off-key? What if those rosebushes I planted all die off?* Until eventually we're so caught up in what might happen that our creativity gets crushed before it even gets off the ground. But guess what? How your self-expression "looks" or "sounds" doesn't matter. Being creative is all about freedom. It's got nothing to do with right or wrong. Let's go back to those famous artists. You think Maya Angelou never tore up a few poems, or Picasso never produced a dud? Failure doesn't mean you're stupid. It means you're brave enough to let yourself grow.

One of my old school friends, Maya, always had a real interest in quilting. She loved going to craft museums and looking at the old Amish and Shaker quilts, but she'd never so much as sewed up a hem. She'd pretty much convinced herself that any quilt she tried to make would be so embarrassed about looking bad it would run off and hide under the bed. Friends kept urging her to give it a try. One of them even bought her a quilting class for Christmas, but Maya was too intimidated to go. Finally, the next year that same friend bought both of them a class and personally dragged Maya into the room the first day. Well, Maya took to it like a rooster to a hen. When the first class finished, she signed up for a second and then a third. The first few quilts she produced were a little uneven, but she was enjoying the process so much that she kept on going. These days she's sewing quilts she's proud enough to hang on her wall, and she's even attempting some of those same patterns she used to go look at in museums. She's discovered a whole well of talent that wouldn't have even been touched if she'd let the fear of failing rule the way.

As a society, we've been trained to think of failure as the worst possible thing, and as a result we've lost our appreciation for the learning process. Instead of deciding to grow from our mistakes, we let the prospect of not getting something right stop us dead, not just creatively but in many aspects of our lives. Exploring our creativity is a great place to begin working our way through such fears. Maybe, like Maya, you'll uncover a real hidden talent. Or maybe you won't be the best in the world at whatever you choose to do. I know there are plenty of people out there who can turn a phrase much better than I can, but that doesn't keep me from opening up my journal every day. Being creative isn't about the results. It's about the joy we take in getting there.

Another thing that sometimes blocks our creative flow is the feeling that taking time out for self-expression is just plain old selfish. We've all got busy lives to lead, splitting our hours between work and family and other responsibilities. I've got one friend who tells me she figures it's a day to rejoice when she gets to the dry cleaners on time. Even if we do have a few minutes here and there, we've gotten to feeling guilty if we don't fill them tending to others. After all, someone's got to help cure cancer and feed the hungry. But even if you must force yourself to write in your journal, visit new art galleries, or explore some other creative outlet, it's worth it. In the end, you'll be a stronger, more giving, more loving person for taking that time to develop yourself. Working the virtues is a great first step, but I hope all of us remember to keep going. Spending time with ourselves, tending to our spiritual and emotional health, is one of the most important things we can do to create balance in our lives. And often our creativity winds up bringing joy not only to us but also to the people we love.

Embracing your creativity is the greatest privilege you own. It's a way of saying, *I'm powerful and unique.* And as soon as we stop judging ourselves and start celebrating, we're taking a major step toward bringing our lives back into harmony. I bet you've been waiting a lifetime to hear these words, so here we go.

When it comes to getting creative, you can do no wrong.

Journal time

In our journals this week we're going to spend some time freeing our creativity. First of all, meditate on the page about what role creativity plays in your life. Do you have a hobby or artistic pursuit? Is there something creative that interests you but you haven't taken the time to explore? Why not? Often the excuses we use, like not having enough time or money, are just standing in for something deeper. Try to be as honest with yourself as you can.

Using your journal to explore your creative ideas is a wonderful way to start yourself on this journey. Use these pages as a first step in getting to know your artistic self. Play and have fun with it. Here are just a few ideas:

- Write a poem in tribute to a friend or a story about your childhood.
- Compose a funny song.
- Draw or doodle. Use stick figures if you have to.
- Are you inspired by cooking? Try designing a menu for your dream dinner party.
- Do you like to sew? Use your journal to sketch a new outfit, making it as outrageous as you want.
- Do you enjoy gardening? Search magazines for the type of flowers you'd like to plant. Cut them out and paste them in your journal for inspiration.

As you explore, be aware of that little voice inside your head that tries to pass judgment on everything you do. Keep reminding yourself to focus on the process, not the results. Give yourself the freedom to explore.

WEEK 46
Finding Your Creative Outlet

❖

Imagination is more important than knowledge.
ALBERT EINSTEIN

My friend Vanessa was always real creative when she was young. Growing up, she was the type who starred in the school play, made paintings you'd want to hang on your walls, designed her own clothes, the works. But once she left school and got married, she found less and less time for creative expression in her life. She had three kids one right after the other, the family had some money problems, and then her oldest daughter got sick. Vanessa figured the last thing she had time for was tending to anything creative. Honestly, I think she forgot that side of her even existed.

It wasn't until Vanessa was seriously unhappy, gaining a lot of weight and starting to take antidepressants, that she remembered her old love for art. Although finding a creative outlet had been easy back when she was in school, with plays to audition for and art classes to take and her mother's sewing machine always nearby, now that she was an adult with her own life, she was kind of at a loss. She knew she had to find something to bring beauty and pleasure back into her life or she was going to drop right off the deep end. But what did she want to do?

Vanessa got her answer by opening her eyes to the creativity going on around her. She still loved clothes and design, and one day she noticed a friend wearing a unique pair of beaded earrings. Vanessa asked about where she'd bought them, and it turned out the friend had made them herself. She helped hook

Vanessa up with all the right supplies and Vanessa set up a table in the corner of her basement. These days she's making earrings and bracelets for all her friends and family. She's also a whole lot happier, she's lost some weight, and she's got the patience and love to deal with her family problems. She claims finding her creative outlet literally saved her life.

I think a lot of us run into Vanessa's problem. Even if we're willing to admit we're creative—and remember, we all are—we're not sure just what to do to explore this side of ourselves. I certainly had no idea I was going to exercise my artistic side by becoming a collector. But don't worry. In fact, finding your creative outlet might be the most enjoyable part of all.

Maybe you've always expressed yourself in a certain way, by writing or taking photos or doodling all over the backs of envelopes. Now's the time to stop jamming this stuff into the corners of your life and really devote some time to developing your talents. Or maybe you like doing something that seems weird or unconventional—that's okay, too. Remember, we're not making judgments anymore. Just follow your heart. I've got friends who are into antiquing, photo collage, African dance, juggling, knitting. My mother makes the most amazing collages for family members on special occasions. In the vast spectrum of creative endeavors out there, one must appeal to you. And if it does, go for it, no matter how outlandish it might seem.

This week we're going to take some time to figure out what inspires us. Just relax and have some fun with this. The only rule is that there are no rules. Anything goes. This is your time to explore what really speaks to you and for you. How do you want to express your creativity?

Try as many different things as you want to. And don't feel you have to narrow it down or make a decision right away. Maybe you want to pursue a couple of creative paths at the same time. Or maybe you can combine them—like performing with a community theater group and helping design the costumes. As long as it makes you happy, explore wherever you want to go.

Finding your creative outlet is essential work. It's part of figuring out who you are. Creativity adds beauty to our lives. It lets us recharge the battery that gets drained by spending all day, every day out there in the world. When we get in touch with our imaginations, we feel inspired to pursue our dreams. You owe it to yourself to invest the time to do it right.

Journal time

This week, we're going to use our journal time to explore what really moves us creatively. Make an effort to put aside a chunk of time that's all yours. Hire a baby-sitter, postpone a meeting, do whatever you need to do to find a few hours. Then start your creative exploration by developing a soothing atmosphere. That might mean lighting candles, making a mug of hot tea, or running a bubble bath. It definitely means closing the door.

Once you're feeling relaxed and ready, use the pages of your journal to meditate on what inspires you creatively. If you're stuck, think back on what you used to like to do when you were younger. Most of us were creative as kids. We had the time and the freedom back then to really indulge our artistic selves. If you used to like to draw pictures, then now's the time to buy yourself a sketchpad. Did you get into singing at church? Go ahead and look into joining the choir, or just buy a gospel CD and start singing along at home.

Jot down different areas that interest you now and think of ways you might pursue them. Make some sketches. If you're feeling lost, try looking through some magazines to help you come up with fresh ideas. Let your mind roam. Travel anywhere. This is your time to just get creative with you.

WEEK 47
Creative Inspiration: Finding Your Muse

🔲

I saw the angel in the marble and carved until I
set him free.

MICHELANGELO

When it comes to deepening our relationships with our creative
selves, some of the most powerful sources of inspiration we'll
find come from other artists. I know I got back in touch with my
creative spark by taking in the works of others. The Black Arts
Movement was charged with so much creative energy you
couldn't help but feel a part of it, even just as an audience member. After performances, groups of us would gather at a coffee-
house or restaurant talking until all hours about what we'd seen
and how it had moved us. Later, I started drawing inspiration
from the artistic works I hung on my walls. Just looking at those
images can fill me up with a sense of hope and purpose, and get
me moving in creative directions of my own.

Since way back in history, all kinds of artists—from the famous
names to the ones no one's ever heard of—have been drawing inspiration from other artists, studying up on their works and their
lives. They use that creative energy to give them fresh ideas, and
new avenues of expression. It's called finding your muse.

As you set out on your own creative journey, take the time to
absorb the creative energy going on in the world around you.
Start thinking about other artists and creative people you admire.
They might be world-famous actors, writers, and artists, or they

might be family and friends. As soon as you open your mind to a creative place, you'll discover that such inspiration is everywhere. Learning to appreciate others' works helps make space for creativity in our own lives.

There are all kinds of ways to spend time with your muses. Are you moved by the great jazz musicians or singers like Billie Holiday and Nancy Wilson? You could start playing their tapes or CDs during your daily commute. Do you have favorite novelists or poets? See if you can spend half an hour with their writing before you go to bed at night or check into whether their works are available as books on tape to listen to in the car or while you go for a walk.

Try finding some time during the day to connect with the creative works of others, and restore your own energy and emotional balance. Go off by yourself and read a biography of an artist you admire. Put on your headphones and listen to a comedy tape. Spend your lunch break or a weekend afternoon at a museum or art gallery. Seek out new artists, people you've never heard of. Often young artists have a fresh, unconventional kind of energy that can get you thinking in different directions. Pause to listen to musicians playing on the street or in the subway (and don't forget to put a couple of bucks into the hat). Read poetry and pay attention to the language and how the words make you feel.

When we take time to absorb other artists' work and read up on their lives, we often pick up on some of their creative energy and funnel it into our own self-expression. That's one of the reasons great artists are so powerful. They really do change our lives. I have a colleague who's a budding photographer. To help keep herself motivated, she designed an entire work space at home that's plastered with pictures taken by her muses. One wall is entirely devoted to pictures taken by her own aunt, a professional photographer who traveled through West Africa in the 1950s shooting people and landscapes. Whenever she gets to feeling tired or flat about her own pictures, all she has to do is look around her to get inspired.

This week, start thinking about people, especially other creative women, who might serve as your muses. Come up with some women who really get you moving and excited. Women who've chased things, dreamed dreams, and found their voices. If you're unsure, try browsing in the biography section of a bookstore or picking up an arts magazine to give you some ideas.

Some of the powerful creative women I find inspirational include Zora Neale Hurston, novelist, anthropologist, and member of the Harlem Renaissance; Faith Ringgold and Dr. Tracey Rico, gifted quilters; and Judith Jamison, dancer, choreographer, and muse to the great Alvin Ailey. Such women don't just provide inspiration through their work, they do it through the struggles they've overcome and the way they've lived their lives. Who are the creative women who move you? What are their stories? How did they get in touch with their creative souls? How can they help you get in touch with yours?

Journal time

This week, devote some time to developing your own sources of inspiration. Make a list of artists or other creative people you admire. It could be a chef, a poet, a dancer, a musician—anyone who speaks to you. How can you find out more about these people? Can you get prints or copies of their works? Check the library for articles or books about their lives? If your inspiration is someone you know, take the time to talk to her about her work and her life. Ask questions about who and what inspire her.

Also this week, set aside some space at home where you can gather all these sources of inspiration. You could hang a bulletin board on your wall, set aside part of a desk or table, or create a collage in the pages of your journal. Try cutting pictures or words from magazines, finding old photos, and gathering books, CDs, or fabrics—whatever it is that provides you with creative fuel.

WEEK 48
Creativity at Work

The creative thinker is flexible and adaptable
and prepared to rearrange his thinking.

A. J. CROPLEY

Writing is a legitimate way, an important way, to
participate in the empowerment of the community that names me.

TONI CADE BAMBARA

Even as we start to make creativity more a part of our everyday
lives, it can be hard to feel inspired in some settings. Like the office. For a few lucky people out there, their creative pursuit is
also how they make their living. I've been fortunate to know
many professional artists in my life, and though the good ones are
probably the hardest-working people around, they also tend to
be some of the most fulfilled. They get to spend all day doing
what feeds them, and bringing joy and beauty to the rest of the
world. As for the rest of us, we've got to find some other way to
deal.

For a lot of people, arriving in the workplace—or just the
working mind-set—means leaving creativity behind. Creation
and the office just don't seem to mix. All those fears about looking stupid start resurfacing, and we become cautious and
guarded. We play it safe. And to make matters worse, sometimes
the process of waking up the other parts of our lives can make the
workday seem longer and less fulfilling than ever. But it doesn't
have to be that way. There are all kinds of ideas for bringing cre-

ativity into your workplace or turning your job into something creative. I see it happen all the time.

One of my favorite designers spent years struggling with how to incorporate her creative soul with the need to put food on the table. Anita always had a serious love for fashion, including designing her own clothes and crocheting cute little hats for all her friends. But somehow she'd gotten the message early on that you couldn't make a living doing something so frivolous. Instead, she got a job in an upscale boutique selling other people's clothes for a whole lot of money. She got unhappier every year, getting real down on herself and her future, but she didn't know how to make a change. Then one day she spotted an ad for weekend design classes at the local art institute. So she decided to test them out.

Though the classes covered the fun part of fashion design, they also showed the more "serious" business side of things. And Anita realized there was a way to combine her creative talents with making a living. She decided to go to design school full time. After graduation, she started out small, just selling those crocheted hats of hers to boutiques around town. Gradually she expanded, and now she has her own shop selling her line of accessories plus those of other small, independent designers who are trying to make their way. It's been a real labor of love for her. It took years of scrimping—no vacations or nights on the town—before she was turning any sort of profit. But these days Anita is one fully fulfilled woman, happier than she even thought she could be.

Stories like Anita's prove that work and creative pursuit don't have to be two separate things. There are many ways of combining the two. These words you're reading now are a perfect example. Writing this book is my work, but it's also an expression of my creativity.

Now, not everyone can or wants to do what Anita did, making their creative outlet into their work. But that doesn't mean your artistic side has to go into hiding. Sometimes it's just a question of bringing a more creative mind-set to the job you already have. You might discover that your office or workplace is a whole lot more creative than you think.

A few years ago I met Rita, who'd worked her way up from secretary to the manager of a small cosmetics company in just a few years. I was curious about how she'd made such an impression, and she told me that when she started working for the company they did everything in a real dry, conventional way. They were competing against huge cosmetics lines with products in stores all over the world. And they were struggling. At first Rita was tempted to just phone in her work and make sure to leave at five on the button every night. But after a few months she decided that eight hours a day was just too much time for boring herself to tears. She might have been "just a secretary," but she knew that company was going to have to get more creative or die.

Rita had always liked to draw and sketch things, including making fancy cards for birthdays and posters for her walls. So when her boss asked her to organize some information on their new color line, Rita decided to take it on as a creative project. She drew pictures of women wearing the company products as they led exciting lives, then bound the whole thing in beautiful paper, tied it with ribbon, and made a copy for each of the managers in her department. Not only were her bosses impressed with Rita's hard work and initiative, but they also loved her presentation so much it became part of the package they sent out to all their prospective clients. The company as a whole has grown more innovative with its products and its advertising, and sales have risen. So has Rita, who's now working as a manager herself and loving her creative and exciting new job.

Though you may not wind up changing the company or your career, finding smaller ways of injecting creativity into your job can help make for a more exciting and personal work experience. I know a nurse who always had a yearning to be an actress. She didn't have to change careers! Instead, she brings her love of performing to her work on a hospital children's ward. Whenever she appears in the doorway of a kid's room, she's wearing a funky hat or putting on voices or telling jokes to make them giggle. The patients love her. Not only does she enjoy her job more, but the kids are less scared and anxious about their time in her care.

Creative thinking in the workplace is getting more and more popular these days. Some of the trendiest companies are putting toys in the office, scheduling informal brainstorming sessions, or arranging the desks in a more creative way to keep employees excited and stimulate fresh ideas. If your office feels kinda stale around the edges, maybe there are some suggestions you could make to loosen things up. What would it take to make it a more creative space? Is there a way you could decorate your work area? Things you could bring in? Ideas you could present to your boss?

Getting confident with our creative selves was just the first step. Now it's time for that artistic soul to spread inspiration into the rest of our lives.

Journal time

This week, meditate on the page about different ways to bring creativity into your workplace. What are your creative strengths? Are you a good writer? Artistic? A frustrated actor? You might want to design new office stationery, or think up an exciting and different way of giving a presentation. They can be big ideas or little—it doesn't matter. Make a list of four or five things you might want to try.

If you really feel like you'd like to devote your life to your creative pursuit, know that this is a serious commitment that takes a lot of hard work and many years of effort before you see the rewards. Still interested? Use your journal to explore some ideas. What would you have to do to make this happen?

WEEK 49
Creative Celebrations:
Sharing Our Creativity

▣

Happiness is not a destination. It is a method of
life.

BURTON HILLS

One of the most rewarding things about working the creativity virtue is the fact that we can use our inspiration to bring joy
not just to ourselves but also to the other meaningful people in
our lives. Creativity is an important part of enhancing any ritual or holiday gathering, from the biggies like Thanksgiving
and Christmas to smaller events, like a birthday celebration for
a friend.

For many of us, holidays and celebrations mean Stress with a
capital S. Our lives are busy enough without having to deal with
cooking a turkey, trimming a tree, or shopping for gifts. I sure
used to feel that way. But taking the time to focus on the personal, on creating this balance in my life, has made me see such
occasions in a different way. They allow us to slow down and
spend time with our loved ones. After all, we shouldn't forget
that special events are special for a reason. They are blessed occasions, our chance to express our feelings to those people we
love most in the world.

When I was growing up, Christmas was always a real fun time
of the year. Sure, I loved unwrapping all those presents under the
tree, but that was only a tiny part of it. What really got me excited
were the activities our family did together. Every December,

about a week before Christmas Eve, we'd all bundle up in our coats and hats, pile in the car, and go out and buy ourselves a tree. When we got home, my mother would make hot chocolate and my father would build a pretend fire in the pretend fireplace. Then we'd spend the whole afternoon in the living room together, opening up the boxes of ornaments that had been sitting in the basement all year long. We'd search for our favorites, like the felt stars and Santas my sister and I made in Sunday school. And we'd argue about what to hang where. There was always a whole lot of laughing and teasing and loving going on. I don't know if my parents meant for it to happen that way, but a family tradition was born.

Lots of us have nice memories of the holidays when we were children, but in today's faster-paced world it can seem hard to recreate such homey, joyful celebrations. No one has time for lazy afternoons or the energy to get all excited about decorating the house. But it doesn't have to be that way. In fact, taking the time to inject some real creativity into our holiday celebrations is a wonderful way to pass traditions on to our own kids.

Think about ways in which you can make the holidays truly special for your family and loved ones. Kwanzaa is a perfect time to begin celebrating both the virtues and your creativity. This year, plan a special feast for one of the seven days and get your kids involved in all the preparations. Make harvest decorations, or design collages using pictures of your ancestors. Find a cookbook with traditional African foods and prepare the meal at home. Let your children help choose some music to play during the celebration, maybe some African drumming. Getting involved will make the occasion much more enjoyable, and meaningful, for them.

Children always love Christmas. Though it sometimes seems like all they care about is unwrapping the right toys, most of them will really get into celebrating in more shared and creative ways. My friend Khadijah throws a little Christmas party every year for her daughters and their friends, and she and the girls do all the prep work as a team. That means spending an entire weekend baking and decorating dozens of Christmas cookies. The girls take over as designers, mixing the colors for the icing, sprinkling on the decorations, and arranging all the platters. When it comes time for party day, Khadijah sets out bowls of frosting and a bunch of naked cookies so the guests can get into the fun, too. She and her daughters spend some creative, quality time together planning the day, and the party is a big hit with all the families. Even better, she's creating memories that her girls will cherish their entire lives.

Whatever holidays you celebrate—Kwanzaa, Christmas, Hanukkah, Easter, Fourth of July—including your family and friends in the preparation can make the event a real shared and loving time. It's a way of stopping for a moment and just letting everyone know how much you appreciate their being a part of your life. Even if you're not up to tackling the major events, you can add creativity to any holiday in a smaller, more intimate way. Instead of buying a birthday cake at a bakery, spend an afternoon baking and icing one yourself. It may not look quite as pretty, but it's a far more meaningful gift. If you and your romantic partner usually just exchange cards and flowers on Valentine's Day, this year try cooking an intimate candlelight dinner together instead.

Of course, you don't have to wait for the next holiday to start celebrating your creativity. You can bring your artistic side to dressing up any special occasion. Plan a lunch in honor of a high school graduate, making special diploma-style place cards for the table and decorating the room with photos of the graduate through the years. Or splurge on a nice bottle of champagne, lay a special table, and pick some jazzy music to pay tribute to a mini milestone, like a promotion or a new job.

Creative celebrations don't have to involve spending a lot of money. In fact, often the personal touches cost far less and mean more than just running out and buying up a lot of stuff. Instead of sending store-bought holiday cards this year, you and your family could design and make your own. Try filling Easter baskets with homemade cookies and candies, or making your kids' Halloween costumes together instead of buying them at the store—you'll be amazed by the clever ideas you can come up with.

Holidays and rituals are occasions we can set aside for sharing the bounty of our lives. Whether we're celebrating something small and intimate, or big and extravagant, such times are all about giving, creating a warm and inviting space to share with our loved ones. Creative celebration gives us a chance to pause and give tribute to the many blessings of our lives.

Journal time

This week, use your journal time to come up with a creative way to celebrate an upcoming holiday or special event. Start by making a list of your favorite holiday memories. A Kwanza activity that I've participated in with my own friends and family, often before or after saying grace at mealtimes, is the historic or ancestral roll call, i.e., calling out or raising the names. I've found that calling out the names of our ancestral heroes, heroines, and departed relatives is in itself a prayer. Standing beside and holding hands with the people in our lives we both love and are proud of, sharing our heritage and its innate strength, reinforces and cultivates community bonds, inspiring and spurring on community and individual growth. Bearing witness to those whose lives have given and continue to impart us with spiritual and civic instruction reaffirms the goals we have for our own lives, and the hopes and prayers we have for the members of our community. And that is in fact, possibly, the most dynamic aspect of the roll call: it asks us to acknowledge the love and responsibility people have shown us through the purpose of their lives, most without ever really knowing us at all.

Start thinking creatively about the events you want to celebrate. Plan a Kwanzaa arts-and-crafts day so you and your kids can prepare holiday games and decorations. Throw your spouse or best friend a birthday party, design your own birthday cards, or write funny songs or poems to give as gifts. If there are no special occasions coming up, then make one up. Hold a Christmas in August barbecue, or an appreciation party for someone who plays a meaningful role in your life. There are all kinds of things you could do to share your creativity with those around you. It's one of the most powerful ways of also spreading your love.

WEEK 50
Creative Healing

Art hurts. Art urges voyages—and it is easier to
stay at home.

GWENDOLYN BROOKS

Creativity is a powerful tool. It can boost our confidence, bring
us pleasure, and make us feel strong enough to take on the world.
It can also arm us with the courage to go places we don't necessarily want to go. Artistic expression is all about getting in touch
with our emotions, getting out of our heads, and spending some
time with our hearts. And though our hearts hold a lot of love and
generosity, they also usually contain some pain. Creativity can
help us start working through that pain. It can provide us with a
way of expressing feelings so deep we don't yet know how to put
them into words.

In the past few years my friend Beth has become a dancer. She
started with some classes at the local Y, hoping a little physical
activity might help knock her out of the depression she'd been
sinking into. Something in the movement, the ability to express
herself with her body, really spoke to her, and she decided she
wasn't satisfied with just showing up for two hours three nights a
week. She got permission to work alone in one of the studios and
began bringing along music, hoping to choreograph her own
piece. As Beth began working on her dance, she found herself
returning to movements that revealed lots of vulnerability and
pain. She gradually came to realize that this creative outlet was
giving expression to a lot of repressed pain she'd been holding
inside for years.

As a child, Beth had been sexually abused by her uncle. Though she'd done her best to block those painful memories, recently a deepening relationship with a kind and loving man had made the hurt resurface in the form of a general depression. It was through dancing, the creative connection with her body, that Beth was able to get in touch with that old hurt again and slowly begin the healing process.

Many of us still struggle to deal with the pain of childhood baggage or trauma. As the years go by, it can feel like those events get locked deeper and deeper inside us. Creativity can provide a direct link to such difficult emotions, sometimes giving expression to things that are alive only in our subconscious. Professional therapists often use art and drama as avenues for their patients to explore issues and events that are too powerful to confront head-on. They might have them draw pictures or act out scenes that show what they're feeling.

Creative journalling can be another powerful tool for dealing with the hurt. I often use my journal to explore painful emotions. My aunt died recently, and I found myself spending a lot of time exploring my feelings about her and about loss. It was tough to work my way through that stuff, but now that I've done it I can say I truly feel at peace with myself. Sometimes issues I'm that not even aware I'm dealing with will come pouring out on the page. In the past I might have dealt with my pain by turning to another old friend—the ice cream spoon. But learning to express ourselves creatively can help wean us from those old coping mechanisms, habits that, as you probably know, don't really help us heal very much at all.

If you're working on any issues, if you're in a twelve-step program or going to therapy, your creative journey can help facilitate the growth and changes you're trying to bring to your life. See if you can use the pages of your journal to explore some of the difficult issues that begin to come up.

Creative expression can also help in dealing with painful situations that may be going on for you right now. It's a way to turn down the static from all the other demands in your life and get one-on-one with your emotions. Recently my friend Daniel's four-year-old daughter was diagnosed with brain cancer. For eighteen months, while she went through chemotherapy, he and his wife devoted every moment of their lives to tending to her. They neglected everything else, especially themselves, in the process. Once she was out of the woods and they began trying to resume an ordinary life, their marriage started feeling the strain. Neither of them had taken the time to process the personal pain they'd suffered during their daughter's illness.

Dan's creative outlet had always been rebuilding old motor-cycles, and he usually had three or four of them at various stages in the garage. But with his daughter's illness, he hadn't allowed himself time for anything else. Now he found himself wanting to spend every moment he could in his workshop. He'd often be there tinkering until one or two in the morning. Sometimes he'd find himself starting to cry for no reason and he'd have to stop working and just sit a while with his pain. As the weeks went by, Daniel started to process his own grief and reach out again to his wife and begin rebuilding their family. For Daniel, getting in touch with his creativity again was his way of starting the healing process.

Connecting to our pain by exploring our creativity can make us feel less victimized by the world. By discovering the ability to express ourselves, we begin to generate positive energy and even a whole new outlook. It makes us feel stronger. We realize we're powerful enough to overcome.

*J*ournal time

This week, try using your journal time to begin working on some painful issue in your life. It could be something from your past that you've had trouble dealing with or something going on in your world right now. For many of us, this is the most difficult work we will have to do. Stay patient and move as slowly as you need to. Creating peace and harmony in our lives is a process, not a race.

If you're having trouble writing about your emotions directly, try expressing yourself in other ways. Write a poem. Draw a picture. Anything that might help you get in touch with those feelings is fine. Pay attention to how your emotions begin to change as you find the courage to release them. Creative self-expression gives us a chance to finally find peace with the painful issues in our lives.

WEEK 51
Creatively Working the Virtues

Do all the good you can, by all the means you
can, in all the ways you can, in all the places
you can, at all the times you can, to all the people
you can, as long as ever you can.

JOHN WESLEY

Working the virtues is an ongoing process. We'll never stop
growing and we'll never stop finding ways to apply the lessons
the virtues teach us to our lives. As we work toward peace and
harmony, we'll be calling on our creative selves all the time.
Learning to balance the needs of ourselves and others, learning
to be both strong and nurturing, learning to speak our minds
even as we're respecting the wishes of others—all this will provide many opportunities for incorporating creativity into our
lives.

Remember what we said at the beginning of this section? Creativity is the ultimate expression of who we are. The fifty weeks
we've already spent working the virtues have given us the
chance to get to know that person, to develop her, and to provide
her with plenty of space to grow. It's been quite a journey, and it's
one that we'll continue for the rest of our lives.

Of course, sticking to the virtues can be difficult, especially
when we're feeling anxious or stressed. Sometimes I'm over-
worked or overtired or just not in the mood. Some virtues come
harder than others do—I still get stuck on that taking responsibility for my body—and I've really got to pay close attention to
not letting them slide. I find the biggest challenge is just show-

ing up, day after day, trying to keep the virtues at the forefront of my mind. This week, let's look at some ways in which we can use our creativity to incorporate all of the virtues into our everyday lives.

The first rule here is to be realistic. If you're aiming to spend two hours every day writing in your journal, chances are you're not going to get there. You'll just wind up letting yourself down, and after a while you might even be tempted to quit. So keep setting goals, but make them goals you think you can reach. While it may not work to write in your journal every single day, it does make sense to have a regular check-in time—maybe Sunday afternoons—to make sure you've written something each week. I also like to have a little personal check-in time with myself every morning when I get up. It takes only a minute and it helps me focus on the issues I might be dealing with that day.

I also find it's just too overwhelming to think about working all the virtues all the time. There's only so much improving a self you can get your mind around. So I like to pick a different virtue to focus on each week. Often, at the beginning of the week I'll jot down the virtue I've chosen and list a couple of points that I want to work on. Then I'll stick it on my bathroom mirror so I'm reminded of my goals at the start of each day.

You might want to keep a list of the virtues handy in the places where you spend your time. Write them up on a pretty card or with colored pens, anything that'll make them seem special to you. Then make a copy for the office, your bedroom, your kitchen drawer, your car, maybe even your locker at school or at the gym. This is a great way to keep the virtues constantly present in your life.

There may be other people in your life who are working on the same issues as you are. A "virtue buddy" can be a valuable way to keep you focused and excited about your work. Maybe you and your friend could schedule a weekly check-in time to talk about what's going on in your lives. Try making up new journal exercises for each other. You might even want to give her a copy of your special list of the seven virtues to start her on her way. Then keep checking in with each other regularly to see how you're doing. Sharing the virtues is a wonderful way of also sharing your love.

These are a few ideas to get you going, but they're only a start. Keep coming up with other creative ways to make sure your efforts stay fresh and present in your life.

Creation is cyclical, like the harvest. What you create in turn makes others feel creative, and opens up new possibilities for all of us. So keep growing. Keep loving. Keep being true to who you are. And remember, creativity is just like all the other virtues. It doesn't work unless you work it.

Journal time

This week, meditate on the page about how to incorporate creativity and all the other virtues into your life. Make a list of the seven virtues: Calling, Thrift, Responsibility, Community, Love, Spirituality, and Creativity. Come up with one or two creative ways in which to continue working each one.

For love, you might write a letter or a poem to someone you care about just to let her know how you feel. For responsibility, you could think up a creative way to start taking charge of your body, like signing up for a karate class or learning to salsa dance. As you're working on developing your relationship to your community, come up with some ideas for gathering your neighbors, like a holiday party or food drive. For some people, finding a calling will be straightforward: They want to become a lawyer or a teacher. For many of us the path isn't quite so clear. If you're still figuring out what your calling might be, think up ways to test-drive a few interests. If you know a writer or chef or doctor, ask if you can spend a day in her shadow. Open yourself up to some new worlds.

One of the most important things you can do as you continue to make the virtues a part of your life is to keep journaling. Fill these pages with your thoughts and feelings. Use them to work through your problems and celebrate your successes. I hope you continue to love yourself and love what you can achieve in this world. I hope you always succeed in finding the plenty in your life.

WEEK 52
Reaping the Harvest

回

> Whoever sows generously will also reap generously.
>
> 2 CORINTHIANS 9:6

There are times when working the virtues can seem like just that, a whole lot of work. But there's another, equally important side to this journey we're taking, that of harvesting the rewards. We're going to devote this final week—and part of each week that follows—to honoring all the truly amazing things we've accomplished as we've brought the virtues in harmony with our lives. Over the past year, we've searched and struggled, journeyed and journaled and come to a better understanding of who we are and how we face the world. Now it's time to take stock of all the fantastic growth that's been going on. It's time to reap the harvest from those powerful seeds we've sown. Honoring the work we've put in is just as important as the doing the work itself.

For us women, I think it can be especially hard to remember to harvest those seeds we plant. We tend to spend a whole lot of time focusing on what we haven't achieved and on all those things going wrong in our lives. We feel like we've always got to be making sacrifices and playing small instead of rewarding ourselves for that glory waking up inside us. Of course, it's good to want to grow. But part of becoming a whole and balanced person includes acknowledging all the ways in which we've expanded our lives so far. So this week, take some time out to truly celebrate what you've accomplished in the past year. Honor your healthy relationships, your spiritual growth, the giant steps you've made in discovering your creativity and your calling. And promise yourself to make harvesting a regular part of your future.

The harvest cycle is part of our history as human beings. It provides one of our strongest connections to the earth. For generations, our ancestors survived by planting seeds, nurturing, watering, and waiting patiently to see what those seeds would yield. Because both my parents and grandparents were sharecroppers, I've always felt a special tie to the cyclical nature of growth and the seasons. But unlike farmers, our personal growth cycle isn't dependent on the seasons. We're planting the seeds and reaping the harvest all the time. Think of all the ways in which you might celebrate such growth just in your daily life. When you stay true to a commitment you've made to a job or a relationship, you're harvesting responsibility. When you pause to give thanks for the blessings in your life, you're harvesting spirituality. When you take time out of a crowded day to write or sew or paint or dance, you're harvesting creativity.

Harvesting is one of life's most important cycles, but sometimes it's hard to recognize just when and how to honor all this bounty we've sown. Though I've put this harvesting time at the end of the book, that doesn't mean anything has come to a close. Harvesting will always be part of the growth process. Really, we should be thinking about harvest throughout the year. It's never the wrong time to celebrate our strength and love, or to stop long enough to praise our progress. Try to make honoring your achievements a regular part of your life, just like you've made working the virtues. Take time each week, or even each day, to get in touch with those things that are going well. Use your journal to record all the changes. The harvest is the most joyous and rewarding of celebrations. It's when we take time to love ourselves, respect our challenges and our losses, and honor our potential to grow even more.

As I continue to work the virtues in my own life, I've come to realize that there will never be a time when I no longer have to challenge myself. The work is hard, and there will always be places where I feel stuck or frustrated or even tempted to give up. Part of what keeps me inspired is the time I take to assess and honor what's going right. Recognizing how far I've come keeps me motivated and focused on restoring the balance in my universe, no matter how much hard work that requires. Harvesting keeps me closer to life's natural processes and rhythms. It reminds me that those knots I feel in my stomach are a sign that I'm challenging myself every day. When I see how far I've come, that's when I know this is one journey I never want to end.

Remembering to harvest what we've planted in ourselves can also make us more aware of the bounty of the universe. When we begin recognizing our own goodness—our ability to be disciplined and loving and patient—we can start seeing the goodness in others as well. Think of the ways in which your work in the past year has opened you up to the universe. Maybe you've started to feel more compassionate and generous toward those around you. Maybe you've discovered a deeper appreciation for the beauty of nature and the power of God's love.

When we get in touch with the loving aspects of the universe, problems that once felt overwhelming can suddenly seem solvable. Things like stress and depression aren't as likely to get us down. By celebrating all the good we've brought into this world, we begin to see the possibilities for spreading even more. We begin to understand that even when we're going through tough times, we continue to learn and grow. Our lives are always moving forward. This too is the power of the harvest.

I hope that this past year has inspired you to continue your work with the virtues. And I hope that, in the course of that work, you will always remember to honor the cycle. Take time to both plant the seeds and reap the harvest. Celebrate the changes you make and all the positive new things that enter your life. Love the person you are and the person you can become. Each day of our lives will be filled with the work we must do, sowing the seeds of the future. But we're also surrounded by great good fortune; by the love of God, our family, and our community; by spiritual strength and creative expression. The gifts the world has bestowed upon us are also the gifts we will bestow upon the world. Those gifts are our greatest blessing. They are our reason for being. They provide the joys of a plentiful harvest.

Journal time

This week's journal is about reading, not writing. Go back through the entries you've made throughout the past year. Where have you grown? What have you accomplished? Allow yourself to reap the rewards of all your hard work by appreciating your commitment, growth, and strength. Honoring your achievements will help give you the pride and sense of self you need to continue on this virtuous path.

Books That Have
Touched My Heart

The Highly Sensitive Person by Elaine Aron
Look In, Look Up, Look Out! by Joyce Vedral
Illuminaia by Marianne Williams
When Food Is Love by Geneed Roth
Simple Abundance by Sarah Ban Breathnach
God on a Harley by Joan Brady
Tuesdays with Morrie by Mitch Albom
Fathers Aren't Supposed to Die by T. M. Shine
Lessons for Living by Susan L. Taylor
The Bible
A Cherokee Feast of Days by Joyce Sequichie Hifler
This Far by Faith by Linne Frank and Andria Hall
In the Meantime by Iyanla Vanzant
Moment of Grace—Meeting the Challenge to Change by Patrice Gaines
The Next Place by Warren Hanson
On My Own at 107 by Sarah Delany with Amy Hill Hearth
Long Winter's Night by Sista Souljah
The Color of Water by James McBride
My Life Is an Open Book by Bill Zimmerman
The Cherished Self by Michelle Morris-Spieker

ACKNOWLEDGMENTS
Every day I thank God for you . . .

Family
Mom—for planting the seeds and for always being there to help me reap the harvest. I love you.

My dad, Charles Williams—for building the foundation on which the Williams women could go out into the world and make a difference and know that we'd always have a safety net.

My loving sister and brother-in-law, Lani and Tom Johnson—for being an example and teaching so many the power and majesty of our Creator.

Roc, the light in my life—for teaching me many lessons and the true meaning of unconditional love.

Xavier—for guiding me to step into my name and for teaching me new dimensions of love, patience, sacrifice, and commitment. Thank you for renewing my spirit.

Khalilah—my spiritual daughter. The way you share yourself is extraordinary. Love you.

Aunt Jo (Mom #2), Aunt Ethel, Aunt Louise, Aunt Bea, and Uncle Floyd (you are a rock for us).

My godparents, Aunt Daisy and Uncle William—for helping to set the foundation.

My cousins—Let's elevate
Alex—chairman of the board; Pat—you are the shining example for us all . . . family first; Gaddy—you are my heart; Rev. Betty Jean—you pleasantly surprise me; Tony Gaddy—for keeping the line of communication open and strong. Persevere.

Bernice, Valerie, and James, Tony Simmons—for reminding me to breathe—Regina, Toya, Twanna, Wes, Nathan, and Andrell.

"A Plentiful Harvest" journey
Tanya McKinnon—thank you for "seeing" me, for your vision and infinite wisdom. You walked through fire for us on this journey—and we are still standing. My faith has been strengthened and my soul rejuvenated. I consider it my personal mission to fill your closet with Manolo Blahniks.

Donna Marie Williams—for your voice and patience and for going the extra mile. Thanks to Ayanna and Michael for sharing your mom with me.

Joann Davis—for your wise and generous counsel . . . your friendship helped carry me through this journey. You were a beacon of light.

Susan L. Taylor—don't know what on earth I would do without your friendship and loving guidance.

Khephra Burns—for your time, your patience and gentle spirit, the words, and the haven so I could complete this journey . . .

even though you left me hanging with no password to the alarm. I love you.

Iyanla Vanzant—for your loving and generous spirit, words, and trailblazing ways.

Anita Diggs—what a gift you are to me and to the universe. Thank you for your insight and vision.

Nan Mooney—thank you for your skill and dedication.

Robyn McClendon-Jones—thank you for your time and creative, life-affirming artistic vision.

Damali Smith—for the loving spirit, and for sharing the harvest message.

Carol Taylor, Joy Duckett Cain, and Felisha Bell—for your words and your vision.

Faith Evans (and Cheryl Fox) for the heartfelt words.

James McBride—for your friendship through the years and for the wonderful gesture.

Jackie Joyner-Kersee—for being a shining example of humanity and humility. I love you, girl.

India.Arie—for the words and the wisdom and the sharing.

Laura Jorstad—for your gift.

And to Ron Karenga for giving us such a wonderful path to celebration.

Warner Family
Jamie Raab—for your faith in my work and for the vision.

Caryn Karmatz Rudy—for coming in like a champ, making the tough calls and lovingly sifting through the chaff to find the wheat—what a treasure you are. What a harvest we shall reap.

Larry Kirshbaum and Maureen Egen—for your support and leadership.

Jackie Merri Meyer—for your friendship, encouragement, and guidance.

Diane Luger—for bringing *A Plentiful Harvest* to life on the page.

Karen Torres—I shall never forget our first journey together.

Linda Duggins and Emi Battaglia—for your ability to get the message out as we uplift our fellow sistahs who are challenged to "get a life."

Jimmy Franco—I appreciate your generous spirit and fortitude.

Linda Jamison—for embracing me so warmly.

Harvey-Jane Kowal and the rest of the Warner family whose voices and faces I've not yet met but who will, I trust, see that this work reaches the hearts of those who need it most.

Blessings from Above
Joe Cooney—I will always love you for helping me in so many ways to carry out the sacred mission God has foreordained. The work we do is part of His whole great and gracious work.

Jon Tisch—I have no words to tell you how much I love and appreciate you for your support and extraordinary generosity of spirit.

Johnnie Cochran—for helping me to fulfill the mission. You are a Godsend in my life.

Loreen Arbus—for being a gifted and generous spirit and for using your light to impact my life so profoundly and so unexpectedly. You are an angel. I love and thank you.

Charlie and Tonja Ward—for gently and patiently taking me by the hand to find my own walk with Him. The love, encouragement, commitment to strengthening me, and the Bible studies have set me firmly on the rock and give me a solid place to stand. (Tonja—don't know *how* you juggle it all—thanks for reaching out and for fitting me in. You inspire me.)

Stephanie Dyer—for your love, friendship, and guidance

Butch Lewis—you are my inhale; I am your exhale. Together, we breathe life into empowering youth. I know He knows who you are, still I can't wait for the world to know. I love you.

Sir Shadow—for taking such amazing care of all your "patients": me and all of us at TWA, PGP, and The Stay Strong Foundation, and for making my life immeasurably easier as we carry out His work. You are *always* there when I call and *always* on time.

The TWA & PGP Family—The wind beneath my wings
Burgess Harrison—for the gift of your friendship and honor; Renee Gilbert—you have always been there for me. I love you; Priscilla Clarke—together we can. Love u much. Veronica Jones—the voice and spirit that soothes my spirit when I enter #502.

Greg Boyea, Edgerton Maloney, Patti Butler, Major Scurlock, Laila Keith, Penelope Bishop, Tola Ozim, Dominga Martin, Courtney Myers, Tiffany Edwards, Huda Mumin, Derrick Long.

Guardian Angels
Thank you for your love and for helping me to stay strong in ways I cannot explain. We are standing the test of time.

Shellie Anderson—what a gift you are to the universe. Wait till you find out what we all know. Thank you for hearing me when I don't want you to and listening when I don't think you are.

Doug Brown—my safe haven, always.

Chris Cathcart—I'm glad we're friends because spirits are transferable.

Vernon Slaughter—thanks for taking such good care of me forever.

Ken Carter, Jackie and Bob Kersee, Lori Adams, Susan Nowak, Rachel and Khari Noerdlinger (and Yusef), Helen Goss, Rita Ewing, Tony Wafford—for life lessons only you could teach; Leon Carter, Linda Stasi, Tyree Guyton, Jenenne Whitfield, Jae Je Simmons, Cicely Tyson, Alan Gansberg, Hilary Heath—you are a treasure in my life—thank you for your gentle and loving reminders; David Charles—what a loving and giving spirit you are. You will do great things in this life. My life is richer because of you. Bob Law, Lester Conner, Becky Gatling, Carol Jones, George Moses, Joy Thomas Moore, Wes Moore, Ray Gerald, Michael Hickson—for showing me a way of life and love I never knew. Thank you for the amazing gift of friendship and the lessons. Donald Singletary, Ken Smikle, Ruth Clark, Gil McGriff,

Tanya Odums, Bernard and Shana King, Traci Richards, Regina Kulik, Brenda Blackman, and Robin Avrum—what an unexpected blessing and treasure you are in my life; Alex English, Elly Tatum, Bridget Isaac, Melinda Chatman, Bill Lynch, James Mtume.

For your wisdom and teaching and prayer . . . and for opening my heart to understand who the Holy One of God is in my life.
Zeke Mowatt, Joyce Meyer, Rev. Lester Taylor, Rev. Suzan Johnson Cook, Warrington Hudlin, Carl Davis, Lonise Bias, Master Prophet Tomblin, Danielle Carr-Ramdath, Rev. Al Sharpton, Leon Carter, Mark Jones, David Grand, Rick Godwin, Rev. Calvin Butts, Cynthia Powell, and Dr. Yvonne Butler.

Thanks for being in my corner
Lillian Lynch, Nancy Wilson, Jeanne Ashe, Hezekiah Walker, Terry McMillan, Lucille Harrison, Ayala Donchin, Latifa Whitlock, Sonny Ray, Lisa and Christian Ray, Lucille Harrison, Erieka Bennett, Chris Curry, Halima Taha, Teresa Lyles Holmes, Bertice Berry, Janet Hill, Lewis Brown, Tanya Madison, Regina Ross, Mrs. George, Dawn Langfield, Allen Morgan, Carol Passariello, Judy Rosemarin, Adeyemi Bandele, Leon Carter, Debbie Miller, Gerald Peart, Chrysa Chin, Susie Greenwood, Jan Goldstoff, Yolanda Brooks, Darrell Walker, Richie Parker, Dr. Deborah Simmons, Frank Mercado, Rosita Parker, Julia McClure, Ruth Rabb, LiRon Anderson Bell, Marc Pollick, Al Morgan, Ilyasah Shabazz, Eric Adams, Frank Murphy (you are one in a million), Harry Dedyo, Gayle King, Roxanne Johnson, Kimm McNeil, Justine Simmons, Walter Greene, Zambga Brown, Audrey Bernard, Jane Kendall, Blanche Richardson, Leah Wilcox, Marilyn Artis, David Thornhill, Gina Gates, Sandra, Shanisha and Tiara Artis, David Stern, Faye and Karl Rodney, Joy

Halloway, Jim Gilbert, Tony Epps, Marva Smalls, Curtis Bunn, Mike Glenn, Keith Miles, Sharon Paige, Wanda Croudy, Art Thompson, Jesse Harris.

Finally, a heartfelt thank you to all of you who have embraced my work. There were times when I felt like I could not go on and you threw me a lifeline . . . a word, card, hug, prayer, or phone call that literally breathed life into me at that moment.

In loving memory of Vernon Lynch Sr., Mildred Ray, and dear sweet Aunt T, and Aunt Willa Mae. Gone too soon—I love you and miss you. Rarely does a day go by that I don't think of you and feel strengthened by your love and presence in my spirit.

And to Lauren Thompson, Aaliyah Haughton, and Michelle Thomas . . . your life and your spirit continue to inspire a generation of phenomenal young women.

O.M.T. (One More Thing)

I'd like to know how you're staying strong. Reach out to me at:

Terrie M. Williams
The Stay Strong Foundation
Columbus Circle Station
P.O. Box 20227
New York, NY 10023

Or

e-mail: tmwms@terriewilliams.com

THE PERSONAL TOUCH
What You Really Need to Succeed
in Today's Fast-paced Business World
by Terrie Williams with Joe Cooney

Terrie Williams owns and operates one of the premier public relations agencies in the country today. Over the past decade, her firm has handled some of the biggest names in entertainment, sports, and business, including Eddie Murphy (her first client), Miles Davis, Janet Jackson, Jackie Joyner-Kersee, Sally Jessy Raphael, Twentieth Century Fox, AT&T, HBO, and many others. Her key to success in today's impersonal world is personal consideration: treat people with respect, be there for them, and conduct yourself with integrity and compassion. Now in an insightful book full of surefire strategies and down-to-earth advice, Terrie will show how you, too, can apply these simple principles to both your career and your personal life. Because whether you're starting out, starting over, or just trying to improve your life, this book will help you get there . . . successfully.

"One of the most refreshing, practical, inspirational, and informative books I have read."
—Stephen R. Covey, author of
7 Habits of Highly Effective People

CPSIA information can be obtained at www.ICGtesting.com
Printed in the USA
LVOW11s1447250714

396034LV00001B/69/P

9 780446 691208